COHESIVE FORCE

COHESIVE FORCE

Feud in the Mediterranean
and the Middle East

Jacob Black-Michaud

With a Foreword by E. L. Peters

ST. MARTIN'S PRESS · NEW YORK

Printed in Great Britain

Library of Congress Catalog Card Number: 74–83518
First published in the United States of America
in 1975

AFFILIATED PUBLISHERS:
Macmillan Limited, London
Also at Bombay, Calcutta, Madras and Melbourne

Hélas! mon fils . . . , pourquoi se massacrent-ils
ainsi?

—Par esprit d'association, mon père, et prévision
de l'avenir, répondit Bulloch. Car l'homme est
par essence prévoyant et sociable. Tel est son
caractère. Il ne peut se concevoir sans une certaine
appropriation des choses (France 1908: Livre II,
Chapitre III).

To the women in my life

A. M. and B. W.

Contents

Foreword

Some years ago I had the pleasure of examining a thesis of Jacob Black-Michaud, out of which this comparative study of feud in the Mediterranean and the Middle East has come. Although we were well aware at the time that a deep understanding existed between us, we were also conscious of the fact that some of our views were contradictory. Since then we have discussed the matter in conversations and correspondence, without resolving all our differences. When Jacob Black-Michaud paid me the compliment of asking me to write a foreword to his book, and I agreed, neither of us had it in mind that I should write something vacuously laudatory; nor did we think it would be appropriate or fruitful for me to attempt a commentary on the points he makes. My intention is no more than to give an account of the Cyrenaican bedouin feud, and its pre-requisites, derived from my field research among the bedouin. In doing this, no attempt is made to take up the specific issues in the book, nor to debate the author's views, his views of the writings of other authors, nor, for that matter, his views of my writings on the feud. The divergences between us are evident in what we both have to say, and we thought it would be more profitable to expose rather than conceal them.

Homicide is not necessarily feud. This has to be stated flatly, because, in the literature, particularly the literature on the Middle East, evidence of killings and the inevitable disruption of social relationships which follow is seized upon as evidence of feud. Where an effective state organization exists, whatever the sentiments of people may be, homicide of any kind is an offence against the law, and it is dealt with accordingly. Thus, in a Lebanese Christian village, where two men fought at work, one of them died from his injuries and the culprit was arrested and put on trial. Although he was connected to people with strong influence among the country's leading politicians, he was convicted and sentenced to a long term of imprisonment, some thirteen years of which he served. In circumstances such as these, the idiom in which discussion is couched includes phrases which ring of feud-talk, like 'the boiling of the blood', 'the owner of the blood', 'vengeance', 'blood between them' and so on. Indeed, of two brothers born in a south Lebanese Muslim village, while they were both employed as miners in the U.S.A., one was killed in an accident and the other was paid what was described as *diya*, blood money, by the American company for which they worked. This use of idiom, the proverbs and saws which go with it, all appear in abundance where feud is practised, but their presence does not necessarily point to feud. The ascription of feud to contexts where its pre-requisites are wholly absent is perverse romanticism, evidence of deficient data, lack of understanding, or permutations of all three defects.

Feud is defined in the Shorter Oxford English Dictionary as a state of bitter and lasting mutual hostility; especially such a state existing between two families, tribes, or individuals, marked by murderous assaults, in revenge for some previous insult or wrong. One of the main issues to be discussed is the nature of feuding groups; consequently the terms for them, used loosely anyway, in the definition, are to be discounted. As a description of the relationship, the definition of feud, as given in the dictionary, serves the purpose admirably.

Bedouin corporate groups are based on the joint ownership of the natural resources, land and water, by men gathered together as descendants of an ancestor, said to be common to them all, within a genealogical framework of some four to six generations, including the living. Recruitment to these corporations is not by birth alone: evidence is available showing that incorporation has taken place, sometimes on a substantial scale, within living memory. While it is true to say that actual descent in a patriline is by no means inconsequential in an analysis of the nature of these bedouin corporations, they are composed essentially of a body of men with shared interests in parcels of property and the wells they include. The exploitation of these resources requires men to share well-water for domestic purposes, to agree to arrangements for watering their animals; to accept that in most years only parts of their homeland receive sufficient rain to grow a crop and that, therefore, cultivable land must be divided for ploughing purposes, in a spirit of amity; and that pastures, abundant after rain has fallen, are available for shepherds and herdsmen without hindrance. Simple as these activities may seem, they are, nevertheless, the source of constant friction, usually trivial, but occasionally becoming serious. Tempers fray easily in mid-summer, especially in August when the temperatures soar to 120°F and higher for weeks on end, because, when they arrive at the well with their animals, men are fractious with tiredness, and it sometimes happens that one insists on being given priority over others in the rota of users, for they are all anxious to have the job done to get away for a short rest. When drawing water for domestic purposes, assistance might be requested, and if this is withheld anger might flare between two men and a nasty fight ensue. Ploughing is another occasion when men are required to work hard throughout the hours of daylight for two or three weeks continuously; quarrels of varying intensity break out during this period. On any of these occasions, and on others also, fights might result in death, or death from injury: a man shot another at a well during a quarrel about the order of watering animals; a man bludgeoned another to death with a large stone for similar reasons; a third man's back was broken in similar circumstances; a man shot his first paternal cousin during a quarrel over the ownership of a newborn kid; and this list of examples, illustrating some of the circumstances in which homicide occurs between fellow members of a corporation, can be extended considerably.

Homicides committed in the heat of the moment do occur amongst those groups of people who are daily thrown together in the pursuit of the essential economic activities. It sometimes happens that the quarrels which occur among men, and lead to death, are between close kinsmen, first paternal cousins, mothers' brothers' and sisters' sons, fathers' brothers and brothers' sons, and between brothers themselves. Cases are reported of a man killing his father, but this is thought to be so heinous that it is said of this man that he could not have been his father's son. Permanent expulsion is the only course the bedouin take for an offence the sinfulness of which defies any possibility of arbitration: a father can deal with fratricide, but brothers, jural equals, undifferentiated by rules of primogeniture or ultimogeniture, and all equally subordinate to the father's authority—even though in practice they are differentiated among themselves, while their father is alive, and more clearly so immediately he dies—cannot

deal with patricide. Save in the case of patricide, members of a
corporate group act to prevent a perpetuation of the disruption
homicide causes, by conniving with the offender to allow him to
escape to a distant group, but are ready to receive him on his
return, years later, by which time, it is said, the memory of the
killing will have been obliterated. Suppressed is a better word to
describe what happens: the memory is deliberately suppressed in
the sense that people say that a mention of this kind of homicide
is sin in itself. They know all about it, of course they do; but it is
one thing to know and quite another to parade the knowledge.

Rationally, people argue that neighbours are likely to quarrel
amongst themselves, and come to blows. Their *intention*, however, is not to inflict permanent injury or cause death. Should
either occur among neighbours, contrition is assumed, and there
are conventional means for showing it. Circumstances prompt
men to do evil deeds, not the natures of men. *Jīrān*, neighbours,
are people who have chosen to live together in the small camps,
because they can co-operate, and it is in their interests to do so.
The *jār*, neighbour, is sacred, and the obligations of mutual
succour, protection and devotion are among the most impelling
recognized by the bedouin. Good neighbourliness is as much the
staff of social relationships as barley is the staff of life. If, therefore, a killing should occur between close kin or neighbours, the
definition of their social relationships excludes the possibility of
its being intentional, however deliberate the act itself.

Neighbours, perforce, get along well together. If they did not,
the routine activities of making a living in this harsh and economically marginal environment would be put in jeopardy.
Herding, watering animals, drawing water for use in the tents,
and ploughing, are activities which cannot proceed successfully
if there is a constant threat to life and limb. They are planned on
the assumption that it is not necessary to be on the watch all the
time against possible attacks from people with the best opportunity of making them. Most of the time bedouin go about their
tasks reasonably confident of their security, not in fear. They are
far too susceptible to attack from kith and kin to allow for this
possibility in their arrangements. Hence their sentiments are
heavily weighted against killing within the corporate group: they
have a rich collection of execrations and proverbs condemning
men who kill within this range of relationships.

Feud is excluded from the corporate group because the activities its members perform, and the social relationships which develop out of them, make it imperative that serious breaches of the peace, whether homicide, physical injury, adultery, sexual misdemeanours, gross insult or false accusations, are dealt with at once, to prevent a spread of hostility. Sentiments do not exclude feud; they grow out of the social relationships in which people come to be involved in the course of making a living together, but they serve as a buttress of great strength. The act of homicide does not determine the presence or absence of feud. Homicide within a corporation is the same kind of act as any other homicide; what makes the difference between homicides is the group or groups of people they implicate.

In circumstances where co-residents need to co-operate in their exploitation of the natural resources, whether the producing groups are very small and very many, or large and few, and where their activities necessitate the movement of people to and from their gardens, plots, or fields, without let or hindrance, homicides may well occur, but feud will be absent. Hamlets and villages are residential units from which feud must be excluded. It is possible to envisage a condition of things in which quarters of, say, a village are sufficiently detached to permit feud to occur, without, at the same time wrecking the basis of ordinary, day-to-day, economic pursuits; but, then, why should people trouble to live together in a single village if the relationships between the quarters they inhabit are sufficiently discreet to permit feud to flourish, when their interests could be equally well served were the village to be split into a number of smaller villages or hamlets?

Vendetta, akin to feud in some of the forms of behaviour which characterize its hostility, is distinctively different, and appears where feuding relationships cannot be tolerated. I have not worked in a community where vendetta is present, and, consequently, I am not familiar with the conditions in which it makes its appearance. From reports I have received of two cases, in two villages in different parts of the Lebanon, there are two matters of immediate interest. First, a vengeance killing takes place on the exact spot where the previous victim met his death: the latter's blood is washed by the blood of his killer. If the reports are correct, vengeance is exacted in a public place, the centre of a village market, or some other meeting point. Second, it is the killer who is killed in vengeance, or a direct heir; and he is killed by a son of his victim or the nearest surviving male relative.

Neither of these two conditions is compatible with bedouin feud. The fixity of location for exacting vengeance is an impossible condition to fulfill for herders-cum-cash-croppers, living a romany way of life. The rule of vendetta limiting vengeance to a particular place is consistent with sedentary life. The further rule, limiting responsibility for vengeance, and liability for homicide, to a single patriline, runs counter to bedouin behaviour: among them, all members of the corporate group are liable to be killed, and the responsibility for exacting vengeance falls on them all equally. It is quite true that there is often purposeful selection of a victim in bedouin feud, but this had to do with a person's status, his advanced age, or his very young age, and it is a process of selection deliberately intended to exacerbate relationships, quicken the tempo of the feud, or throw down a challenge. Selection is not based on a rule of descent which makes an individual an heir of liability. Members of a corporate group inherit the 'debts' of a feud as 'one body', corporately. For the exclusion of feud from the corporate group is not negative; its exclusion has the positive effect of binding its members together as a feuding group, so that they move together against like groups, undivided.

On the small amount of evidence I possess, I cannot say why hostility of the kind occurring in the vendetta should appear in some villages and not in others. The conditions which permit vendetta have not been adequately explored. Other forms of hostility have also been descriptively recorded, but they still need to be isolated analytically. Brief reference has been made, here, to vendetta, only to detach one form of hostility from the feud, with the aim of giving its meaning greater precision.

In his book, *The Nuer*, Evans-Pritchard made the obvious but important point that feud presumes social relationships of some sort. Among the bedouin, while the corporate group is the feuding group, this is not to say that all corporate groups are at feud, nor even potentially thus engaged. There are always combinations of corporate groups among which feud relationships are excluded, since the homeland of a corporate group is insufficient in its extent to capture the micro-ecological diversity produced annually by the vagaries of the marginal climatic conditions. The latter demand that the bedouin have access to the resources of corporate groups other than their own, for cultivating a crop and watering animals; freedom of movement is also a necessity to allow for the wanderings of animals, and to enable men to travel —sometimes long distances—to their nearest markets, to travel across the country to sell their surplus animals in Egypt, and to travel to the oases for dates. Economic activities impose conditions of peace between certain corporate groups. The same activities stimulate competitive relationships between them and other corporate groups. Feud between any two corporate groups is, therefore, a calculatingly selected relationship.

Lying adjacent to any particular corporate group are the territories of four others, as a rule, although in a few instances there are less. Of these four others, one at least, is politically a collateral segment in the lineage structure, and it shares the same micro-ecological conditions. A second of the four could be in a similar relative position; or, it could be one of three which are disparate with regard to the micro-ecological conditions in which they are situated, and each of these three could be a segment of any of three different political orders in the lineage structure. This disparity in the ecological and political statuses of corporate groups, and the permutations in relationships invited by this variety, constitute the basis of selection for feuding relationships or alliances. The possibility of extending the pattern of relationships beyond the territories of the immediate neighbouring groups of a particular corporate group must be available, because connections with some of the groups in the immediate vicinity does not offer sufficient economic security, against the maldistribution of ecological resources from year to year and from place to place in any one year, to meet the recurring bedouin needs to water animals and grow a crop. It remains now to examine the ways in which corporate groups are brought together in co-operating combinations, and how these combinations compete with like combinations for scarce resources.

Two corporate groups linked genealogically as descendants of a pair of brothers—their respective founding ancestors—occupy adjacent strips of territory, which are ecologically virtually the same in the sense that if the rainfall of one, in any given year, is adequate to raise a crop of barley, it is adequate for the other as well. The same remark applies to pastures and sources of water.

That is to say, when one is in surplus the other is enjoying similar conditions; likewise a deficit in the resources of one is suffered in similar measure by the other. An alliance between two such groups merely serves to multiply surpluses and deficits. The need for co-operation between two such groups is not urgent on this count, but this does not necessitate hostile relationships either. While the aim is always to achieve the neutrality of a *modus vivendi*, the relationship is more complex than this. In order that animals and their shepherds and herdsmen may move freely in the pastures, and also to allow for the strayings of animals, a condition of general peace must prevail. If, therefore, a killing should occur between them, the apprehension it causes must be quickly dispelled for life to resume its even tenor. Arrangements exist for the early negotiation of compromise, and if, before this is achieved, a vengeance killing is exacted, vengeance itself can be contributory to a restoration of amity. On this count, there is an urgent need to co-operate with regard to pastoral activities. Moreover the camps of the two groups are often close together, sometimes within earshot, and often within sight. Out of this propinquity springs a camaraderie which gives texture to the otherwise thin relationship of a material need. But, if a corporate group, because of its population increase and a favourable demographic structure, is poised to expand its resources, one of the several available possibilities is expansion by force into the territory of a collateral corporate group. Stability in the economy of a corporate group is achieved if its territory spans two or more micro-ecological areas, since the vicissitudes affecting a single micro-ecological area are considerably reduced, with the consequent advantage of a lessening of the urgency of external connections, and the greater choice this implies. But, while granting the urge to diversify the assets directly controlled by a corporate group, an accumulation of existing assets is critically advantageous in some situations. Thus, in a year of deficit, to acquire access to the surplus resources of another corporate group, the wherewithal to meet demands for a share of surplus, in opposite conditions, must be readily available. Also, if a local group is to increase its population it must gain the power to increase its surplus in productively good years, enabling a greater sloughing off in periods of plenty to make good the increased deficit of bad years. During a stay of over two years with the bedouin, the only direct evidence I have of two corporate groups preparing for armed combat, was an occasion when one attempted to seize the territory of its collateral. Nevertheless, the conditions for a successful seizure are so complex that the attempts are few and far between; most of the time a *modus vivendi* obtains between corporate groups occupying the same micro-ecological area.

In years of insufficient rainfall, it is still possible to meet the domestic needs of people from the small amount of local well water, but it might not be possible to meet all animal needs. To ensure a regular water supply for animals, connections into different micro-ecological territories are made. In practice the area of territory which these connections must cover to secure supplies of water for animals is not very great: the area spanned by the territories of neighbouring corporate groups is sufficient. Marriage patterns show links into one or two proximate and different micro-ecological areas, but missing out collateral corporate groups of the same micro-ecological area. It would be an inefficient use of the available marriage 'capital' to invest it all in this one kind of resource; to do so would also entail a thin spread of frail links over several groups; and it would also mean denying a collateral group the opportunity of such links, since there is a low limit to the number of links a corporate group is able to tolerate from the same micro-ecological area—in a poor year, when all the groups of people inhabiting it would be suffering insufficiency, the simultaneous demands they would make on their linked partners would be overburdensome. Consequently, if group A is maritally linked to group X, its collateral B will be maritally linked to Y. In other words a line of clear cleavage is drawn by marital links both between collateral corporate groups, and between the two clusters of partners.

The rainfall requirements for growing a crop are much more exacting than those for satisfying either human or animal needs. Rain, whenever it falls, at anytime during the winter and spring months, or even in summer thunder storms, is useful for consumption purposes. If ploughing is to be undertaken at all, the land must be drenched with rain—to enable the soil to congeal—not later than mid-December. After sowing, a further period of heavy rain is required, about a month later, to germinate the seed. A final period of rain lasting intermittently into March, or better still, into April allows the growing plants to absorb enough moisture for them to withstand the severe drought and the high temperatures of the ripening period. Such optimum conditions do not occur widespread in one season. This year might bring plenty to, say, five or six localities distributed unpredictably over a relatively large area; next year these areas may be experiencing insufficient rainfall, and other localities may be reaping the benefits of optimum conditions. Good years produce bumper crops, but the surpluses do not all accrue to the corporate group on the territory where they are produced, because the abundant resources of a good year, here, must be shared with the partners who are having a bad year, there. The area of territory in which optimum rainfall, in amount, in its onset, frequency and duration, is available in any year is very much larger than that in which optimum conditions are achieved for satisfying human and animal needs.

All bedouin plan to grow some grain each year. Access to the territories of corporate groups, distributed over a wide area, must be available without elaborate negotiations or argument, if advantage is to be taken of the rain when it falls. The link securing this access must possess the strength which allows men to move hurriedly from their homeland to, perhaps, a distant territory, with the confidence that, when they arrive, they will be able to get on with the job of ploughing without further ado. For this reason a number of marriage links are widely flung. This does not mean that they are haphazardly distributed. They fall within the area which gives each group the security of a barley crop, of sorts, annually. Like the pattern which is to be seen within the range of rainfall required for animal water supplies, numbers of collateral corporate groups do not marry into the same corporate groups within the crop growing range of rainfall. Thus if group A is maritally linked to groups M (say 10 miles away), O (say 20 miles away) and Q (say 30 miles away), then its collateral B will have marriage links with groups N, P and R at similar distances away. The line of cleavage between two collateral groups, and between the two clusters of partners referred to already, is deepened as it extends to divide them and their more distant partners severally. Confederations of corporate groups are thus formed within which there is co-operation, and between which there is competition.

The boundaries which delimit these configurations are drawn

by marriage connections, but it would be misleading to envisage them as a tenuous single line of links. Bedouin tend to concentrate their marriage links. Of the total marriages available, almost half of them are expended within the corporate group—the amount used up in this way varies between groups, but this is not relevant to the discussion. The remainder is not dispersed over the maximum numbers of corporate groups. It is concentrated in relatively few spots, lying mainly within the two areas of major economic interests, previously cited. Thus, to give a specific example, a particular corporate group has external marriage links to eight other corporate groups. Affinal anchors are dropped into corporate groups the territories of which are nearby, but which are micro-ecologically disparate, and it is this disparity which gives stability to animal water supplies, and which permits the planned expansion of flocks and herds. Affinity also connects three more corporate groups in territories which are further removed: they are the connections which represent the paths along which some amount of grain travels to the grain store each year. The total number of corporate groups to which connections lead, through external marriages, within the territorial range of major economic interests, is six. The number of corporate groups available within this range is twenty-seven. Of the remaining two links, one is thrown out to the south-west, terminating in a date oasis; and the other stretches far away to the east, a single link to guard against the possible but infrequent contingency of a protracted and widespread water shortage.

The concentration of external marriage links into only seven corporate groups (the eighth long distant link was only given earlier to complete the distribution, and it is no longer relevant) is sure indication of their significance. Moreover, these links are reciprocated, albeit not on a strict one-for-one basis. Genealogical evidence shows that over three generations there are instances of abandoned affinity—links that were tried, found unsuitable, and left to wither. Where an initial link has been successful, affinal renewal has given added strength, and several others have been planted around it. Individual links, that is to say, are built into a structure of kinship locking corporate groups together, thus creating a plurality of kinship connections, with their accompanying different modes of behaviour, expectations, jural relationships, and so on, opening multiple channels of approach between corporate groups, for a variety of purposes. Plurality of links converts stranded connections into a durable structure, and when this is achieved the quality of durability is injected into the confederations. It also leaves them discrete: competition is not strangled by the dense tangle of kinship links which apparently characterizes certain societies.

The total population of corporate groups held together by the elaborate kinship structure built on multiple affinal connections, sometimes renewed in several successive generations, runs into a few thousand souls. Confederations of corporate groups are, in some cases, numerically strong enough to constitute a war-making unit. Numerical strength, and an appropriate demographic structure, are both essential for this purpose, since war presumes a population sufficiently large to provide a labour force for the maintenance of an army in the field. Bedouin, when they talk about war, think of the tribe as the minimal unit which can go to war, and distinguish any other mass attack as a *ghazi* (by which they mean an armed raid), or what they call a war of sticks. The last tribal war lasted for four years from 1860, and is referred to as the war between the Bara'asa and Abaidat tribes. Information for that period in history, and earlier, leaves little doubt that the two main corporate groups of the Bara'asa were at enmity, as they have been right up to the present; and in recounting the events of that war only certain corporate groups on both sides are said to have been committed in battles. Although it is impossible to estimate with any accuracy the number of corporate groups engaged on both sides—and it seems likely that elements from other tribes joined in the fray— it is safe to say that the number substantially exceeded that of the confederation of corporate groups referred to earlier.

One of the major difficulties in deploying a confederation for purposes of making war is that it is not a unit. Territorially the corporate groups of a confederation are dispersed, some of them clustering if their borders happen to be coincident, but others of them disposed in several directions at varying distances away. Mobilization of an army in these circumstances is well nigh impossible. Members of allied corporate groups are always willing to help, whatever occasions the need, and this help is especially effective in disputes over land and water, when members turn up in strength to give support in an argument. In armed combat, however, members of a linked corporate group may help as individuals but not as a group. Also, when vengeance is exacted the killing is, occasionally, actually carried out by a maternal kinsman of the avenging group, not by one of its own members. So too, when a corporate group moves to seize a neighbouring well and the territory in which it is situated, it does so sure that its strength is sufficient to subdue the opposition in a short sharp skirmish, ending in the loss of only a small number of lives and the surrender of the resources; help in this might be given by individuals, on a personal basis, from linked groups, but they would not be assisting compulsorily as co-members of a political unit.

Help given on an individual basis in avenging a death, in disputes, in moots and in peace-making is disparately different from mobilizing warriors and producers for a period of war. Indeed, I very much doubt whether the relations between bedouin corporate groups permit the development of the organizational apparatus necessary for war, despite the evidence that a pro-longed war did take place in the 1860s—we do not know whether the war was a series of skirmishes between the same groups, or between different groups; or whether on either side there were two small cores of men continuously engaged in fighting, while the rest of the two armies changed their composition; still less do we know about the structure of leadership which gave the war its direction, which planned the strategy, which dealt with problems of logistics and so on. This leadership was available during the period of the wars against the Italians from 1911–31, provided first by the Turks, and subsequently by the Sanusi Order, a religious fraternity at the outset of its Cyrenaican career in 1842, but which developed political functions and assumed military responsibilities once the Italians had forced the Turks to with-draw. During my fieldwork among the bedouin there was no evidence that corporate groups were able to combine in segment-ary order to span the kind of unit, with a total population of between 10,000 to 30,000 souls, referred to as a tribe. War, if it ever does occur on the organizational basis of segmentary fusion, assumes a sense of unity able to withstand serious loss of life, constant fear, waste of very scarce products, and the attendant privations. It is intelligible that people fought the Italians for twenty years, and suffered appallingly—better that than life behind barbed wire fences. Also, if the aggregate population increased, or the natural resources contracted over a period, or both, it is possible that large groups were forced to fight wars to maintain a realistic relation between the carrying capacity of the land and the total population living off it. But the bedouin know and say that the effect of prolonged armed conflict between clusters of corporate groups would mean such a catastrophic loss of males that there would be few left to benefit from the extra water and land which a victory would make available.

What unity there is among corporate groups which combine to form confederations is not of the sort that is expressed in a permanent political structure, having in it the power to compel men to action. Men of corporate groups combine after preliminary probings suggest that it would be advantageous for them to do so; and, if their relationships prosper, affinity is used as a commitment to continue them. Further success leads to more affinity. But if at any time relationships deteriorate, affinity is not renewed and the strength of kinship ebbs away. At any moment, therefore, the links between the corporate groups of a confederation are not evenly distributed. Between some there are many more than between others, and they are of longer standing. Between others the links have been made among people of the contemporary generation, and they have yet to be weathered by time. While these links are still extant, however, co-operation of some kind remains active. When they become defunct, it is possible that the groups between which relationships have thus been severed, enter into feuding relationships, but there is no genealogical evidence for stating this with certainty. Genealogical evidence does show clearly that affinity has lapsed in some cases, and lapsed affinity is a sure index of hostility in contemporary relationships.

The content of the pattern of feuding is liable to change inasmuch as the actual groups engaging in strife might alter; but since feud is competition for preferential access to natural resources, as long as these resources are scarce and competition continues, the pattern of feuding stays. While resident among the bedouin, I happened to be living in a camp at a time when its members were intent on escalating their feud with a nearby group, and the senior men had already been called to the administrative offices to account for their behaviour, several times. Undeterred, they continued their active hostility, causing a serious fracas in a local market on one occasion. The British officer in charge of their district, a man with a predilection for travelling widely and frequently in the area under his control, met me and complained about the recalcitrant behaviour of the people with whom I was living. An explanation, attempting what was an analysis of a feuding relationship, he found interesting, but it did not give him the information he wanted to make an administrative decision which would terminate the business. Almost by way of soliloquy, I said that there was no way of ending a feud, unless, perhaps, the two groups concerned were to be separated by such distance that there would no longer be any relationships between them. To my chagrin, he thought this a good idea, and acted on it promptly, but heeding my plea not to banish the people with whom I was then living. He banished a group without removing the cause. Other people would come to inhabit the vacated territory and the same recalcitrance between two groups of people, in the same area, would reappear.

Like a suppurating sore, the hostility in a feud comes to a head, bursts, festers anew, and the process is repeated. Whenever rain falls, it is likely that men at feud will contest the right to plough a border strip of land; before the watering season begins they are likely to clash over the use of a particular source of water; if camels stray into the ripening barley, although the herdsman may be of an uninvolved group, blame is immediately attached to a feuding group; if animals stray into the territory of a feuding group, protests are shouted at those who come to recover them, and shots may be fired in their direction; if men of a feuding group visit the market when it is not their turn, a disturbance— sometimes serious—is most likely to occur; when men travel across country they are careful to keep out of sight of the camps of the people with whom they are at feud, to avoid the volley of shots aimed at them if they are spotted. Finally when a homicide does occur, no attempt is made to settle the matter, no offer of blood-money is made, and the behaviour on both sides is calculated to keep the enmity alive, even though further killings may not occur for many years.

Feud is only one form of competition. Among the corporate groups which combine to co-operate there is competition of a different sort for the same kind of resources, but this competition is patterned by the behaviour appropriate to the diverse categories of kin: nevertheless when a man uses a mother's brother's link to place some of his animals for watering purposes, or to plough an extra few strips of land to plant barley, he is adding to his assets as surely as he would be doing if he used coercion to acquire these gains. Feud, however, is actively hostile competition, and it is pursued by groups unconnected affinally or consanguineously—by groups, that is, whose members are not placed in known positions of relationships, and who, as 'strangers' behave unpredictably.

Relationships of the kind characterized as feud, obtain between paired corporate groups. This is not to say that assistance in prosecuting a feud is not tendered by a linked corporate group. It does mean, however, that responsibility for the actions fall on the feuding groups, not on their linked groups. The feuding group is the corporate group, not a combination of such groups. The significance of combinations of corporate groups to form confederations is partly the mutual assistance that flows between them in feuding, but also that feud is excluded from among them. Released from the task of guarding against the groups in a confederation, each corporate group is, to that extent, freed to concentrate its hostile energies on a relatively small number of opposed groups; it is because of this ability to concentrate hostility that the feud is so persistently intractable and vicious in Cyrenaica.

Discreteness is the most important single characteristic of the bedouin corporate group, in understanding why it is that feud is present in Cyrenaica. There are four main aspects of this discreteness relevant to the present discussion.

1. Territorially each local community—the camps of the corporate group—is separate from the nearest community to it, even if the latter is a collateral segment occupying the same broad trough of land. Nowhere throughout the territory are the residential units of corporate groups indistinct. Each is associated with its own homeland, and the proprietory rights to its resources are vested in all its members equally. Although the territorial discreteness is obvious once it has been stated as a fact, it is no less important for that. In another part of Libya where I have worked the type of dispersed settlement found on

a plantation militates against the growth of a sense of community, and the inhabitants explicitly think of themselves as members of several different kinds of groupings, without ascribing priority to any one of them. Where settlements are strung out in a line, one settlement merging with the next, the problem of defining a residential universe can be difficult. A village in south Lebanon, where I also worked, as it is approached, looks splendidly isolated, perched on the top of a mound in the hills; but in parts the houses are built on the site of the mound, and the inhabitants of these parts are nearer neighbours to people living in a hamlet at the base of the mound, or to the inhabitants of a smaller village on another side, than they are to the residents of the core area of their villages. The ambiguities which these residential patterns create are absent among the bedouin.

2. Each corporate group bears a name. Every man belongs to a corporate group, and to one only. There is, therefore, no confusion about identity. When an act of hostility occurs between two corporate groups, it is the names of the groups which are used for reference purposes, not the names of the individuals directly concerned in the act, so completely is the identity of a man fused with that of his group.

3. Ownership of the natural resource is vested in a corporation of agnates. Residual rights to resources are said to belong to lineage members, in other societies. If these members are dispersed, some living on territory to which they have these rights, and others—perhaps the majority—living in settlement where they do not have these rights, then an almost inevitable consequence is that ambiguities in loyalties arise. Among the bedouin the concentration of agnates is exceptionally high: the average of around eighty per cent would be much higher were it not for the very low figure for the few camps of upstart shaikhs, who tend, in the first place, to recruit non-agnates as their followers. This concentration obviously reduces the significance of divided loyalties which appears to stultify decisive action among other peoples.

4. The rules of marriage do not compel bedouin to seek spouses from other corporate groups. It is doubtful whether, for demographic reasons, all marriage needs could be satisfied by taking spouses from within the corporate group. In any event there

are pressing economic reasons for marrying into other corporate groups, as argued earlier. Politically, also, a situation in which all external relationships were of hostile competition would be untenable. But since external marriages are concentrated into a relatively small number of other corporate groups, bedouin are able to satisfy their needs without compromising the discreteness of their groups.

Compromise inheres in a multiplicity of cross-cutting ties. Discreteness means it is possible to dispense with compromise: it is the basis for decisive action. Feud is present in Cyrenaica because any one corporate group is sufficiently discrete in relation to a limited number of others that its members can take the decision not to compromise. The ability to take this decision is central to the feud. Where groups are discrete, the possibility for feuding is also present; but where an entanglement of ties precludes decisive action, threat of feud may be used to arrive at compromise but the pursuit of feud will be thwarted.

The feud is not peculiar to either Cyrenaica or the bedouin way of life. Wherever there is sufficient discreteness of groups, the feuding relationship is a possible means of competing for definable sorts of assets. Moreover, the indices of discreteness for bedouin groups are not necessarily the relevant ones in other communities: for example, the concentration of agnates is critical among the bedouin, whereas agnation might be inconsequential or absent elsewhere. A close parallel to the bedouin of Cyrenaica, in some respects, are the Nuer. It has been said of them that they cannot feud because their agnatic groups are dispersed, and the rule of exogamy, together with the additional rule that closely related males cannot marry closely related females, imposes a maximum amount of inter-connectedness. This view is acceptable only if agnates and external marriage connections are widely dispersed. If they are not, then it is possible to appreciate that the feud, about which Professor Evans-Pritchard wrote so extensively, exists among the Nuer. Rather than seek comparability between two peoples who have a number of cultural characteristics in common, it would be more profitable, perhaps, to compare culturally dissimilar peoples, using social anthropological definition for analytic purposes instead of culturally determined categories only. It is greatly to his credit that Mr. Black-Michaud, taking cognisance of highly differentiated situations spread over an extensive geographical area, has attempted the task.

By focussing the attention on homicide in discussing the feud, the interest has been deflected away from what is essentially a specific mode of competition in definable conditions. Looked at from this point of view, the feud ceases to be an anachronistic barbarism, now rapidly disappearing, and is instead critical to an understanding of competition between villages in the southern Sudan, and perhaps between villages in certain areas in Spain, and perhaps, too, in urban areas in western Europe. For feud is not necessarily manifested as a number of serially linked homicides. Feud is also advanced without a gun being fired or the loss of a single life.

E. L. Peters

Introductory Note

A few preliminary remarks are necessary for the sake of clarity and in order to avoid tedious repetitions in the text:

(1) This book is principally concerned with feud as it is practised in the Mediterranean basin and the Middle East. I take the latter term to include two marginal regions—Somaliland and the Swat valley in northwest Pakistan—in which feuding activities are not dissimilar to those to be observed elsewhere in the area under consideration. When making general assertions about feud in the Mediterranean and the Middle East so defined, I shall not always repeat my terms of reference, which should at all times be regarded as implicit, unless I specifically state that I am drawing upon material from other areas or formulating hypotheses which are universally valid.

(2) In attempting to analyze the sociological mechanisms which underlie the wide range of apparently disparate phenomena I collectively qualify as manifestations of the 'feud', I have on the whole confined myself to an investigation of violent interaction in a number of tribally[1] organized lineage societies for which ample ethnographic information was readily available in published form. The occasional references I make to feud-like practices reported from Corsica, Anglo-Saxon England, Merovingian France and in the Icelandic sagas do suggest, however, that my conclusions concerning the nature of violence in the absence of an efficient centralized state apparatus are not totally invalid for some bilateral societies as well. Although I am convinced that further sociological research on the feud in kindred based societies would yield interesting results, this is not a subject to which I can claim to have given any serious attention in the present book.

(3) In the first four chapters I shall be ignoring the role of women and treating feud as if it were an almost exclusively 'all-male' pursuit, which, to a certain extent, it is. The rationale for this procedure will become apparent in the last chapter.

(4) Whenever it has been necessary to quote works published in

[1] For my usage of the word 'tribal' cf. p. 38.

languages other than English, no effort has been made to translate the passages in question. For the original (which often dates
from the nineteenth century or earlier) frequently communicates a
unique savour of feuding societies observed at first hand, before
the introduction of a certain measure of governmental control,
which would be entirely lost in translation. Where words and
proper names from Arabic and other languages not normally
written in the Roman alphabet occur outside quotations, I have
sought, wherever possible, to use the spelling given in the first
edition of the *Encyclopaedia of Islam*. When the *Encyclopaedia*
does not mention the particular word or name, I have copied it as
it stood in the system of transliteration employed by the author
quoted. This method has led to numerous inconsistencies, but at
least has the merit of making it relatively simple for arabists and
others to check words in their original context, so that they may
form their own opinions as to a correct transcription.

(5) I have drawn heavily in this book, both for ideas and ethnographic material, upon the work carried out among the Bedouin
of Cyrenaica by Professor Emrys Peters (of the Department of
Social Anthropology at the University of Manchester), from
whose theories most of my own ultimately derive. Whenever I
have occasion to refer to the Bedouin of Cyrenaica, I shall be
speaking of the camel-herding nomads of the southern *barr*, or
semi-desert, among whom Peters made most of his observations
on the practice of feud. I shall nowhere allude to the culturally
similar tent dwellers of the *jabal*, or northern plateau, where
lusher pastures and a different terrain have been conducive to the
development of other social conditions.

(6) Although the final version of this book was completed in
spring 1972, the theoretical propositions on which it is based had
already been elaborated in a draft dating from three years earlier.
All references are consequently to sources published before 1969.

I

A Typology of Violence

Any discussion of the feud in the Mediterranean and the Middle East must almost immediately encounter a major obstacle, for although travellers, administrators and anthropologists have reported a mass of often very detailed material describing sporadic outbreaks of violence of one sort or another, they have in the main studiously avoided formulating an exact definition of what they mean by the word feud. A study of the occurrence of the term in the literature on both the Middle East and the more familiar preserves of social anthropology, like tropical Africa, yields a bewildering variety of interpretations ranging from individual acts of lethal retaliation for homicide, injury or insult, to repeated acts of full scale aggression between large ethnic groups whose adult male population may number several thousands strong.

Austin Kennett, an administrator in the Egyptian desert, for instance, applies the word 'feud' to an incident in which a Bedouin was killed by three men from another tribe as the result of a quarrel: the victim's fellow tribesmen capture the aggressors and impound as many animals as they can abduct from the enemy tribe's pastures. The small son of the dead man, who witnessed his father's murder, is told to decide which of the three captives delivered the death dealing blow, whereupon the boy is given a loaded pistol with which he shoots the guilty man as he stands bound hand and foot. The remaining two men are then allowed to return with the flocks of their fellow tribesmen to their tents and peaceful relations are resumed between the two groups (Kennett 1925:56–9). 'Feud' stands here for exact retaliation in kind.

On the other hand, von Hahn, the Austro-Hungarian consul

for eastern Greece, who travelled extensively in Albania in the mid-nineteenth century, could write of a case of 'Blutrache [feud] zwischen zwei angesehenen Familien, welche über 80 Jahre gedauert und an 50 Männern das Leben gekostet hatte' (von Hahn 1867:341). The difference between this and the incident reported by Kennett is not merely one of dimensions and time. In the first instance the biblical principle of an eye for an eye was accepted by both sides and the affair is said to have been regarded as closed forthwith, whereas in the second the principle was either deliberately flouted or was even never entertained as a serious alternative to intensive reciprocal murder. Although von Hahn does not go into the causes and the historical background of the 'feud' he records, it is clear that the underlying social mechanism is totally dissimilar to that operative in the Bedouin example of talion. Yet both authors state explicitly, albeit in different languages, that they are dealing with the same phenomenon. This illustration constitutes but a faint echo of the inconsistencies of meaning that surround the word 'feud' throughout the literature.

Those authors who have troubled to define their terms may be divided into two main categories. On the one hand stand the British social anthropologists, whose increasingly sophisticated definitions of feud have suffered from a twofold limitation: firstly, they are elaborations of the original model developed by Evans-Pritchard with the specific purpose of describing Nuer patterns of self-help and inevitably show strong signs of this influence; secondly, their own field of application was hardly wider, restricted as it was to the analysis of violence as a means of social control among acephalous tribes of tropical Africa. In the other camp are situated those authors who have attempted to create a sociological typology of conflict. This division into two categories is largely a reflection of the divergent interests of the two groups of authors, the social anthropologists seeking in the main for a typology that will accommodate conflicts on a fairly reduced scale, and the sociologists being concerned with the smaller scale manifestations of conflict only in as far as they could shed light on their principal problem, the nature of war in western society.[1] For these reasons, the anthropologists tend to concentrate upon an

---

[1] Due to the extent of his emotional engagement in the issues of the Second World War, Malinowski stands somewhat incongruously in the sociological camp.

exact definition of the feud, whereas war is acknowledged as a vague residual category over and beyond feud with no clearly specified limits. The sociologists, on the contrary, attempt to define warfare with precision, but neglect feud. The possibility of the existence of intermediary categories is in general ignored by both camps. On one point, however, all are implicitly agreed: the really important criterion to distinguish between one form of conflict and another is the size and structure of the groups involved.

I shall now examine some of the typologies of conflict proposed by both anthropologists and sociologists. I shall discuss their validity and point out their blind spots. By reference to the work of Lewis, Nadel and Peters, I shall subsequently suggest some ways in which they might be amended to accommodate a more refined analysis of violence in tribal societies.

(1) SOME PREVIOUS ATTEMPTS

A deceptively lucid definitional statement of intent is made by Middleton and Tait in their 'Introduction' to *Tribes without rulers*:

> By feud we refer to fighting between people as groups, usually undertaken as response to an offence, the groups being in such a relationship that although they fight they both accept the obligation to bring the fighting to a close by peaceful settlement there being machinery to achieve this conclusion. . . . If there is no such obligation or machinery to settle the fighting we refer to it as warfare. Feud is thus a condition that flourishes typically within the same jural community (1958:20).

For Middleton and Tait, therefore, the decisive criteria to distinguish feud from warfare are the possibility of concluding hostilities through 'machinery', by which it seems they mean recourse to arbitration, and the (what they elsewhere term) 'moral' (1958:9) obligation to do so.

Although they do not express it in so many words, Middleton and Tait postulate a third criterion which is implicit in the phrase 'jural community'. As this is one of the concepts that they admittedly (1958:9) derive from Evans-Pritchard's theoretical work on the Nuer, it is reasonable to surmise that they have retained its original meaning. Evans-Pritchard's use of the term applied to the unit he called a 'tribe', which he defines (among other things) as the largest group within which compensation is paid and accepted as a surrogate for self-help in cases of homicide or injury (Evans-Pritchard 1940:121).

Middleton and Tait's division of the whole field of violence into only two sub-categories is quite deliberately restrictive, for although they are aware that 'Existing accounts of political systems in Africa refer to various types of overt expression of hostility between groups as warfare, feud, blood-vengeance, fighting or vendetta,' they prefer to regard them all as forms of 'self-help'. But they offer no reason for this disinclination to differentiate between them other than that 'It is often difficult—and often pointless—to distinguish them clearly' (1958:19). In these circumstances the reader is left wondering why they made the attempt in the first place.

A similarly self-defeating exercise in definition is to be found in a doctoral thesis entitled *The political organization of an Arab tribe of the Hadhramaut* (Hartley 1961). The author provides a list of Ḥaḍramī conceptual categories of conflict: 'Hostile relationships are set out on a continuum of increasing intensity, from a simple quarrel (*khiṣām*), to killing (*gatal*), "blood" (*damm*), the right of talion, to revenge (*nagā*), to war (*ḥarb*). One leads to the next, especially once a killing has occurred' (1961:175). This material seems to offer a wealth of possibilities for the accurate delineation of feud and other types of physical conflict. Yet the author inexplicably refers back to Middleton and Tait's tripartite definition of the feud based on arbitration, compensation and relative size, or structural distance between the contestants. Like them, he is also content to contrast feud with war, which term he reserves 'for hostilities between groups of a certain order, generally larger groups, the sub-clan, clan and tribe' (1961:175). Hostile relationships between groupings of an order inferior to that involved in warfare are placed indiscriminately under the heading of feud. The categories of *gatal*, *damm* and *nagā* would appear to have no further significance. It would be difficult to be less precise.

In 1941, Malinowski published, as a contribution to a symposium on the sociological background to the European conflict,

'An anthropological analysis of war', in which he also distinguished all other forms of violence from warfare by the stress
he laid on the *political* aspects of the latter. His 'minimum definition of war' is 'an armed contest between two independent
political units by means of organized military force, in pursuit of
a tribal or national policy' (1941:523). Thus, he rules out 'raids
for head hunting, for cannibal feasts, for victims of human
sacrifice to tribal gods . . . this type of fighting . . . is not cognate
to warfare, for it is devoid of any political relevancy; nor can it
be considered as any systematic pursuit of intertribal policy'
(1941:538).

For Malinowski warfare is characterized by the size of the units
engaged and the extent to which the conflict can be said to be the
result of a consciously implemented policy. Though he is unwilling to be specific, the tone of the whole article is transparent and
belies the title: Malinowski is here more concerned with a sociological analysis of international wars in the mid-twentieth century
than with a definition of the general phenomenon of war in
anthropological terms. If he does quickly sketch in the lines of
an overall typology of violence, this is more for the sake of com-
pleteness and to provide points of reference to enhance his main
theme, than because he regards other categories of conflict as
important *per se* in this context.

In what are, for Malinowski the 'functionalist', terms with a
curiously evolutionistic ring to them, he lists six items culminating
in the definition of war as an instrument of conscious national
policy referred to above. Two of these 'cultural phase[s] in the
development of organized fighting' are of interest here. They are
the lowest and the most 'primitive':

(1) private fighting, on the impulse of anger, within a group
    'countered and curbed by customary law . . .'
(2) collective and organized fighting as 'a juridical mechanism
    for the adjustment of differences between constituent
    groups of the same larger cultural unit . . .' (1941:541).

Both these items fall within the Middleton-Tait tripartite definition of feud, for they apply to fighting within the jural community, and in as far as one is 'countered and curbed by
customary law' and the other is a 'juridical mechanism for . . .
adjustment' they may be assumed to allow for arbitration and,
possibly, compensation, although, again, Malinowski is not

specific. They are similar in that they postulate the operation of an impersonal legal principle that exists over and above the conflict itself. But if both, as Middleton and Tait would have it, are regarded as types of self-help, they nevertheless differ in the application of this principle: in the case of 'private fighting' it would seem that the penal element of customary law is exercised coercively against the defaulting individual by the society at large, whereas in the second case it is the inter-action of the fighting groups that itself constitutes the 'juridical mechanism'. The importance of this distinction will become more apparent in the discussion of vengeance killing later in the present chapter (cf. p. 29).

Malinowski cites one other category of violence that often attains important proportions in western and non-western societies alike: 'military expeditions of organized pillage . . .' (1941:541). Anthropologists are familiar with this category under the generic term of raiding. But Malinowski collates it with modern inter nation state warfare under the rubric of politically regulated violence, because political organization and large-scale military ends are, in his opinion, coextensive. Raiding at the 'lower levels of culture' is for him 'a type of man hunting sport'; and he explicitly denies that primitive and semi-primitive peoples can ever undertake raids for economic motives. It is for this reason that he eliminates even the largest and most planned of head hunting raids from his category of politically significant forms of conflict, yet includes, as proximate to warfare, the 'organized robbery' indulged in by the majority of nomadic pastoralists. Now, one of the points that I intend to make in the course of this book, and particularly in the last chapter, is that the reverse of what Malinowski says is nearer to reality: in as far as raiding can be ascribed to purely economic motives, it may be said to constitute an oecological necessity in conditions of scarcity and is relatively free of political overtones, for in this type of raiding the aggressors seek to empower themselves of a material prize (e.g. flocks) which they carry off to their home territory to enjoy; military defeat of a 'foreign' enemy and organized political dominance by enduring territorial occupation are superfluous and unpracticable in the pastoral situation. I shall show, on the contrary, that apparently gratuitous violence, raiding or homicide for 'glory' and trophies of little material value, or to avenge insult and injury with no goals of an economic nature, are more akin to the sphere of 'policy' to which Malinowski, in my view mistakenly, imputes raiding.

However, at this juncture it is sufficient to register disagreement with Malinowski's typology for two reasons: firstly, it displays a notable lack of precision in all but the last two categories which deal with 'political' phenomena. By providing four categories to Middleton and Tait's one at the bottom of the scale, Malinowski attempts to refine his concepts but is prevented from going very far by his vague phraseology and use of terms. Secondly, the distinction he makes between politically motivated hostilities and other types of fighting, in which the political element is absent, is superficial and misleading. For whereas, on the one hand, he makes the implicit assumption that primitive society exists beyond the pale of political action, he labels, on the other hand, as 'political' certain patterns of aggressive behaviour— like some forms of raiding—which in reality have little or no political content.

Whereas Middleton and Tait, and Hartley, after a short skirmish with the difficulties of definition, surrender to the forces of confusion and indifference, Malinowski has endeavoured to bring order to the concept of violence, but fails. Alvin Johnson, in his article on 'War' in the *Encyclopedia of Social Sciences*, states that 'The term war is generally applied to armed conflict between population groups conceived of as organic unities, such as races or tribes, states or lesser geographic units, religious or political parties, economic classes. Armed conflict between states that legally enjoy complete and unlimited sovereignty is in modern thought treated as typically war.' This concentration on the integrity of the group proves, however, somewhat abortive, since Johnson is forced to admit that, if this is regarded as the principal criterion, 'there are numberless boarderline cases often treated essentially as war' (1935:331).

Johnson was writing in 1935. Fifteen years later the definitional controversy had made little headway and Joseph Schneider felt bound to concede in the first lines of a 'note' in the *American Sociological Review* that 'The literature of primitive warfare is acknowledged as being in an unsatisfactory state' (1950:772). One of the causes of this he ascribes to 'the tendency to classify under primitive war all forms of group sanctioned violence whether the fighting can be properly called war or not. The fact that blood vengeance is nearly everywhere an attribute of primitive fighting has encouraged the view that fighting within the group cannot be distinguished from fighting between groups . . . no criteria are available by which crime and punishment may be distinguished from war' (1950:772). It is clear from what follows that by blood vengeance Schneider means any form of publicly recognized and accepted physically violent reaction in retaliation for a wrong inflicted in the absence of more sophisticated penal institutions and a means to enforce them. For Schneider there is only one way out of the terminological *impasse* created by this ubiquity of 'retaliation or self-help' 'in cultures where there exist scant forms of public justice': 'whether one method of redress is called punishment and another war depends upon the social unit of classification employed as basic or primary' (1950:774).

This insistence upon the definition of the social units involved provides the *Leitmotiv* of all the attempts at the construction of a typology of violence quoted above. Whatever the other criteria taken into consideration a dilemma is encountered when a hard and fast rule is sought to distinguish the level at which feud becomes war and *vice versa*. Reliance on absolute numbers of combatants implicated on either side is obviously far too arbitrary. Malinowski circumvents the problem by referring to the criterion of political independence as a necessary prerequisite for war. But he proposes no means of establishing whether a given group can be considered totally independent or not. Nineteenth-century Cyrenaican Bedouin tribes paid tribute to the Sublime Porte and were nominally subjects of the Ottoman Empire. By absolute standards they were not politically independent. But this did not prevent the occurrence of large scale hostilities on an intertribal basis that tribesmen themselves do not hesitate to qualify as war (Peters 1967:269). Johnson, with certain misgivings, it is true, postulates that war occurs between 'organic units'. Schneider refuses to commit himself by identifying any particular type of unit. Middleton and Tait, together with Hartley, on the other hand, emphatically opt for the 'jural community' beyond and outside which they regard any fighting as warfare.

(2) ACCESSIBILITY TO COMPROMISE AND THE 'FINITE' FEUD

I have already mentioned that Middleton and Tait's definition of the jural community is derived from Evans-Pritchard's use of the term in his book *The Nuer*. The phrase describes the maximal group within which there exist both an obligation to bring fighting to a close by peaceful settlement and machinery to achieve such a conclusion; the group is furthermore identical with that within which compensation or blood money is paid and accepted for *all* torts and injuries (except those occurring within the nuclear family and between certain very close relatives).[2] All definitions are to some extent arbitrary, and, at first sight, the acceptance of mediation and the principle of compensation would appear as good criteria as any by which to draw a necessarily arbitrary line between feud and warfare. Nor was Evans-Pritchard the first author to do so. More than thirty years before the publication of *The Nuer* Simmel had emphasized this aspect of conflict: 'In sharp contrast to the termination of conflict through victory is its end in compromise. In a classification of conflicts one of the most important characteristics is their intrinsic accessibility or inaccessibility to such ending' (1966:114).

Simmel unfortunately does not pursue this remark. Although he discusses the nature of compromise at length and even goes so far as to call it 'eine der grössten Erfindungen der Menschheit', he shows reticence in suggesting how accessibility or inaccessibility to compromise could be used in practice for the classification of conflicts. The incompleteness of Simmel's argument is especially vexatious when viewed in the light of certain ethnographic facts. For Lewis, in his excellent account of arid zone pastoralists in the Horn of Africa, gives the following information: 'Since all Somali recognize the payment of compensation for injuries all disputes at every level of segmentation can be composed.' In Simmel's terms, since in this case *all* conflict is accessible to compromise, no classification is possible on this basis. Indeed, Lewis is quite unambiguous: 'It is not therefore useful to make a rigorous sociological distinction between war and feud; and I use these terms here in much the same sense speaking rather of war, however, when hostilities are general and involve large

[2] Cf. p. 29.

groups' (1961:242). And the terminological fancy of the anthropologist is sustained by that of the people he is studying, for the Somali themselves 'do not make any rigorous distinction between "war" between large groups structurally distant, and "feud" between small closely related lineages' (1961:248).

Quite contrary evidence can, however, be produced for other parts of the Middle East. Dr. Kadhim, an Iraqi jurist, has, for example, studied a series of documents recording the norms of tribal law in different parts of Iraq that were drawn up by tribal councils in 1937 and have lain untouched ever since in the archives of the Ministry of the Interior in Baghdad. The documents specify the amount and type (whether money, animals, women etc.) of compensation to be paid to effect the conclusion of different categories of conflict. But no compensation is due in cases of *damdoum*, that is an inter-tribal affray in which fighting in general and casualties on both sides are numerous but not necessarily equal in number and gravity (Kadhim 1957:81). Kennett alludes to the same practice among Sinai and Arabian tribes who recognize what he calls a 'state of war' during which no compensation can be claimed for deaths caused by the enemy (Kennett 1925:51).

If all Somali conflicts are, in the final analysis, accessible to compromise, this is certainly not the impression given by the bulk of ethnographic literature on the Mediterranean and the Middle East. This disparity between Somali practice and that of other tribal peoples in the area could to a certain extent be ascribed to the marginal geographical situation of Somaliland in relation to the rest of the Middle East and its cultural prolongation westward into the Mediterranean. Nonetheless, the Somali are ardent and, sporadically, fanatical Muslims[3] and have always remained in close cultural and commercial contact with southern Arabia whence their major clans trace descent. Moreover, tribal peoples in the interior of the African continent having, unlike

[3] An unusually strict adherence to the norms of the *sharī'a*—which in principle forbids all armed conflict within the *umma* or Muslim community—were it proved, might just account for the widespread acceptance of compensation in Somaliland, if this were seen by the tribesmen as a compromise with Muslim precepts enjoining non-violence. But this seems improbable, as on other points of Islamic law—such as the legal right of women to inherit—the Somali are as irreverent as other Muslim tribal peoples in the Middle East.

the Somali, until recently suffered very little interference from without, follow, with no exception that I am aware of, the same principle of ignoring the payment of compensation in battle at a high level of segmentation, as described by Kadhim and Kennett. Lewis' information is, then, inexplicably atypical.

This enigma apart, however, the criterion of accessibility to compromise and its concomitants, in manifestations of violence among tribal peoples, of arbitration and compensation, to distinguish between feud and warfare, is not entirely satisfactory for one further reason: throughout the literature on the feud in the Mediterranean and the Middle East it is affirmed that in all circumstances in which compensation is a recognized means of bringing about a reconciliation between the offended party and the offenders, retaliation in kind is an acceptable and frequently recommended alternative. Kadhim, for instance, whilst conceding that the majority of conflicts are brought to a peaceful settlement, nonetheless insists that 'It must be borne in mind that the prevailing custom among the tribes is "a soul for a soul" or, sometimes, "souls for a soul". The tribesman considers it his first duty to take revenge.' But 'prominent men on both sides' intervene 'to establish peace; and the tribesman tries to escape from being forced to accept compensation, so that he can vaunt his pride by taking his revenge and killing the offender or any man of his tribe or sub-tribe as the case may be' (1957:74). Similarly, Peters states that among the camel herding Bedouin of Cyrenaica compensation for a homicide should ideally be refused by the victim's close agnates, who should exact vengeance (1951:302). From Albania on the opposite shore of the Mediterranean it is reported that only 'On rare occasions the aggressors might confess their guilt and the aggrieved forgo their pound of flesh for an indemnity in cash or kind' (Amery 1948:8). Hardy, who travelled within the last ten years in the Syrian desert, found that the acceptance of compensation in lieu of vengeance 'is still . . . regarded as dishonourable' (Hardy 1963:22), although the area is now well policed and provided with modern courts. One of the most remarkable aspects of the whole vengeance complex is the high degree of consistency, throughout the regions in which it is practised, of beliefs relative to talion and even the vocabulary used to describe them, for sentiments identical to those of the Syrian Bedouin were voiced in nineteenth-century

Albania: 'Bei den Mirediten und Pulati wäre es sogar schimp-flich, seine Rache zu verkaufen' (Gopčević 1881:71).

To resume my objections to the criteria for distinguishing be-tween feud and war proposed by Evans-Pritchard, Simmel and others of like persuasion: in the first place, there is at least one well attested case of compensation being payable at *all* levels within the same society in spite of marked inner divisions between tribes, sub-tribes and clans. The different sections of this society do not refrain from indulging in unmitigated physical violence with each other. Since the numerous casualties on either side can always be accounted for by the payment of blood money, this is not a universally valid test of where war begins and feud ends. In the second place, talion is in most cases expressly preferred to the acceptance of compensation, which fact implies that, although compromise may conclude even a majority of conflicts, the ideology behind compensation is in reality vengeance. In illustration of this can be cited the Cyrenaican Bedouin dictum that a horse bought with blood money will be used to ride when 'bringing vengeance' (Peters 1951:303). In other words, com-pensation is not a substitute but a palliative.

In order to give the *coup de grâce* to the criterion of accessi-bility to compromise as indicative of a real distinction between feud and warfare, it should be sufficient to enlarge upon this last point. Not only is the ultimate exaction of vengeance the ideal behind the acceptance of compensation, but there appears to exist enough evidence to suggest moreover that this also con-stitutes actual practice.

Ever since Evans-Pritchard's remark in *The Nuer* to the effect that 'corporate life is incompatible with a state of feud' (1940:156) a protracted controversy has raged among social anthropologists as to whether or not the feud can ever be con-cluded other than by extermination of one of the parties. Evans-Pritchard's words seem to have been taken too literally at times and not enough attention has been paid to an equally telling statement made two pages earlier in the same book: 'All Nuer recognize that in spite of payments and sacrifices a feud goes on for ever, for the dead man's kin never cease "to have war in their hearts"' (1940:154). I shall enter into the intricacies of the debate that arose from these two apparently contradictory positions in the next chapter. For the present moment I shall limit myself to showing briefly from the ethnographic facts that neither ceremonial reconciliation after the exaction of vengeance nor peaceful settlement sanctioned by compensation can be truly said to terminate a violent episode whether by talion or by compromise. If this can be satisfactorily proven, *none* of the criteria for the classification of conflicts so far cited can be said to be individually valid.

Peters, who is perhaps the most cogent champion of the 'interminable' feud, makes the assertion that payment of compensation among the Bedouin of Cyrenaica can prevent the wreaking of immediate vengeance, but in no way precludes further homicide when the agnates of the dead man, who have allowed themselves to be bought, finally 'awake' to vengeance. A peace settled with *diya* (blood money) is, in Peters' belief, never more than temporary (Peters 1951:303).

Peter Lienhardt, in a doctoral thesis entitled *Shaikhdoms of Eastern Arabia*, writes similarly that in this area blood money 'does not necessarily end a feud, but is considered a worthwhile step towards a settlement' (1957:159).

After a strong panegyric of the rationalism and good sense of Albanian customary law dealing with homicide, the celebrated British traveller Miss Mary Durham, who spent many years of her life among tribal peoples in the Balkans, deplores that:

Even the laws of Lek[4] are not always obeyed in Nikaj [a district of north Albania]. In a recent case the feud had ceased for years. And when the son of the man who had ended it grew to be fifteen years old and was now head of the family, he declared that as the honour of the family had been sold when he was an infant, he was not bound by the oath [to keep the peace], so went forth with his gun and shot a man of the other house. And the feud began again (1909:199).

In a later version of the same story Miss Durham adds, in a more romantic vein, that the young man,

[4] Lek Dukagjini, a fifteenth-century older contemporary of Skanderbeg, who is credited with the reform of the body of Albanian customary law that, until the foundation of the second Republic in 1945, constituted the only repository of legal knowledge in the mountainous north of the country.

according to the ideas of the land, [was] sent out by his mother on the deadly errand. She knows she may lose her son . . . and be left lonely and destitute. But the soul of her dead husband has cried to her night after night. Blood-gelt gives it no peace. Blood alone can do that, and her son must go out to slay or be slain for his father's sake (1928:164).

The Reverend Henry Fanshawe Tozer, another upstanding British observer of imperial times, reports a tale told him by a Dr. Finzi, secretary to the Prince of Mirditë in the Albanian mountains, the grisliness of which is by no means atypical of the hundreds that make the nineteenth-century literature on the Balkans such entertaining reading:

Fifty years ago [*circa* 1820] two men of this country quarrelled and fought so desperately, that both of them died of the wounds they received. Time rolled on, until it might have been thought that the event had been forgotten. But it had happened that as they lay wounded on the ground, one of them had managed to deal the other a blow over the head, which caused him to die first. The recollection of this circumstance had been preserved, and only the other day a descendant of the one who had died first presented himself before a descendant of the other and reminded him of the fact, threatening at the same time to burn his whole village unless he gave him one hundred goats by way of satisfaction. The Prince heard of the affair; and, sending for the man, persuaded him to delay his vengeance; but beyond this he could not proceed, for the laws of blood are superior to every other law. Thus the matter stood at the time of our visit (1869:310).

European historical texts reveal numerous examples of old feuds that have been composed through arbitration and compensation but then revived. One such case is to be found in Gregory of Tours' *History of the Franks*. The original feud and its composition are described in chapter 47 of the Seventh Book. In the Ninth Book (chapter 19) one of the principals in the earlier conflict, Sichar, and the son, Chramnesind, of one of Sichar's murdered enemies have become bosom friends and are drinking together:

But Sichar, letting the wine go to his head, kept making boast-
ful remarks against Chramnesind, and is reported at last to
have said: 'Sweet brother, thou owest me great thanks for the
slaying of thy relations; for the composition made to thee for
their death hath caused gold and silver to abound in thy house.
But for this cause, which stabilished thee not a little, thou wert
this day poor and destitute.' Chramnesind heard these words
with bitterness of heart, and said within himself: 'If I avenge
not the death of my kinsmen, I deserve to lose the name of
man, and to be called weak woman.' And straightway he put
out the lights and cleft the head of Sichar with his dagger
(Gregory of Tours 192:387).

With reference to this particular episode, the historian, J. M.
Wallace-Hadrill, has commented that the renewal of dormant
violence is a pattern familiar in the literature of the period, and
'To work through the seven volumes of the *Scriptores Rerum
Merovingicarum* is to be made aware that feuds are like vol-
canoes: A few are in eruption, others are extinct, but most are
content to rumble now and again and leave us guessing'
(Wallace-Hadrill 1962:143).

For the last instance of how neither vengeance nor compensation can truly conclude a feud, I return to the field of social
anthropology. Lewis relates the case of two sons of brothers who
were working in a field in Somaliland:

One took up a cudgel to kill a rodent but the other accidentally
caught his arm deflecting the blow upon himself and received
an injury from which he subsequently died. Both men belonged
to the same *jiffo*[5]—paying group and compensation valued at
thirty-six camels was gathered by the group and given to the
children of the deceased . . . Thus the matter appeared to be
successfully composed and forgotten. But three years later . . .

[5] *jiffo*: a type of compensation mainly paid by and accorded to close
agnates. The *jiffo*-paying group is a situational core of the more com-
prehensive *dia*-paying group, which among the Somali constitutes the
basic solidarity unit beyond the minimal lineage. Cf. p. 110 for examples
from other societies of analogous types of compensation the effect of which
is to accentuate the discreteness of component lineages within the basic
solidarity unit.

this accidental death was being represented as deliberate murder by the deceased's brother, and tension was mounting between the immediate kin of the two cousins.

And Lewis remarks: '... as this case illustrates although dia-paying solidarity inclines disputants to make peace and often forces them to do so, it does not necessarily lead to the complete dispersal of hostility and resentment' (1961:245–6).

The preceding examples show that although there may exist, in Middleton and Tait's words, 'machinery' to achieve a peaceful settlement in the majority of what, for the sake of convenience, I shall for the moment call 'feuding' societies, it is difficult to prove that the parties to a hostile relationship can be either physically or morally 'obliged' to avail themselves of this machinery. Nor is it certain that such an obligation would of necessity also entail compulsion to abide by the verdict. Recourse to arbitration, pay-ment and acceptance of compensation may arrest a feud in cer-tain circumstances, but will not 'conclude' it, as Middleton and Tait maintain. Indeed, there are good grounds for the belief, as I shall demonstrate presently in my discussion of Peters' work, that feuds are by definition eternal.

One of the reasons for the persistence of attitudes akin to those displayed by Middleton and Tait may lie in a fundamental trait of human thought. The mind, as Simmel has pointed out, imposes a teleologically oriented structure upon perception, so that order is conceived of as an evolution out of chaos and movement as a development out of rest. '... because of the way in which our conceptual categories happen to function, we think of the undif-ferentiated state as of the first. That is, our need for explanation requires us to derive variety from unity much more than *vice versa*' (1966:108).

I would argue that Middleton and Tait's postulate that the provision of machinery for its conclusion must enter into a valid definition of the feud is the involuntary consequence of this type of thought pattern. Their error arises out of the same kind of process that induced Talcott Parsons to lay an exaggerated emphasis upon 'those elements of social structures that assure their maintenance' (Coser 1965:21). With a functionalist philo-sophy as his point of departure, he could hardly do otherwise but view conflict as disruptive, dissociating and dysfunctional, for functionalism is essentially the induction of a self-buttressing system of social order out of a mass of chaotic and self-contradictory social facts. Similarly, Middleton and Tait seem to make the implicit assumption that a society and the internal peace they regard as necessary for its continued existence are the end product of an evolutive process tending towards the progressive resolution and elimination of violent confusion. For them the word society implies a predominance of peace over conflict. Yet, as Simmel says, there is no reason why either should be assumed to have priority over the other. Peace and conflict together create an unending rhythmic alternation through time. 'Both in the succession and in the simultaneity of social life, the two are so interwoven that in every state of peace the conditions of future conflict, and in every conflict the conditions of future peace, are formed' (1966:109). Middleton and Tait perceive the necessity and means of achieving peace, but they neglect the fact that the social rigidity which is a frequent result of peace itself may, in certain conditions, become intolerable and prove the source of renewed conflict.

If, instead of exclusive concentration on absolute criteria (like machinery for arbitration, the acceptance of compensation and accessibility to compromise) which all stress the supposedly chronologically finite nature of feud, prominence could be given to the processual aspect that comes out so forcefully in the examples given above, it might be possible to formulate a typology of violence that would take into account all three of the critical factors that I have been careful to keep conceptually distinct in the discussion so far: (1) the size and structure of the units involved; (2) the possibility of achieving (temporary) reconciliation; (3) the continuation of serial killings or acts of outrage long after the principals are dead.

(3) THE CYRENAICAN SOLUTION

Such a definition of feud has been elaborated by Peters in the context of the material he gathered during fieldwork among the Bedouin of Cyrenaica. His method of proceeding was not to allow himself to be shackled by a list of arbitrary criteria which could be applied in any given instance to provide the cut and dried answer

whether or not the case in question was one of feud or, alternatively, something else (such as vengeance, warfare or raiding).
Instead, he took as his point of departure the observed fact that
the vast majority of conflicts of any type outside the nuclear
family sooner or later invariably resulted in one of two consequences: either the two parties had recourse to geographical
separation and ceased to live within a range at which the conflict could be daily pursued, or else one of the two parties resorted
to physical violence against the other. As the Bedouin all carry
rifles, homicide was the most frequent outcome of the latter course
of action. But homicide itself was an inexorable prelude to fission
for the following reasons: as *all* Cyrenaican Bedouin think of
themselves as of 'one womb', that is descended from a single
apical ancestress (Peters 1960:29), they are *all* related. Since
residence is also in the normal course of events genealogically
defined, save in exceptional circumstances, a man will live and
herd with his closest agnates. The effect of this territorial distribution is that the resolution of conflict through one of the parties
moving away from the other is strictly equivalent to genealogical
segmentation,[6] since the two parties would not have lived in
proximity in the first place had they not been genealogically proximate. However, vested interests in possessing a share of the *watan*
(1967:262) or home territory (with watering points, arable and
pasture land) of the section into which one is born are such that
segmentation, that is abandonment of their birthright by one of

[6] I am aware of the distinction frequently made in anthropological kinship literature between segmentation and fission which postulates the
abandonment of any notion of corporate identity by the sections concerned
as a necessary condition for the latter, whereas the former is considered
to apply in cases where the 'group merely divides in certain contexts but
retains its corporate identity in others' (Middleton and Tait 1958:7–8).
Although both processes may occur in the Mediterranean and Middle
Eastern segmentary lineage societies that I mention in the course of this
book, the distinction is of little relevance to the discussion of feud in the
area. For segmentation and fission are both terms which describe the
ramification of political relations between groups within a framework of
reference provided exclusively by the notion of kinship. Since it is my
object in the next chapter to show that kinship is only one among a
number of pertinent factors acting as incentives to the formation of
alliances and the dissociation of groups, a distinction between the words
segmentation and fission would serve no useful purpose in the present
context. I shall therefore use the two terms indifferently.

the two parties, is not a course of action upon which any Bedouin would enter lightly. Thus the motives for separation have to be very strong indeed if segmentation does in fact take place. The only motive of sufficient force is homicide—whether threatened, supputed, actual or of generations past is, as Peters shows, almost totally irrelevant as long as it serves to promote the end in view, which is the creation or confirmation of genealogical distance between the parties.

Observing, then, that all conflict was ultimately expressed in terms of homicide and that the Bedouin referred to a variety of conceptually distinct types of homicide when presenting the model they themselves hold of inter-group relations, Peters came to the conclusion that homicide might be visualized as a kind of cursor sliding up and down the scale of genealogical history:[7] at whatever date the cursor is stopped there can be read off a level of segmentation, the names of persons involved, a well defined list of stereotyped reactions to homicide and, at the levels at which they exist, the modalities of composition and compensation or the type, rules and extent of endemic inter-group hostilities. This image is not only valid for a given homicide at a given moment in the development of a given genealogical framework, but if the cursor is slid down the scale to a later date the information that can be read off at that point indicates the effects that the same homicide would continue to have at a later point in time.

By regarding homicide as an historical fact that becomes distorted by distance and its passage through time, Peters is able to obviate the rigidity imposed by the chronologically finite criteria that others have used to construct a typology of violence. For, in his scheme, what may have initially been accepted as an accidental death can quite well blossom after a generation or two in the minds of the victim's kin into a deliberately gory atrocity seen as the first step in an eternal feud. Alternatively, if it is thought by the kinsmen of both the victim and the offender that the interests of both sides will be best served by mutual co-operation, the accidental nature of the death will be emphasized and the incident passed over with the minimum of commotion, though not forgotten. Peters demonstrates that it is consequently rather inappropriate to speak of vengeance killing, feud, raiding and warfare as

[7] The image is my own.

separate categories of violence (1967:275 *et passim*), since an unintentional wound inflicted, whilst harvesting, by a brother in one generation may be retaliated for by a homicide between first cousins, which is then composed and 'forgotten', a generation later; the same homicide may subsequently serve after forty years as the pretext for fission and the initiation of sporadic but lasting hostilities between two groups of descendants of third cousins.

In the Middleton–Tait conspectus, the homicide between first cousins is a 'feud', because it is accessible to compromise and can be 'concluded' thanks to the peace-making activities of arbitrators and the recognition of compensation as a substitute value for the life taken. The same criteria applied at a subsequent point in time give somewhat different results. If in a later generation the kinsmen of the deceased choose to repudiate the reconciliation negotiated by their forbears and take 'revenge' on the pretext that the compensation received was insufficient and the decision of those responsible for its acceptance degrading, the same homicide, seen as an ill-starred episode inaugurating a chain of killings that has no ending except in the total extermination of one of the groups, is liable to two contrary interpretations according to the light in which it is examined: either it must be regarded as conceptually unconnected with the acts of violence that follow, or else it necessarily qualifies, in terms of the same typology, as an act of 'warfare'. As the second suggestion is manifestly ludicrous, it may be hoped that the other alternative corresponds with the facts. Unfortunately, it does not, for the Bedouin speak of the original homicide as a 'debt' and vengeance, though it be 'brought' generations later and despite prior acceptance of blood money by the victim's group, is commonly said to constitute 'a redemption of the debt' (Peters 1951:iii). The initial homicide and the serial killings that follow are seen by the Bedouin as events logically connected. Viewed in this light the Middleton–Tait definition is quite inept, since it ignores the dimension of time.

The elements for this kind of analysis have always existed in the literature. The examples from Albania and Somaliland quoted above are ample proof of this and also the fact that the phenomenon does not occur only in Cyrenaica. But no one before Peters had taken the trouble to determine the parameters of a model that would accommodate all the different aspects of violence within a single analytical framework. It is Peters' merit to have shaken himself free from the criteria-bound definitions of feud that had, on the one hand, so restricted certain of his colleagues and, on the other, encouraged the type of definitional anarchy displayed by Lewis in his treatment of the Somali material.

Peters' analysis of the mechanisms of conflict, whilst clearing the structural ground, nonetheless left him to face the issues of nomenclature, that is, of attaching the labels vengeance, feud and warfare[8] to categories of social facts. This amounted to establishing a satisfactory shorthand usage in order to avoid the necessity of cumbersome repetition. The solution he adopted, for Cyrenaica at least, was to base his nomenclature quite simply on an examination of the categories employed by the Bedouin who *themselves* see the nine noble tribes[9] as split at three major levels of segmentation. Each tribe has primary, secondary and tertiary sections in numbers varying according to the birth-rate and the carrying capacity of the land. Relations of hostility between groups are conceived of as quite different in quality to those within groups. Thus the phrase 'to redeem the debt' referred to above is typical of relations between secondary sections but is not used between or within tertiary sections of the same secondary section. A homicide committed by a member of one tertiary section against a member of another collateral section of the same order of segmentation is described by the Arabic word for vengeance, *thār*. Homicide within the tertiary section has no specific name,[10] because ideally it should never happen. Consequently, no recognized means of obtaining redress exists at this level, although 'A reprisal exacted in hot blood is always a possibility, but this is not referred to as *thār*, vengeance. Even if, at a later date, the closest kinsmen of the victim should slay the offender, the act would not be referred to as *thār* and any connection with earlier homicides would be denied' (Peters 1967:263).

[8] He omits nearly all mention of raiding, probably because he considers that the Bedouin of Cyrenaica do not indulge in it.

[9] There exist also a number of client tribes and grafted on sections, the members of which are regarded by 'noble' tribesmen as second-class citizens.

[10] If pressed to, however, the Bedouin will obliquely refer to it as *fitna*, that is, civil war, disturbance, sin or calamity (Peters 1951:263; 1967: 264, 269).

A 'state of feud', on the other hand, is preliminarily defined by Peters as

> a set of relationships between two tribal [secondary] groups which are characterized by hostility whenever two or more of their members meet. These hostilities are of a sort that cannot be terminated; feud is not a matter of a group indulging in hostilities here at one moment and there the next, but a sequence of hostilities which, as far as the contemporary Bedouin are concerned at least, know no beginning and are insoluble (1967:262).

> It is a form of behaviour associated with a specific structural order, and it is as persistent as the structural order itself; in this sense it is eternal (1967:268).

Whereas vengeance killing between collateral tertiary sections can, after an appropriate lapse of time, if the deaths incurred are thought to have cancelled each other out, be brought to a temporary halt by attendance at a ritual meal shared by the groups concerned and followed by communal prayers, or, alternatively, if a life remains outstanding, the promise to pay compensation, in the feud no quarter or respite is ever given or accepted (1967:265).

Actual contact between collateral primary sections of the same tribe are rare, because they occupy geographically distant territories. If a homicide does occur between two such sections, only a small scale raid is undertaken against the offender's own camp by a group recruited from the victim's kinsmen, for although a logical conclusion of the tendency to structural limitation of violence in Cyrenaica would be the possibility of warfare between primary sections, the Bedouin recognize the destructive potential of such action and restrict warfare to inter-tribal relations (Peters 1967:269).

In short, Peters' terminology relies upon a single criterion to differentiate vengeance killing, feud and warfare: the criterion of levels of segmentation. As long as homicide within the tertiary section does not lead to fission it is classified as an accident and has no precise name.[11] If homicide precipitates fission in the tertiary

[11] See note 10, p. 21.

section or occurs between tertiary sections, it is known as vengeance killing. Homicide between tertiary sections that results in the creation of two separate secondary sections or homicide between secondary sections qualifies as feud. Hostilities between tribes can only be warfare.

By concentrating on the structural aspects of homicide as reflected in inter-group relationships, Peters has managed to incorporate into his typology of violence the three factors that I enumerated prior to discussing his contribution, that is

(1) the size and structure of the units involved;
(2) the possibility of achieving (temporary) reconciliation;
(3) continued resort to violence after the principals are dead.

Peters is the only author to have succeeded in formulating a definition of the feud and ancillary types of conflict which synthesizes *all* the variables alluded to by others. But, although (or precisely because) it is based on Bedouin concepts, this is only a model, and, as he confirms in the second half of his 1967 article on 'Some structural aspects of the feud . . .', 'there is a far greater range of possible consequences to a homicide than those summarized' in the paradigm of violence he initially presents.[12] Some of these I shall examine in the next chapter.

(4) VIOLENCE AND POLITICAL STRUCTURE

Peters' perception of the feud as 'a set of relationships' (1967:262) and its importance as an outward sign of imminent fission among the Bedouin will also provide the germ of much of what I have to say in later chapters on the ritual nature of conflict regarded as a qualification for leadership in unstratified societies. But his ascription of the terms vengeance killing, feud and warfare to certain categories of physical violence recognized by the Bedouin themselves is so narrowly dependent on conditions prevalent in that

[12] Peters calculates that the Bedouin model in fact only accounts for roughly one half of all homicides committed in the Cyrenaican *barr*. The other 50 per cent are treated by the Bedouin as 'special cases', because they countervene the postulates of their own *conscious* structural model of the society in which they live. For a discussion of the 'unsegmentary behaviour' implied by the inability of the Bedouin model to accommodate a number of traits to be observed in the reality of Bedouin social life cf. p. 54 ff.

society that it is not possible to claim a wider validity for his typo-logy. In fact, the only tangible result that can be said to have emerged from this whole inquiry into what other authors have written on the nomenclature of violence is a considerable measure of doubt as to whether the construction of a universally valid typology possessing any degree of precision is at all feasible.

Yet this conclusion compels retreat into vast and unprofitable generalizations of the type dear to Middleton and Tait, for whom all violence in acephalous societies may be classified under the undifferentiated heading of 'self-help'. This sort of thinking is merely an evasion of the definitional problem. The difficulty, as I see it, is somehow to formulate a typology which will be simul-taneously both specific and flexible enough to allow, on the one hand, for the degree of precision reached by Peters in his treat-ment of the Cyrenaican material and, on the other, to cater also for the analysis of types of self-help in societies that are neither segmentary nor pastoral.

As definitions are necessarily arbitrary, their usefulness is on the whole strictly limited to the argument in the context of which they are elaborated. Their validity in other contexts is thus directly proportional to the range of the argument to support which they were originally conceived. The validity of the definitions that I am about to propose is consequently a function of the cogency and scope of my main line of argument: if credence is given to my principal contentions as regards the nature of feud *in general*, my typology of violence may, with some reservations, be accepted as universally valid. The bare bones of my argument are set out below. A detailed discussion of the same theme will follow in chapters IV and V.

(a) The argument

Like Peters, I regard feud as a *relationship* between the feuding parties. But since 'feud' among the Cyrenaican Bedouin is con-fined to relations between groups at the same level of segmenta-tion, there is an implicit and possibly unintentional emphasis in Peters' analysis on the egalitarian nature of relationships expressed in feud, for feud constitutes not only a relationship between equals, but also—paradoxically—a means of affirming authority in the absence of an institutionalized power structure conceived to this end. Feuding societies are everywhere character- ized by a fiercely egalitarian outlook. Yet the object of feud is to acquire a position of authority by worsting the adversary and commanding his submission. The relationships created and main- tained through feud are thus fundamentally ambiguous. But the presence side by side in the feud of elements as disparate as equality and hierarchy is not as contradictory as it might at first seem. Some insight into the logic behind this situation may be gained from an analysis of the structural implications of the notion of relationship itself.

Few social theorists would contest the statement that a relation- ship cannot be maintained unless some form of communi- cation, that is transaction, takes place between the two parties. Transaction implies interaction. A complete transaction comprises two stages, each (in the etymological sense) a *trans*-action in itself: one party proposes, the other reacts. For this reason a transaction cannot be initiated simultaneously in both directions at once without there resulting confusion and a subsequent loss of com- munication. Each stage must be followed by a lapse of time, however short, to allow the receiving party to assimilate the infor- mation transmitted, so that this information can be taken into account to modify the reciprocal *trans*-action. Thus, although the positions occupied by the two parties to a relationship may appear, over a long period marked by a series of interconnected complete transactions, to remain relatively stable *vis-à-vis* each other, at any given moment in time one of the two parties is always in possession of a greater value than the other. The word 'value' stands here as an abstraction for whatever objects or quan- tities change hands in the course of a single *trans*-action. In the present context it is exactly synonymous with 'information'.

The conclusion that I wish to draw from this short excursus is that, if it is accepted that feud constitutes a relationship, then a feud may also be regarded as a series of transactions. The value transmitted by one party to the other in the course of this series is negative: death. It follows that the party to the transaction which at any given moment has managed to impart more of this value than it has to date received is in a more advantageous position. In more concrete terms: the party in a feud which has inflicted more deaths than it has received is 'winning'.

The comparison between feuds and games may be taken further. Competitive games have the following salient characteristics: the play is initiated from a situation in which both sides enjoy rough equality of status, skill, equipment and numbers, for if the pre-play situation is one of inequality, one of the sides will refuse to compete for fear of the result resembling a massacre rather than defeat; competitors seek dominance, but not extermination of the adversary; a game ending in the defeat of one side frequently leads to a 'return match' to afford the loser a chance to 'equalize'; games are played according to a set of rules.

If the word 'feud' is substituted in this list for the word 'game', the sense is but little changed, and all the characteristics attributed to games could well apply to, for instance, the Cyrenaican feud: equality of status, skill, equipment and numbers is provided for by the segmentary restriction of feuding to relations between collateral secondary sections, since hostilities between two groups of different orders would invariably result in the defeat of the one endowed with a smaller fighting potential; feuds result in a series of situations of temporary dominance that last until a fresh killing (return match) again tips the scales; lastly, the manner in which feuds are prosecuted is, as will be seen, rigidly prescribed (rules), and there always exists an inventory of provocative 'fouls' that can be appealed to if it is desired to change the nature of the contest from that of a game to that of a more serious encounter with less inhibiting rules.

If feuds resemble games so closely, it is reasonable to assume that the objectives of both are also analogous. The primary reason for playing games is, by winning, to gain honour and prestige which may be converted into social advantage in other fields. Once victory has been achieved, the identity of the adversary may be forgotten: the victory as such is more often exploited than the defeat of a given player. Similarly, the reason for indulging in feuding relations is not so much the desire to inflict a loss on a given section, as to use this victory to enhance individual and group prestige within the home community and in the eyes of the world. The prestige thus acquired is the foremost ingredient of leadership in a situation in which egalitarian ideals and a lack of opportunities for economic differentiation prevail.

Feuding relations may thus be seen as the raw material which provides the foundations of internal political hierarchy and serves to engender external ties of temporary dominance. It is this political factor that I propose to use as the ultimate criterion to distinguish, within the general category of self-help, between feud and vengeance killing.

(b) *The typology*

Politics is essentially a matter of the manipulation of the relationships between *groups*, for even if the manipulators are individuals, they can achieve nothing without the support of numbers. If feud is a means to political ends, the term feud must, then, necessarily refer to, among other things, a means of recruiting personnel to carry on the feud: it is an intrinsically collective phenomenon.

Vengeance killing, on the other hand, is, in the opinion of the only anthropologist who has thought it necessary to define the term, characterized by a total absence of any reference to collective solidarity. I submit, therefore, that perhaps the simplest way to draw the line between feud and vengeance killing is to examine the significance of the collective factor in cases of physical violence.

The anthropologist alluded to in the preceding paragraph is Fredrik Barth who, in his book on *Socal organization in southern Kurdistan*, affirms that in the Kurdish areas of northern Iraq 'the blood feud is not found' (1953:73), though vengeance killing is. In making this statement Barth had in mind the description of the blood feud 'in its most characteristic form' as reported by Nadel from the Nuba Hills of the Anglo-Egyptian Sudan (Nadel 1947:151). I shall use Nadel's account of the Nuba blood feud as a point of departure in the discussion which follows of the distinctions that I myself draw between vengeance killing, feud, raiding and warfare.

The crucial traits of the blood feud as enumerated by Nadel are:
    (1) collective responsibility of all members of a group for the behaviour of one of its members;
    (2) collective duty of all members of the injured group to avenge this injury;
    (3) retaliation governed by considerations of equality, or,

subsidiarily, by compensation in terms of traditionally stipulated blood money.

The reference to compensation I have already disposed of as
being beside the point (cf. pp. 12–16). Considerations of approximate equality in the choice of the victim to be killed in retaliation
may be said to constitute the principal criterion to distinguish
feud from warfare, which is collective but not selective: if equality
of sex, age and status is not respected and a venerable old man of
high status and numerous progeny is killed for an unmarried
adolescent with no political standing, this may be regarded as
extreme provocation and warfare in the sense of *damdoum* (cf.
p. 10) may ensue. The ideal condition for warfare is that all killing
should be thought of as legitimate, though this is rarely the case.

The first two characteristics enumerated by Nadel correspond
with Peters' localized definition of the feud in Cyrenaica. They
furthermore provide a valid means of recruiting personnel in what
I argue is an essentially political situation. Together with the
criterion of rough equality in the selection of victims they constitute the parameters of my own definition of feud. Between feud
and warfare lies raiding.[13] Raiding is intermediary between feud
and warfare in that, like feud, it is, in general, not a haphazard
manifestation of predatory greed but a relationship between quite
distinct traditionally earmarked social groups. Like feud again,
raiding is subject to an often very elaborate body of rules conceived to limit the extent of material damage and to reduce to a
minimum the loss of life on both sides. As in warfare, however,
little or no account is taken of the 'score' in either camp, and the
raiders will consequently attempt to carry off as much material
property as they can safely seize without fear of encumbrance
in case of attack on the return journey.

With feud, raiding and warfare thus circumscribed, vengeance
killing might appear as a residual category. But although the principal characteristics of vengeance killing are, as Barth asserts, the
almost total absence of any kind of solidarity with either the
killer or the victim and the lack of recognized norms or rules,
the category as it stands includes two quite different types of
homicide.

[13] Institutionalized raiding will be examined in more detail in the
discussion of the relationship between violence, oecology and ideology in
chapter IV.

In the first place, there is murder of an individual by another individual to obtain redress for a wrong inflicted when judicial machinery to achieve the same ends is lacking. The murderer in this case is not supported by his kinsmen or associates. Nor are the victim's kinsmen under any socially recognized obligation. The second type of homicide which, by Barth's definition, may be included under the general heading of vengeance killing is the murder, in a feuding society, of an individual who is a member of the same compensation-paying group as the killer. Since compensation-paying groups are everywhere in the Mediterranean and the Middle East defined as those who agree to 'pay and take together' (Peters 1951:298) and also represent the minimal unit for offensive and defensive action, the differential support of one member by part of the group as against another would automatically lead to fission. Solidarity is thus withdrawn by the collectivity from the intra-group killer; and he is usually exiled and left to fend for himself in a hostile environment.

The fundamental difference between the two types of vengeance killing is that, in the second, group solidarity provides an embryonic form of judicial machinery in normal conditions, that is when legal action is confined to inter-group relations. But in the first, no judicial machinery exists at any level of the social structure. The second corresponds to some extent to Malinowski's category of 'private fighting ... countered and curbed by customary law' (cf. p. 5). It occurs in societies that practise the feud as I have defined it, yet recognize a category of anti-social behaviour within the solidary group which is sanctioned by the withdrawal of solidarity and annulment of the birthright. I shall refer to it as intra-group killing. However, in a few cases, when the victim is from another group, but the crime is committed by an habitual offender (Peters 1951:282; Lewis 1955:104) or is for other reasons (e.g. the killing of a mother's brother in Cyrenaica (Peters 1967:272)) regarded as an enormity, the same penalty is incurred. I shall call this anti-social killing.

True vengeance killing, in my sense, is encountered rarely in acephalous tribal societies and is the result of a particular pattern of historical circumstances which are well illustrated by its occurrence in southern Kurdistan. Vengeance killing, as I have suggested, may be seen as the action of an individual who decides quite literally to 'take the law into his own hands'. It thus presupposes that no legal machinery of any kind whatever exists to resolve conflicts. This was in fact the situation in southern Kurdistan when Barth did his fieldwork: until the mid-nineteenth century, when the vigorously centralized and powerful Baban Pashalik was suppressed by the Ottoman government, the area had been relatively orderly and well policed. The inability of the Ottoman government to replace what it had destroyed with a substitute executive for the administration of justice had as an almost immediate result the promotion of total anarchy and inter-village warfare. In conditions like this, it is not difficult to understand how homicide came to be the *ultima ratio* in any clash of interests. A previously 'anti-social' form of behaviour became the only means of satisfying certain needs when more adequate institutions suddenly failed.

Vengeance killing is consequently not to be regarded as a typical development in conditions of minimal government, but as a reaction to the collapse or disappearance of previously extant institutions and coërcive means to enforce adherence to cultural norms. It may also continue in force as a 'habit' contracted in times of anarchy in an area which has only recently once again submitted to the effective control of a modern centralized government: in his 1957 thesis Kadhim records dozens of cases of vengeance killing in the non-tribal areas of rural Iraq that came before the Courts of Sessions over a period of only two or three years. He ascribes this high frequency of vengeance killing in peasant communities to 'a long absence of law and justice' (1957:185).

To recapitulate, my typology of vengeance killing, feud, raiding and warfare shows certain correlations between these categories of physical violence. Feud, raiding and warfare share the factor of collective action, whereas vengeance killing, together with intra-group and anti-social killing, is restricted to individual initiative. Feud and raiding constitute hostile *relationships* with structurally or geographically defined partners, in which the goals pursued are on the whole indirectly political.[14] Vengeance killing and warfare, on the other hand, are characterized by hos-

---

[14] Some types of raiding referred to in the discussion of Malinowski's typology of violence (cf. p. 6) are, it is true, to be seen as means to a primarily economic end. I shall examine these in more detail in chapter IV.

tilities in which the end envisaged is the achievement of an immediate material advantage over the adversary. When this is accomplished, the conflict ceases and the relationship between the parties is at an end, whereas each episode of violence in feud and raiding perpetuates the relationship through time.

It may be objected that warfare, except when it is accompanied by genocide, is rarely as finite as vengeance killing and that the alternation of overt hostilities and uneasy peace at this level makes the relationship between belligerents in a war indistinguishable from that between the parties involved in feud and raiding. There is a difference, however, for 'revenge' in warfare is rarely carried out by a group structurally identical to the group originally defeated, where as retaliation in feud and raiding is always the affair of the kinsmen or close associates of those who were worsted in the first encounter. The outbreak of warfare tends to be an exceptional event occurring between two unrelated parties, ulterior manifestations of hostility having but tenuous connections with particular incidents in the past,[15] whereas the essential trait of both feud and raiding is, on the contrary, that they constitute permanent relationships and incorporate the idea of continuity.

Feud postulates persistent rough equality between the 'scores' on both sides. Vengeance killing, raiding and warfare do not. Raiding and warfare contain but little to suggest that they act as a legitimate means of obtaining redress for wrongs previously inflicted upon the aggressor. They are predatory rather than remedial. But vengeance killing and feud may be said in different manners to approximate to substitutes for legal machinery where this does not exist. They thus suppose a seminal development of the notion of penality.

So although the terms vengeance killing and feud are usually associated with homicide, or attempted homicide, the incident (or series of incidents) which finally provokes violence is not necessarily itself characterized by physical aggression. The homicidal aspects of vengeance killing and feud constitute the ultimate penal sanction when all other means of obtaining redress— mediation, compromise, restitution of stolen property or public apology in cases of insult—have failed or for some other motive

---

[15] I am aware that examples abound to contradict this *general* rule: e.g. the Franco-Prussian conflict from 1870 to 1914. I hold that it is nonetheless *generally* valid.

are unacceptable. The homicidal stage of vengeance killing and feud cannot be conceptually divorced from the succession of illegitimate acts or torts which in most instances preceded recourse to violence. It is for this reason that I shall use the terms vengeance killing and feud to refer, in the context of acephalous societies, to a wide range of inter-personal torts and retaliatory acts the gravity of which does not call for reprisals of a violent nature following immediately upon the initial outrage, but which are liable to result in murder if the conflict continues over a longer period of time.

None of the categories discussed above or the criteria that define them are absolute. They can be, and are frequently, combined to produce the most complex situations in reality. This nomenclature is a purely heuristic device intended to serve as a kind of ethnographic shorthand in the treatment of feud that follows.

II
The Course of Feud[1]

It might be thought that the most logical sequel to the discussion in the first chapter would be, at this juncture, to describe several feuds which actually occurred. By examining the ways in which they resemble each other and yet differ substantially it might be possible to isolate a certain number of common denominators which correspond to the characteristics enumerated in my definitional model of the feud. But there is an important objection to pursuing this method: if Peters is right and all feuds are eternal, no unbiased observer has ever been able to follow—let alone describe—the course of a single feud from beginning to end. It may be argued that a series of killings occurring within a fairly brief spell of time provides a good enough statistical run to serve as a reasonable sample of what happens over longer periods. Unfortunately, even such short statistical runs are inexistent, for feuds are normally very intermittent and almost all reports of them come only from such people as travellers, administrators or anthropologists who have rarely been privileged to reside for several years at a time in a feuding community. The very few references to feud made by people who actually participated in them, such as, for example, the history of the hostile relations between Sichar and the family of Chramnesind told by Gregory of Tours, who was himself called upon to mediate between the parties at one point, all without exception neglect to provide an adequately detailed account of the political, oecological and

---

[1] The amount of ethnographic material set out in this chapter may at first sight appear excessive. It should, however, be borne in mind that the same material will be referred back to as evidence to vindicate the argument in later chapters.

genealogical circumstances that led up to the outbreak of hostilities.

Because of the temporal constraints suffered by the majority of observers the historical information on feud that has been recorded is of an extremely fragmentary nature. Accessible accounts of feud are consequently of roughly two main types. The first reflects the interests of a large category of eclectically minded travellers whose main concern was with the bizarre and the 'primitive' and who were not guided by an excessive respect for precision. Thus, Spiridion Gopčević, who visited Albania at the beginning of the last quarter of the nineteenth century, writes of a gun fight resulting in the deaths of twelve men because a member of one of the parties had refused to hand over four cartridges that he had previously promised to a member of the other (1881:71). The literature on the Balkans, an area in which western Europeans travelled widely but did not normally reside before the 1920s when the intensity of feuding had been considerably diminished through the exercise of central government control, yields large numbers of similar accounts of episodes of violence apparently sparked off by such trivial matters as a small debt, the shooting of a quarrelsome dog—one case is reported in which a fight between two sheepdogs belonging to different lineages was the immediate cause of the death of eighteen men in a single night (Hasluck 1954:78)—or an apparently innocuous remark voluntarily taken as a major insult. Such accounts all stress those aspects of the incident that seem the most irrational and unwarranted when seen through western European upper-middle class eyes. The result is a series of sketches of ephemeral outbursts of violence which are on the whole dismissed as the 'quaint' customs of a lawless society. No effort is made to link one episode to another. Each case is treated as isolated in time and space. Nor do these writers attempt to explain the disproportion that so marks what superficially appears to constitute the relationship of cause to effect.

The second type of account of feud that is readily available in the literature on the Mediterranean and the Middle East is characterized by the episodes that I have already quoted from Tozer and Lewis: the dimension of time enters into the narrative; the effects of an initial homicide are related over a period of two or more generations. But the elements for a complete analysis are never all present in the same account at one and the same time. In Tozer's story (cf. p. 14) of the two men who fought until they both died of their wounds, there is no mention of the original causes, though the reader is informed of the effects of the struggle at a later date. Nor does Tozer explain why the descendant of the man who died first decided to press his claim at that particular point in time. Lewis gives more details on the relationship of the parties involved and the circumstances in which the fatal blow was administered. But even he neglects to mention why three years later tension was beginning to mount between the two groups of cousins, although, from the context, it seems probable that the dispute concerned joint rights of the two groups to arable land. Moreover, neither Lewis nor Tozer was able to observe later developments.

The only feud that I am aware of which has been recorded with a high degree of accuracy over a relatively long period of time by an unbiased outsider conscious of the advantages offered by the diachronic approach is quite atypical in that political pressures imposed from above prevented recourse to violence and the evolution of hostilities along traditional lines. The conflict referred to is minutely analyzed by Abner Cohen in his book on *Arab border-villages in Israel* (1965:71–94). But the effective presence, at little distance from the village in which the incident occurred, of the Israeli administration and a highly efficient modern police force so distorted the situation that it is more interesting as an example of the survival of feuding 'attitudes' in a period of accelerated social change than it is illustrative of what actually happens in the course of a feud.

Thus accounts that purport to describe actual 'feuds' either only narrate a single sanguinary episode in a long chain of such events, or, alternatively, provide a much abridged 'history' of feud, which usually ignores several variables without which all attempts to give a sociological explanation of the pattern of hostilities in a particular case must remain abortive. It is for this reason that Peters, who has dealt at length with the feud, of which he had first-hand field experience, deliberately writes of the feud in general and avoids going into the details of *individual* feuds, because he found that it was quite impossible to pin-point in time an initial act that could be taken as the *fons et origo* of a subsequent series of homicides and other manifestations of hostility. 'It was most difficult', he writes, 'to get the Bedouin to give accounts of homicides other than those which had occurred over the past fifty years or so, but they invariably claimed that the origin was earlier than this, although they were wholly un-aware of the identity of the earlier victims' (1967:268). Peters discovered that it was simply not feasible to treat feuds as un-questionable historical entities having a course through time that could be exactly mapped out. Information supplied by the Bedouin was inaccurate and, frequently, intentionally misleading. Different versions of the same events were inconsistent. This state of affairs led him to the conclusion that 'What is interesting is not so much why groups feud, but which groups are involved in feuds' (1951:354).

This concentration on the delineation of the feuding unit and the importance of its structure is fundamental to Peters' con-ception of the feud as a relationship, for in Cyrenaica the size and structure of the group dictate the nature of its relations *vis-à-vis* all other groups. Structural factors do not seem[2] to impinge upon the quality of inter-group relations to the same extent in other Mediterranean and Middle Eastern societies as they appear to among the Cyrenaican Bedouin. But the structure of groups is nonetheless everywhere ultimately, at least partly, dependent upon the set of rules employed for the recruitment of members. Thus, if a straightforward ethnographic description of observed acts of violence reveals little of the propulsive mechanism behind feud, the course of feud may still be reflected in an investigation of the principles according to which individuals unite in mutual defence and the lines along which coalitions are formed at a higher level to parry aggression on a wider scale.

The remainder of this chapter will be divided into four sections. In the first I shall examine the manner in which different feuding societies recruit personnel to form the minimal group which can entertain relations of hostility with others. Having defined the

---

[2] I use the verb 'seem' because it may well be that travellers and ethnographers in other areas have simply not chosen to emphasize, in their accounts of the societies with which they are acquainted, the same structural factors as those which constitute such an important element in Peters' analysis. Similar structural factors may be operative elsewhere. The existent data are, however, inadequate for it to be possible to say where and to what extent.

principles of basic solidarity, I shall then show in what circumstances the group as a whole may repudiate an individual member
and refuse its support.

In the second section, I shall take up the same theme, that of
recruitment, and demonstrate that at the inter-group level in
unilineal tribal societies the process of alliance in the face of
danger between small collateral units of similar structure but
unequal strength does not always invariably follow the lines that
have been traced out for it by the classical theory of balanced
segmentary opposition, which has on occasion been too literally
applied. By reference to the work of Gellner, Lewis and Peters
and a few brief remarks culled from the writings of non-
anthropologists I shall endeavour to place the model of segmentary opposition in a more realistic perspective and prove that
the societies which use it as a conceptual framework to give form
and meaning to the heterogeneity of their social relations are
capable of more subtlety and flexibility than has generally been
supposed.

As a result of this discussion of segmentary opposition it will
come as no surprise to find that in the study of feud it is mainly
those writers who have sought to apply the model of mechanical
solidarity to the feuding situation who have also reached the
sometimes uneasy conclusion that feud can be terminated. Those,
on the other hand, who have taken the bull by the horns and
attempted to solve the contradictions between the sociological
model and the observed facts (which others frequently tend to
pass over as perplexing but minor anomalies), are also in the
main those who regard feud as interminable. The third section
will be devoted to the debate that ensued between these two
'schools' of thought and the ancillary issues—such as the importance of affinity as a mechanism inhibiting the spread of feud
—that arose from it. The section will be concluded by a short
survey of the ways in which feud can outlive the principals and
continue down the generations.

On the assumption that the foregoing discussion will have
convinced the reader that it is in fact *wrong* to see the feud as a
finite series of hostile acts which can be said to have both a
beginning and an end, I shall demonstrate in the fourth section
how the concept of debt is deliberately fostered as a language in
which to express the relationships inherent in feud.

(1) SOLIDARITY WITHIN THE VENGEANCE GROUP

> Suscipere tam inimicitias seu patris seu propinqui
> quam amicitias necesse est (Tacitus: *Germania*,
> XXI).
> You kick one of them, and the rest of them limp
> (an Ulster village saying, reported by Leyton
> 1966:536).

The Mediterranean and Middle Eastern peoples that I shall
be dealing with in this chapter are all tribal—in the sense that
they are all societies in which each individual generally con-
ceptualizes his relationship with every other person who claims
the same ethnic identity as ultimately based on the assumption
that they share the same blood or are descended from the same
apical ancestor.[3] As feuding communities they may be roughly
classified according to whether the basic residential unit is the
village or the herding unit, for the different types of co-operation
elicited by an agricultural or a pastoral economy are mirrored
to some extent in the principles employed to define the minimal
group which can stand as a viable self-sufficient entity over and
against others of the same order.

To illustrate this contention I shall examine the manner of
recruiting feuding personnel at the lowest level in six different
societies. Three are societies in which there exists a clearly
delineated village community. These are the mountaineers of
northern Albania, the Kabyles and the Berbers of the Central
High Atlas. I am aware that large sections of these societies do
also rely heavily upon short range transhumant pastoralism. They
are, however, predominantly cultivators; and I shall concentrate
on that part of their social organization that has evolved in
response to the needs of a population of sedentary mixed farmers.

[3] I am aware that this statement lacks precision and that a number of
other criteria are normally referred to in anthropological definitions of
tribal societies. These are conveniently summarized in J. J. Honigmann's
article on the 'Tribe' in Gould and Kolb 1964. Because they are all in
my own estimation singularly vague, I have confined myself to what may
be termed a minimal definition. Even this is, however, inaccurate, since
certain 'tribal' groups include accretions of an origin different to that
of the majority of their fellow 'tribesmen'. Hence my use of the adverb
'generally'.

I propose to compare the methods of recruitment operating in these societies, in which the local residential unit is the village, with those employed by pastoral nomads in the Syrian desert, in Somaliland and on the desert fringes of southern Cyrenaica.

The principles that I shall enumerate in each case are identical with those that regulate co-operation in the economic field, for in these societies the intensity of the obligation felt to engage in offensive and defensive action on behalf of another is commensurate with the necessity in which the individual finds himself, if he is to survive, to avail himself of the labour, time and good will of those who live near him or are his distant partners in economic enterprise. The principle of active and passive solidarity in the feud is a function of economic co-operation.

I shall demonstrate the validity of this proposition in full for only one of the three sedentary societies I have selected, for there exists on the social organization of Albanian mountain villages an abundance of accurate information conveniently concentrated in the works of two or three authors. Kabylia and the Central High Atlas have been less well served by the ethnographer, and what information there is tends to be very dispersed and often lacks precision. For the sake of brevity and as the basic principles of solidarity at the lowest level of organization are the same in all three societies, I shall ignore minor variations and limit myself to emphasizing those features of the North African situations that bear close comparison with the Albanian material.

The smallest group to engage as a corporate entity in feuding relations comprises, I said earlier, those persons who are prepared to pay and receive compensation as a body, even if compensation is in fact rarely offered or accepted. Among the Albanian mountaineers of the Malësi e Madhe region village communities were composed of a number of what Fortes has called *expanded families* (1949:69–70). Cohen has applied this term to the vigorously patrilineal family organizations of Israeli Arab villages which resembles that described in the literature on Albania (cf. Durham 1908 and 1928; Haluck 1954: *passim*). Cohen lists the following traits as characteristic of the expanded family created by the division of a joint family after the death of its head: '. . . the land, animals, housing units, and other forms of property are . . . divided. The plots of land and the dwellings continue to be adjacent and much cooperation between the households goes on. In some cases the land is too small to divide immediately and so it is left undivided and continues to be held jointly by members of the original joint family' (1965:55).

In Albania, the process of increasing individuation that drove apart the elementary families formed through the successive patrilocal marriages of sons began even before the death of the father, for as each son married it was the custom for the head of the household to build on to the core of the old homestead a new bedroom to house the couple. Centripetal forces, however, also operated to counteract this tendency to division. There were two strong incentives to maintain the expanded family and avoid separation as long as possible.

Firstly, the larger the male labour force an economically in-dependent unit could command the more it could diversify pro-duction. If several brothers, their sons and, in some cases, agnatic first cousins as well continued to live under the same roof and co-operate as a *vllazni* or 'brotherhood' (Hasluck 1954:225), the group as a whole could exploit more oecological niches than if each elementary family had hived off on its own. Subsistence agriculture could be supplemented by logging, muleteering and transhumant pastoralism, whereas a man living alone with his wife and children disposed of barely enough time and energy to fulfil their minimal food requirements.

The second powerful incentive that acted to prevent the ex-panded family from breaking apart at the earliest opportunity was the consideration of mutual defence. An elementary family working its diminutive plot of land alone was not only economi-cally at a disadvantage, but, in the total absence of organized government sustained by coercive force, was also bereft of politi-cal support and a body of riflemen to make it effective. As in all acephalous societies, the best means at a man's disposal for ensuring the safety of his property, his own life and the lives of his wife and children was the support of those men with whom he co-operated in the daily routine of subsistence. The individual needed the group as the group needed the individual. The greater their interdependence the greater their potential gain.

The recognition of the right of all male siblings to inherit equally the estates of the father together with the fact that the homestead itself was indivisible made the option for co-operation with a distant collateral or an extra-descent group stranger, whom there was no reason to trust, an unlikely choice, although in rare cases of total sibling incompatibility this may have occurred.

The institution of patrilineal inheritance, combined with the existence of limited amounts of arable land and oecological and technological circumstances that precluded the acquisition of wealth by the isolated individual, thus militated in northern Albania for a high degree of co-operation between brothers and, subsidiarily, other close agnates. As at least one of the reasons for this co-operation was mutual defence, the expanded family and its dependents could be regarded as the minimal group demonstrating active solidarity in retaliation for an injury inflicted upon one of its members. The corollary to combination for defence was readiness to shoulder collective responsibility for the offensive acts of members of the group, since refusal to support a member over and against outsiders was tantamount to his repudiation by the collectivity. As this brought about his withdrawal and, consequently, an undesirable drop in the number of riflemen for defence, passive solidarity was total except in circumstances I shall summarize at the end of this section.

The duty to avenge a murder fell primarily to the victim's brothers who were also the dead man's nearest collaborators in the field of subsistence, in the acquisition of wealth and the exercise of power in the village community. 'If his father was not too old, and his son too young, to bear arms, they shared the brother's obligation.' So too, 'in slightly less degree', did his father's brother, his father's brother's son and their sons and grandsons (Hasluck 1954:220). The members of the vengeance group were all, theoretically at least, liable to be killed in retaliation for a homicide or an outrage committed by another member of the group. Vengeance tended *on the whole*, however, to be restricted, as elsewhere in the Mediterranean and the Middle East, to the immediate male agnates of the principal. In some of the less remote districts of central and eastern Albania it was felt that a mother's brother was within his rights if he avenged a sister's son despite the fact of their belonging to two totally different lineages, though a man could not avenge his maternal uncle. But in the isolated north, where not only lineages but whole tribes remained strictly exogamous, a mother's brother was thought to be so far removed—both in sentiment and physical distance[4]—from his sister's son, that he could with impunity entertain the murderer in his house (Hasluck 1954:121–2).

As far as can be judged from the copious but often defective information available, it would seem that a pattern of solidarity and vengeance closely resembling that of the Albanian mountain areas is also to be found in Kabylia. In this region transhumant pastoralism is combined with intensive farming. Residence is in large permanent villages the population of which can range, in the sample given by Bourdieu (1965:233), from 500 to 3,000 inhabitants, although further research would probably reveal the existence of smaller residential units as well. The same source states that territorially distinct tribes are subdivided into 'clans' or *zriba*. This feature of the subdivision of tribes into clans is apparently absent in Albania, where there seems to be no group intermediate between the expanded family and the tribe. The Kabyle *zriba* is, according to another source, further divided into *kharouba*[s] or 'associations de famille' (Hanoteau and Letourneux 1893:104–5). Bourdieu states that land is 'indivisible' (1965:208). On the basis of a series of vague affirmations to the same effect made by Hanoteau and Letourneux, it may be surmised that the *kharouba* is a land-owning, economically self-sufficient and internally self-governing patrilineal corporation comprising a number of close collateral minimal lineages. Hanoteau and Letourneux mention that, in many villages, fighting within the *kharouba* cannot be sanctioned by the rest of the community (1893:105). They also give several examples (e.g. 1893:66–7) of 'vendettas' which come to a temporary halt when an *ânaïa* or truce is declared between the *kharouba*[s] concerned. But they are adamant when insisting that 'La dia [blood money] n'est pas kabyle' and attribute its acceptance in a few villages to the penetration of Arab influences from other regions. Bourdieu confirms that vengeance must ultimately always be

[4] Each 'tribe' occupied a geographically distinct river valley divided by a high mountain ridge from the territory of the tribe from which it took wives and into which it married its daughters (Durham 1909: *passim*). I am here using the term 'tribe' as found in the literature on Albania (e.g. *passim* in Durham 1909 and 1928, and Hasluck 1954). The accessible data make it impossible to say whether or not the 'tribal' groups referred to by Durham and Hasluck are in reality better described by the term 'clan' in the acceptance of this word current among British social anthropologists today.

exacted if the honour of the offended group is not to suffer (1965: 214) and supports (1965:208) the surprising information supplied by Hanoteau and Letourneux that it is normal practice for the *kharouba* to demonstrate active solidarity by paying hired assassins to bring vengeance for them (1893:61, 66–7). No stigma is attached to the name of the *kharouba* acting in this manner, for its members remain responsible for the acts of its hired bravos.

Like the Albanian expanded family, the Kabyle *kharouba* is simultaneously both the minimal land-owning, productive unit and the vengeance group. Its defence of economic interests vital to all its members coincides with the duty to protect its honour, which is as much an indivisible possession of the group as its arable and pasture land (Bourdieu 1965:208).

The Berber villagers of the Central High Atlas are similarly organized on roughly[5] segmentary lines into tribes, clans and lineages. Lineages again constitute the land-owning groups in which co-operation between members is essential for economic survival. The lineage is also coextensive with those persons who declare themselves willing to 'pay and take together', although, for once, this does not represent the major criterion of solidarity. Professor Gellner, who investigated the social organization of the sedentary Berbers in this region, has drawn attention to the institution of compurgation[6] which he regards as the ultimate test of group solidarity. Those who are called upon to act as co-jurors to support the claims of their lineage in a dispute with another lineage are in fact identical with those persons whose duty it is to exact vengeance in the event of a homicide or outrage being perpetrated against an agnate (Gellner 1969: 107). Gellner reports that compurgation as an instrument for the temporary resolution of conflict is usually resorted to before vengeance. A man is thus more frequently prevailed upon by his lineage fellows to swear to the innocence of his party in the event of an accusation being levelled against it than he is to exact vengeance. His readiness to use his oath in judicial support of his group, whether or not he wittingly perjures himself, constitutes the primary criterion of lineage membership. Refusal to

[5] The importance of the qualificative 'roughly' will become evident in the next section.

[6] For a further discussion of compurgation cf. p. 103 ff.

give the oath of solidarity is tantamount to the repudiation of lineage membership and the renunciation of rights to land and irrigation water.

This concludes the account of principles governing the recruitment of personnel in the vengeance group in Mediterranean societies practising mixed agriculture. Whatever the precise range of kinship involved, the group in each case comprises a number of agnates who act as a corporate productive unit and combine to defend their common heritage against aggression from outside the group. In Kabylia and among the Berbers of the Central High Atlas the vengeance group would appear to be comparatively large and combines families who, in all probability, do not live under the same roof. Both these societies recognize segmentary subdivisions between the basic domestic unit and the tribe, whereas in Albania there seem to be none. In all three cases the vengeance group regards itself primarily as a constituent part of the village residential unit to which its first loyalties go in defence against aggressors from outside the village, *whoever they may be.*

There now follows an examination of the structure of the vengeance group in pastoral societies in this area and the Middle East.

The classic description of the vengeance group among the Arab Bedouin of Syria and north Arabia has been given by the English nineteenth-century traveller John Lewis Burckhardt. The Arabs, he writes,

> claim the blood not only from the actual homicide, but from all his [agnatic male] relations; and it is these claims that constitute the right of *thár*, or 'blood revenge'.
> This rests with the *Khomse*, or fifth generation . . ., those only having a right to avenge a slain parent, whose fourth lineal [agnatic male] ascendant is, at the same time, the fourth lineal ascendant of the person slain (Burckhardt 1830:85).

He goes on to say that the same is true in reverse of those who are expected to pay compensation for a homicide committed by one of their number and even provides two diagrams to show in anthropological terms precisely who is and who is not involved in the *khomse*.

G. W. Murray, who spent many years in Egypt, Sinai and Syria in British service at the beginning of the present century, identifies the five generations referred to in the word *khomse* somewhat differently. For Murray, the *khomse* does not comprise all the living agnatic male descendants of a great-great-grandfather, but includes (1) the grandfather, (2) all his sons (i.e. the killer's or victim's father and paternal uncles), (3) all the male children of the grandfather's eldest son[7] and the brothers of the killer or victim himself (if his father is not the eldest son), (4) all the male children of the grandfather's eldest grandson and the killer's or victim's own sons, and (5) the killer's or victim's own male grandchildren (Murray 1935:205).

Whatever the basic principles employed to define the extent of the *khomse*, the evidence from a large number of sources dealing with the Arab world and those societies strongly influenced by the popular, as opposed to the dogmatic, aspects of Islamic culture suggests that the vengeance group is in practice much more flexible than might at first be thought. Later in the same book, Burckhardt, for instance, modifies his initial position quoted above and asserts that compensation is only occasionally paid by 'all the individuals comprised within the *Khomse*'. The levying of contributions from all members of the group 'is not a general rule; and the *dammawy* [murderer] in many tribes must make up the sum himself, with his brothers and father only' (Burckhardt 1831:316). The same inconsistency between principles and practice afforded Gellner the opportunity to earn himself a reputation for wit among the Berbers: the Berber equivalent to the *khomse* is the *Ait Ashra'a* or 'people of ten', that is, the murderer's ten nearest agnates who accompany him into temporary exile whilst a truce and compensation are being arranged by meditators. When Gellner asked what would happen to an eleventh near agnate who stayed behind in the village, it was assumed that he was making an hilarious joke, for no near agnate of a Berber murderer, whether elder brother or one of thirty first cousins, would be so foolhardy as to imagine that he was safe from an avenging bullet merely because ten other

---

[7] The killer's or victim's other agnatic first cousins, together with those persons mentioned in categories 1 and 5, '. . . may buy themselves off with a "sleep-camel" *ba'ir en-nom* and sleep safely in their beds' (Murray 1935: 205).

agnates had left the scene of the crime (1969:127). Such allusions to the potential flexibility of systems which, at the ideological level, appear perfectly rigid and predicate clean cut distinctions, portend a wide discrepancy between the stated norm and the observable facts.

Unfortunately, Burckhardt, Murray and authors like Musil (who has written what is perhaps the most complete book on Bedouin life that has yet been published) all fail to perceive the importance of the functional interrelationships between the vengeance group and the minimal unit of economic co-operation in a pastoral environment. Peters, on the other hand, was well aware of the importance of oecological constraints in determining certain aspects of social structure. He also found that, although the Bedouin see their social relations in terms of an elegantly balanced model of segmentary opposition in which all but agnatic links are totally irrelevant,[8] the vengeance group is in reality not entirely composed of near agnates. He traced the origins of this disparity to primarily oecological causes. The Bedouin '*amarā dam* or vengeance group referred to in the last chapter (cf. p. 29) is coextensive with the tertiary section and the dry season camp. Peters says that the Bedouin regard the tertiary section as 'the corporate group *par excellence*, in which "one word does for all". Corporate identity is conceptualized as "one bone" or "one body".' Solidarity is total within this unit; the killing of a member by an outsider elicits the comment 'we all lose blood' (1967:263). Yet the dry season camp is itself composed of a cluster of smaller camps in which the concentration of agnatically related males exceeds 80 per cent of all the males present (1967:262) but does not approach the 100 per cent which might be inferred from a literal interpretation of the Syrian and Arabian materials. The significance of this is that, if, as I have suggested, recruitment to the vengeance group in Cyrenaica is in the first place governed by contractual agreement and only subsidiarily by the principle of agnation, then it is evident that the Bedouin unite for other reasons than 'blood' or loyalty to their agnatic kinsmen.

[8] The model referred to is in essence identical to that proposed by Evans-Pritchard in chapter IV of *The Nuer*, except that the Bedouin only recognize three levels of segmentation, the tribe being subdivided into primary, secondary and tertiary sections. It is so well known that I do not intend to reproduce it here.

Peters makes it quite plain that Bedouin talk of blood and bones is little more than a thin veil to mask the oecological truth. Bedouin naturally tend to stay with the group into which they are born. But if, because of an epidemic or other natural disaster, the adult manpower of the tertiary section falls to below fifty, the group ceases to be an oecologically viable herding unit, can no longer defend itself adequately if attacked and cannot muster enough camels to pay compensation if one of its number kill a member of another tertiary section. The only solution in this situation is expressed in the (Somali) proverb 'If you cannot be a mountain, attach yourself to one.' Put into practice, this usually means that a tertiary section, that has grown too small to remain viable on its own, will make overtures, in the first instance, to a collateral tertiary section and fuse with it. This affects the agnatic structure of the resultant amalgam but little, since the two groups are by definition agnatically related. But it can occur that a tertiary section, which has shrunk to unviable proportions and can no longer defend itself, is forced to leave its *watan* (homeland) by an expanding collateral section of the same order of segmentation. If this happens, or if scarcity of land or water begins to make itself felt within a large tertiary section and a segment declares its willingness to go elsewhere in search of better conditions, it is not unusual for the splinter group to seek refuge with maternal kin in another locality (Peters 1960:43).

The forging of extra-group marriage alliances at a distance is also made necessary by the fact that it may not be demographically possible to find a bride within the tertiary section. Territorially and genealogically adjacent collaterals cannot be considered as possible marital allies, because they are the tertiary section's worst enemies for the control of exiguous local resources (1967:278). The grafting of affinal groups onto matrilaterally linked tertiary sections accounts for a large proportion of the 20 per cent of non-agnatic males within the Cyrenaican vengeance group. Affinally and matrilaterally related sections living at a distance in areas enjoying somewhat different oecological conditions provide, moreover, in times of crisis temporary access to pasture and water. Links through women can thus spell the difference between starvation and survival in periods of prolonged local drought. Other reasons for the presence of non-agnates can be sought in the practice by poor men of uxorilocal marriage (1967:273) and the readiness of most Bedouin to 'welcome, as members of their camps, practically anyone who wishes to join, even, in the case of one group, an Italian' (1960: 42), providing that sufficient resources are at hand. Not only does the vengeance group include a number of non-agnates, but 'Even when a blood money payment has to be made the mother's brother is expected to come forward' (1967:273), although vengeance would not be brought against him for an act committed by his sister's son. Peters lays great stress upon the importance of affinal and matrilateral ties in general and even cites the case of a man who visited his wife's kinsmen to ask them to contribute to compensation owed by his own *diya*-paying group (1951:300). On the other hand, non-agnates actually residing with the tertiary section of a murderer are not normally killed as substitutes for the killer and his agnates. The minimal lineage of the killer himself has most to fear, if the victim's kin bring vengeance. The responsibility for exacting vengeance is also usually theirs (1951: 299).

From the data recorded by Peters it might be legitimate, then, to distinguish two separate solidary groups among the Bedouin of southern Cyrenaica: the larger compensation-paying group which comprises the whole tertiary section, defined as those who live and herd together, whether agnates or not, and frequently also includes the mother's brother together, on occasion, with other matrilateral and affinal kinsmen. This group represents those who are involved in close daily co-operation and their economic correspondents outside the residential unit. The other solidary group is the minimal lineage within the tertiary section which is directly concerned with vengeance as such and becomes the situational core of the tertiary section when one of its members commits a homicide outside the camp. The tertiary section, as a residential unit, unites to fight in mutual defence, whereas the minimal lineage only prosecutes individual acts of vengeance.[9]

A similarly dual principle of solidarity was alluded to in

[9] Peters himself distinguishes two further subdivisions within the tertiary section, which are, however, of no immediate relevance in the present context. These internal divisions within the agnatic corporation coalesce on the basis of (1) matrilateral affiliations, and (2) parallel and cross-cousin marriage patterns, which create cognatic core-groups within the generally agnatic structure of the tertiary section.

chapter I in the incident reported from Somaliland by Lewis (cf. p. 15). The pastoral Somali not only recognize the existence of a situational core within the larger 'dia-paying group'[10] but distinguish it by reference to the name of a particular type of compensation, *jiffo*, due to the immediate kin of the victim who 'are usually male agnates descended from a common ancestor of the third or fourth ascending generation' (Lewis 1961:173). The *jiffo*-paying group normally lives and herds together, but has no 'homeland', although, as a lineage forming part of a clan, it may have rights in certain wells in the less favoured regions (1961:34). Unlike the Cyrenaican Bedouin among whom marriage with the father's brother's daughter is preferred, primary lineages of the same clan among the Somali look upon lineage endogamy with distaste. But this by no means precludes hostilities between affinally linked primary lineages. Stock-theft and feud are indeed endemic between them (1961:6). Affines residing with a sheep and goat herding nomadic hamlet in which the majority of adult males and children of both sexes are agnatically related are regarded with suspicion and are not allowed access to the more vulnerable camel camps guarded by inexperienced youths 'far from the main fighting potential of their lineage-group' (1961:83).

Despite the recognition by the Somali of two types of compensation and a situational core within the larger *dia*-paying group, the latter cannot bear true comparison with the homonymous Cyrenaican unit. The Somali *dia*-paying group is a scattered confederation of lineages and segments numbering anything from a few hundred to a few thousand male members (1961:6). It rarely forgathers as a corporate body except when engaging in major hostilities with another group of the same order. Nor does it represent a unit of economic co-operation like the Cyrenaican tertiary section together with its matrilateral links. The *jiffo*-paying group, on the other hand, does roughly correspond with the Cyrenaican minimal lineage which wreaks and

---

[10] The slightly unorthodox spelling employed by Lewis is in deliberate conformity with British Administration practice in the Protectorate. Wherever the expression '*dia*-paying group' is spelt without the conventional 'y' in this book it will always refer to the Somali unit of this name. The Arabic word for blood money in general will be spelt, as in the *Encyclopaedia of Islam*, *diya*.

bears the brunt of vengeance when conflict arises between two genealogically proximate groups. According to Lewis, homicide between *dia*-paying groups calls for little discrimination in the choice of a victim for revenge and is reminiscent of the type of relations between Cyrenaican secondary sections that Peters calls 'feud'. The wider the structural distance between the groups the more the opposed groups view each other as undifferentiated wholes and the less the identity of the actual victim counts (Lewis 1961:254). Although this seems to be generally true of most feuding societies, this statement calls for a proviso and a corollary.

The proviso is that, whatever the rules relative to passive solidarity, the taking of vengeance always tends everywhere to be the affair of the close agnates of the victim rather than of the group as a whole. This is particularly the case in societies in which the wider residential unit is the sedentary village within which the minimal co-operative group in the economic field comprises only those agnates who hold a patrilineally inherited share in communally exploited resources. In nomadic societies the ethnography is less insistent upon the identity of the avenger, which is rarely mentioned when the homicide occurs outside the vengeance group itself. This may be due to the difficulties attendant upon identification in a shifting population. I would nonetheless surmise that the avenger is nearly *always* a close relative of the victim for whom he is taking vengeance. However, Peters explicitly denies that the active role in bringing vengeance in the Cyrenaican feud is restricted to the close kin of the deceased (personal communication; cf. also p. 22, quotation from Peters 1967:262). But it would seem that the Cyrenaican material is atypical, for the literature from other parts of the world rarely gives examples of killings that were not the act of a man genealogically very near to the person being avenged (e.g. Lewis 1955:107; 1962:24).

Monteil, for example, tells the story from southern Persia of a Qashqai tribesman whose brother was killed by a peasant in another region. He shot a peasant in no way related to the first by way of vengeance. When asked why he had done this, he replied simply, 'Well, they were both peasants' (Monteil 1966: 120). Here, in an admittedly strange and perhaps even pathological case, active solidarity is, as might be expected, restricted and passive solidarity is (involuntarily) total. The Qashqai distinguish, moreover, between active (*mosbat*) and passive (*manfi*) solidarity. Monteil does not pursue this further. But it might be reasonable to suppose that, if the Qashqai do make a distinction, this distinction serves some purpose. I propose that this purpose is to identify a different range of kin who are held responsible in each case.

Evidence to support this conclusion is not limited to ethnographic materials from the Mediterranean and the Middle East. It is interesting to note that Wallace-Hadrill's work on the Merovingian feud reveals a similar double standard of responsibility. He found that 'The Frankish kin was probably less involved as a fighting force than as a compromising one' (1962:126) and reinforces his argument with quotations from Saint Gregory's *History of the Franks* which, he maintains, 'points to the difficulty of enlisting the feud service of more than the closest kin or a very restricted *ad hoc* force' (1962:147).[11]

The corollary to the statement that passive solidarity increases in direct proportion to the structural range separating two hostile groups, is that the reverse is also true: the smaller the structural distance between the groups the narrower the range of persons who will be regarded as fair game, when a killing or outrage is avenged, and the more feud will resemble a 'vengeance killing' in the sense that I defined this term in the first chapter (cf. pp. 28–30).

It will be recalled that a 'vengeance killing' which occurs in a feuding society is classified as an intra-group or anti-social killing. It is obvious that, if the range of passive solidarity extended to the killer diminishes with the structural distance between him and the victim, there will come a moment when the killer has overstepped the threshold of minimum sibling solidarity and finds himself alone with an intra-group (lineage) or anti-social killing on his hands. The progressive withdrawal of solidarity from the killer is a function of the damage he has

---

[11] The Merovingian material might be thought inappropriate in the present context, because the basic solidarity unit in the Frankish kingdom was the bilateral kindred, whereas the Mediterranean and Middle Eastern societies I am dealing with are predominantly patrilineal. But the literature suggests that whether the system of reckoning kinship is bilateral or patrilineal would seem to exercise a negligible influence upon the course of feud.

inflicted upon the structure of the group: if a Cyrenaican Bedouin kills a member of a collateral tertiary section, his own tertiary section will assist him in paying compensation, whilst others will remain neutral. If he kills a member of a collateral minimal lineage within the tertiary section, an armed peace may temporarily ensue; and, unless he is regarded as an habitual trouble-maker not worth defending, the killer's own lineage will on the whole reluctantly side with him in muted opposition to other minimal lineages within the group. These latter will tend, on the other hand, to give moral support to the victim's lineage, since this murder has weakened the internal structure of the in-group as a whole. But to avoid the dire consequences of fission, the majority will, after a period of strained relations with the killer's minimal lineage, eventually accede to a reconciliation sanctioned by nothing more than evidence of sincere contrition on the part of the killer himself. Alternatively, if contrition is not forthcoming or is thought to be inadequate in the circumstances, the murderer himself—not one of his agnates—will be killed in revenge.

If he kills a member of his own minimal lineage or a matri-lateral relative of the importance of a mother's brother, he has, as the Albanians say in the same context, 'killed himself' (Hasluck 1954:210), that is caused the maximum possible damage to his own group, for in both cases he eliminates a person of the utmost importance to the survival of the group. His penalty is the social isolation that he has himself created by destroying his closest allies. An anti-social killer belonging to a tertiary section who, by gratuitously killing a very prominent and influential man in another section, compromises his own group's good relations with the victim's group, is treated in the same manner as the intra-group killer. The penal consequences of both types of homicide are identical: the offender is exiled. In particularly grave circumstances, a recommendation may even be circulated to surrounding camps to warn them not to succour this monster of depravity (Peters 1951:256–7).

The pattern in village communities is basically very similar. A man who kills a close agnate within the economically productive unit is usually expelled from his lineage and the locality and forced to take service as a bondsman elsewhere in order to survive. In some cases, if a man kills his only near agnate and remains, by virtue of patrilineal inheritance, in sole possession of the dead man's property, the village may step in as a body and do justice in lieu of the man's lineage which has ceased to exist. Mrs. Hasluck's book on Albanian customary law cites numerous instances where the village destroys the anti-social or intra-group killer's property and sends him into exile. Kabyle tribal villages appear to act on much the same lines through the *djemâa* or village council (cf. Hanoteau and Letourneux 1893: *passim*). But it seems from Gellner's material that the Berbers are atypical in this respect, for an intra-group killer is said to be able to atone for his crime by the payment of compensation to the remaining members of the minimal lineage (1969:116). It is, to say the least, difficult to imagine how this is possible if property is held in common by all male members of the minimal lineage. This objection would be dissipated if it could be proved either that property is individually inherited or that Gellner's statement was based on a slight misunderstanding and that compensation in such circumstances was due to the village as a whole rather than exclusively to the kin of the victim.[12]

At the beginning of this section I said that I intended to show how the different types of communal interests elicited by an agricultural and a pastoral economy were reflected in the principles used to recruit feuding personnel. The predominantly agricultural preoccupations of the inhabitants of the Albanian, Kabyle and Berber village and the vital necessity of access to arable land which they can obtain only through inheritance in the male line tend to make the agnatic extended or, at a later stage in its development, expanded family the basic unit for co-operation and defence. Nomadic pastoralists, on the other hand—despite the somewhat arbitrary folk model provided by the *khomse*—would seem to possess a generally more fluid pattern of residence and co-operation. Affinal and other accretions modify the ideally agnatic structure of the herding unit. Affinal kinsmen, for instance, frequently reside in Somali nomadic hamlets away from

[12] From statements on pp. 38 and 47 of Gellner's book both hypotheses would seem to be borne out by the ethnography. But Gellner is not at all clear on the issue of land tenure in the Central High Atlas. Thus he implies in yet another passage (p. 62) that the basic corporation, or productive unit, in this Berber society is of greater genealogical depth than his previous statements concerning inheritance would lead the reader to believe. The overall impression is one of confusion, for nowhere does Gellner describe Berber corporations with precision.

their own primary lineages. This was the case in 31.6 per cent
of a sample of fifty-seven hamlet populations taken by Lewis
(1961:67). It is to be regretted, however, that Lewis does not seem
to have given any information in his book as to whether the
presence of affines in the *dia*-paying group affects the course of
feud, and if not, why not. As in Somaliland, Cyrenaican Bedouin
camps also comprise a number of non-agnates. Moreover, great
store is set by the mother's brother as a potential source of
assistance.

In the next section I shall discuss Peters' detailed account of
the manner in which the creation and maintenance of affinal
ties inhibit the development of feud in conditions that might
jeopardize the survival of the group, but nonetheless allow the
vengeance group sufficient political autonomy for it to carry on
feuding relations with others to which it is not allied through
marriage. I shall attempt to relate Peters' conclusions to the
material supplied by Lewis and Gellner in order to establish
whether the same inhibitive principles obtain among the Somali
and the Berbers.

(2) UNSEGMENTARY OPPOSITION

Although the Bedouin claim that relations between collateral
secondary sections imply, by the very nature of things, a 'state
of feud', they hasten to add that they never feud with cognatic
relatives. Bedouin hold that it is a meritorious act to kill a man
from a feuding secondary section, 'but there is no merit whatsoever in it if the tertiary section of that secondary section happens
to contain affines or maternal relatives. This is a sinful act' (Peters
1967:275). Moreover, notwithstanding an explicit preference for
marriage with the father's brother's daughter, as many Bedouin
marry outside the agnatic group as look for their wives within it
(1967:274). This being the case, the number of Bedouin finding
themselves in the relationship of mother's brother or wife's brother
to a man in a collateral tertiary or secondary section must be
almost as great as the number of men whose affinal ties lie within
the minimal lineage and the dry season camp.

This alone would considerably reduce the range of groups with
which it would be feasible to entertain hostile relations. However,

as Peters points out, if all collateral secondary sections, which are by genealogical definition territorially adjacent, were, as the Bedouin maintain, constantly at feud with one another, there would be no possibility of movement even for pasturing purposes. As the camels and other livestock would thus die and all life would cease, the Bedouin obviously do not indulge in the hostilities that their own folk model implies.

Again, according to their own model of balanced segmentary opposition which, as already stated, corresponds very precisely to that recorded by Evans-Pritchard to explain the overall structure of Nuer society, each step in segmentation should be marked by a process of bifurcation. But as human fertility and the carrying capacity of various tracts of land are by no means equal throughout the country, secondary sections are not endowed with equal populations. It is therefore inconceivable that all secondary sections should possess the same number of tertiary sections of the same strength. In conditions of uneven density of population it might just be possible to maintain equal numbers of named tertiary sections, but this would necessarily imply wide variations in the number of adult males to each section. The principle of bifurcation into segments of identical structural constitution is thus rarely, if ever, applicable. But there must exist some means of equalizing the chances of segments to survive, for subjection of the weak to the strong or their expulsion from the land would result in a hierarchical social structure. This is not the case, and Bedouin society is fundamentally egalitarian in all respects.[13] The strongly upheld right of all Bedouin to equal access to land and water and equal political status is guaranteed by the principle of contractual alliance.

In the first chapter I was careful to describe the compensation-paying group as those men who *agree* to pay and take together. As agreements of this nature are restricted in Cyrenaica to the vengeance or compensation-paying group which is synonymous with the tertiary section, it is to be expected that tertiary sections should be of roughly similar size and their defensive force kept up by the accretion of outsiders such as sisters' sons and

[13] —despite the emergence of the occasional petty despot, whose power is nevertheless ephemeral and extremely limited in terms of geopolitical space. Such men constitute a rare phenomenon in Bedouin society and may be regarded as marginal to the social system as a whole.

impoverished daughters' husbands willing to live uxorilocally, or the grafting on to maternal stock of whole tertiary sections that have been so diminished that they have ceased to be viable units on their own.

Links through women and the presence of agnates in other sections are not the only ways among the Cyrenaican Bedouin in which feud is prevented from spreading up the segmentary tree to destroy it root and branch. Other inhibitive mechanisms will be discussed in the next section and chapters III and IV. One of these is, however, relevant at this juncture. If, as suggested above, the system of basic compensation-paying alliances in Cyrenaica is purely contractual in origin and is largely a function of oecological and military viability, then it is difficult to imagine on what principle groups will unite to fight at levels above the tertiary section.

The very fact that this issue should present itself as a problem for solution is the result of centuries of European imperial effort. A long history of experience in the pacification of 'savages' and the 'cleaning up' of regions hostile to colonial rule, particularly in the Islamic world, has impressed the image of the warlike tribe firmly upon the European mind. It is widely assumed that feuding is a kind of minor warfare which automatically blossoms into full scale belligerence between numerically vast tribal groups as soon as the prize at stake attains proportions that warrant the death and suffering to be incurred. It is not generally realized that, although feud may be observed to be endemic at a low structural level, this does not necessarily imply, in the first place, that the groups involved can conceive of any valid reason for the spread of fighting or, in the second, that there exists a mechanism by which the escalation of hostilities may be achieved. As I have already remarked in connection with Malinowski's definition of raiding, it is by no means certain that tribes engaged in nomadic pastoralism are motivated by a permanent Hobbesian frenzy to worst their neighbours and occupy their lands.

In reality, as far as the apparently accurate information supplied on this point by anthropologists goes, neither the Somali nor the Cyrenaican Bedouin are prone to unite of their own initiative to fight each other in *organized* encounters at the tribal level. Peters has, it is true, referred to one such occasion on which there was inter-tribal fighting in Cyrenaica (cf. p. 8), but the precise circumstances are lacking; and Lewis does present evidence for the occurrence of inter-tribal 'war-expeditions' among the Somali, which, however, remains extremely inconclusive (e.g. 1955:104). So even if inter-tribal warfare does occur and there do exist organizational concepts which make prolonged hostilities between numerically vast tribal groups possible, it would seem that the phenomenon is on the whole a rarity. Both the Somali and the Cyrenaican Bedouin nevertheless proved themselves ferociously effective warriors in guerrilla warfare when it came to the organization under charismatic leadership of resistance to British and Italian penetration. In both cases, a *djihād*, or religious war against the Infidel, was declared at the instigation, in Somaliland, of the 'Mad Mullah' who from 1900 to 1920 led a successful insurrection against European colonization and, in Cyrenaica, by the successive heads of the Sanūsī religious order who prevented the Italians from establishing themselves in the interior. Fredrik Barth reports a similar phenomenon from the Swat valley in northwestern Pakistan where, in spite of a constantly changing pattern of small scale alliances between sedentary agricultural households and permanent hostilities between villages and factions, it was nevertheless possible for a man of 'saintly' renown to lead the whole population into massive armed resistance against the British (1965:122–3).

The frequency of this type of colonial 'war' and its suscitation of violence on a 'national' scale have been largely responsible for the widely accepted fallacy that the principle of balanced opposition operates all the way up from the bottom to the top levels of tribal organization in Islamic and African segmentary lineage societies. In Peters' view, one of the factors that make it quite impossible for the principle to work in acephalous lineage societies is that 'there is a lack of instituted authority, there are no chiefs distributed throughout the land as heads of segments of the hierarchical orders . . . there is no one to command the action' (1967:271). As Peters himself adds, an absence of instituted authority in acephalous lineage societies does not necessarily preclude the exercise of *informal* leadership. It is moreover my opinion that some form of leadership does exist in all such societies, as I shall try to demonstrate in chapters IV and V. However, leaders do not, in normal circumstances, attempt to extend their political authority beyond a fairly limited range.

Their satisfaction is gained from presiding rather than ruling over the destinies of their fellow tribesmen: they are influential but cannot dictate war or peace, for if they tried to impose their will against that of the majority, their subjects would desert them.

Without formally recognized leaders, then, and in the absence of even numbers of numerically balanced segments the Cyrenaican Bedouin are unable to follow the rules inherent in their own model. If a tertiary section has no ties of affinity with another section of the same order in a collateral secondary section, the two may live in a state of sporadically overt hostility. But this does not mean that other tertiary sections belonging to the secondary sections on either side will unconditionally support their collaterals. Ties of affinity and other interests (cf. p. 47) will make this undesirable for individual tertiary sections; they therefore prosecute their own feuding relationships alone or in collaboration with allies contracted in the context of a particular enmity and refrain from any demonstration of mechanical solidarity (Peters 1967:277). Even when a homicide does occur across tribal boundaries and a general affray is the result, sections joined as allies in both tribes will mobilize together, but will refuse to fight if they hear of the presence of affinal kinsmen in the opposite camp. 'Consequently', Peters sums up, 'the statement that homicide results in a tribal war when the offender and his victim are members of two separate tribes is not merely incomplete, not merely a simplification, it is wrong' (1967:278).

The situation in Somaliland bears a close resemblance to that of the Cyrenaican Bedouin. Somali pastoralists are organized into what Lewis terms clan-families, clans, sub-clans, primary lineages and, finally, *dia*-paying groups (1961:4). Most clan-families are so vast—one numbers over a million members—and scattered that they cannot operate as 'corporate political units'. The clan is the largest body that acts corporately. Its members are mainly concentrated in a single area, although no precise tract of land is recognized as its territory. The Somali are quite aware that lineages expand at different rates: some grow to inordinate sizes and segment frequently; others enjoy only a low level of fertility and come near to petering out. Prolific lineages, whose very size has caused frequent segmentation, sport longer genealogies than those with only a small number of living male representatives, because '. . . ancestors who are not structurally

important tend to drop out of the genealogies as a lineage pro-
liferates over the generations' (Lewis 1961:147). This is a process
that Gellner has aptly referred to as 'structural amnesia' when
discussing a similar phenomenon among the Berbers (1969:249).
'There is thus a demonstrable correlation between the numerical
strength of a group and its genealogical span' (Lewis 1961:146).
The Somali conceptualize the disparity in genealogical depth
between lineages in terms of the branches, *laan*, of a tree, which
can be long, *deer*, or short, *gaab*. They pride themselves on belonging to a *laandeer*, because this is a direct reflection of the
superior physical force and, consequently, political power of their
lineage.

The fact that the fighting potential of descent groups is related
to their genealogical depth, causes several 'short' branches to
combine by contractual agreement to form composite *dia*-paying
groups of approximately equal strength to those comprising a
lesser number of lineages of the 'long' branch type. Agnation is
counteracted by contract, or *heer*. Such contractual agreements
are drawn up by a council summoned for the purpose at which
all adult males of the lineages concerned have a right to speak.
Contracts are frequently recorded in writing, and, in colonial
times, were sometimes placed in the safe-keeping of the Administration (1961:177–8).

The *dia*-paying group is the most stable unit in the Somali
political structure (1961:6), but it can disintegrate as easily as it
was formed if, for example, rivalry develops between the elders
of constituent segments. As a political unit it acts as a body over
and against outsiders even within the same clan. But when not
engaged in hostilities its members are often widely distributed
over different areas (Lewis 1961:66). Its situational core, the
jiffo-paying group, on the other hand, is a localized herding unit
based on a single small lineage (1961:173). Like the Cyrenaican
Bedouin, the Somali pastoralists will not knowingly kill an affinal
kinsman. Extra-lineage ties through marriage are valued and 'a
man can expect hospitality as a kinsman (not merely as a guest)
from a lineage with which he is either linked personally as an
affine or through the affinal ties of another member of his lineage'.
But this does not prevent heavily inter-married lineages from
indulging in mutual aggression, though '. . . in battle, a man will
always seek to spare his wife's agnates, at least her close kin, and

if captured they will be accorded preferential treatment' (1961: 140; cf. also 1962:25). Similar principles are operative in Cyrenaica if affines are unwittingly involved in a wider conflict (Peters 1967).

Information of this kind casting doubt upon the applicability of the model of mechanical solidarity in a feuding situation is not to be found only in the recent work of social anthropologists. Burckhardt, for example, states that 'If an Arab in battle should meet with a personal friend among the enemy's ranks, he turns his mare to a different side, and cries out "Keep away! let not thy blood be upon me!"' (1830:174–5). It is interesting to speculate whether a 'friend', in Burckhardt's sense, could include an affinal kinsman, as Lewis' and Peters' material would suggest.

Instances of such 'unsegmentary behaviour', as Gellner calls it (1961:42), are frequent in the literature on feud. In his thesis Gellner emphasizes similar features, contradicting the classical model of mechanical solidarity, in the political system of the Berber villages he studied. He estimates that 10 per cent of the total male population in any single community may be composed of immigrants from other villages who have changed their group affiliation, as defined by the status of co-juror, at least once in their lifetime (1969:62–3, 121). Nevertheless, the overall model of social organization that results from an examination of the genealogies given by the Berbers is one of strict segmentary opposition. Even so, it is feasible for people in the same village to 'change their segment, their co-jurors, without changing their habitat' (1961:73; cf. also 1969:121). Since Berber villages are usually divided into wards each controlled by a lineage, this remark bears witness to a degree of flexibility and structural tolerance quite remarkable for a society that would normally be described as segmentary,[14] for it implies that whole families continue to live and work in immediate daily contact with a group with which they have repudiated all ties.

In this examination of the pertinence of the segmentary lineage model to the study of feud among nomadic pastoralists in the Mediterranean and the Middle East, I have shown that little evidence exists to support the theoretical postulate that genea-

[14] Gellner—in my opinion quite unwarrantedly and on the basis of insufficient evidence—maintains that the contrary is true: 'Berber society of the central High Atlas . . . is certainly not very fluid' (1969:62).

logically close collateral segments will always unite to fight against structurally more distant ones. Though not much precise information is available for sedentary societies, it would seem that, unlike the nomads, not all tribally organized cultivators in the area, for whom the range of total solidarity in the feud is coextensive with the land-owning descent group, are given to the practice of contractual alliance. The notion of vicinage frequently overrides that of contract.

In the three tribally organized sedentary societies, for each of which I drew a brief picture of the vengeance group in the first section of the present chapter, the extended or, at a later stage, expanded family is the basic unit of social organization. Among the Berbers there may be a certain amount of intra-village factionalism due to the possibility of shifting one's jural affiliations within the village. But Gellner does not state whether co-jurers do more than lend moral support in feud to minimal lineages which are not closely related as agnates and are only recent accretions to the group of co-jurors. It seems unlikely that a change of jural allegiance should be sufficient to rally the armed force of a family's new allies for the pursuit of a feud in which it had been engaged before the change.

The Berbers, however, appear to be somewhat exceptional in their division into units of a higher order than the extended family within the village. This could be imputed to the fact that many lineages were until comparatively recently still nomadic. In the rest of the Mediterranean—and perhaps the Middle East, although information is again poor here—tribal societies in which the primary means of subsistence is agriculture tend to have no unit of organization between the extended family and the village level. Individual families indulge in feuding relations in general outside the village but within the same tribe. The village itself is organized in north Albania and Kabylia, for example, on extremely democratic lines: a village council, recruited on the basis of an adult male from each house, endowed with the power to levy fines and destroy the property of defaulters is responsible for calling out the whole village for defensive purposes in the event of attack. The emphasis among sedentary cultivators at a level above that of the minimal lineage is on vicinage more than agnation, although the two are not mutually exclusive, for it is clear that in a tribal society the two frequently coincide, since villages may be composed of entire tribal segments. It is said in Albania, for instance, that neighbours are under a moral obligation to seek vengeance if all male members of an adjacent household are exterminated in the course of a feud (Hasluck 1954). A similar trend towards a minimization of agnatic solidarity in favour of the wider interests of the community was observed by Lewis in Somali agricultural settlements (1961:233 ff.).

Thus, to return finally to the conclusions of the preceding section, although the actual externals of feud—killing, compensation, vengeance and the ideology which serves to express them—show a notable similarity from one society to another in the Mediterranean and Middle Eastern area, there exists a marked difference between its structural implications in a nomadic pastoral and in a sedentary agricultural context. In both types of environment, two hostile groups of close agnates constitute the irreducible core in any feud. Among sedentary cultivators recruitment to the vengeance group tends, with a few minor exceptions, to remain strictly agnatic. The interest of agnates in mutual defence coincides with their interest in common proprietory rights in the exploitation of natural resources. Pastoralists, on the other hand, are forced by oecological circumstances to admit a wider range of non-agnates to the basic unit of economic production— the herding camp. Their main concern is to guarantee themselves access to pasture and water. They therefore engage in feud to protect their common interests as a group united on a contractual basis. The ideal of agnation is subordinate to the dictates of survival. At a higher level, pastoralists again give priority to practical considerations and join, in political alliance, with those who can offer them substantial assistance in times of need. The principle of agnation continues to provide the general framework within which allies are sought, but it is of little significance compared with the search for material advantage. At a level above the vengeance group in sedentary cultivating societies the interests of neighbours are vested in the maintenance of the territorial integrity of the village and its agricultural resources. Contractual alliance is made superfluous, because it is clearly to the advantage of all to show a common front in mutual defence against aggressors from outside the residential unit.

(3) FEUD WITHOUT END . . .

(a) *The debate*

If 'unsegmentary behaviour' is as common in what have been called 'segmentary lineage systems' (Fortes and Evans-Pritchard 1940:6) as the examples marshalled in the preceding section would intimate, there must clearly be some doubt as to whether the theory of segmentary opposition is at all valid. To resolve this dilemma, Peters had recourse, as I have shown, to the now familiar dichotomy between the folk image and the model constructed by the anthropologist from the observed facts. The discovery of a very wide discrepancy between the two made it possible for him to accommodate both a diachronic treatment of the feud and the segmentary lineage model within one and the same analytical framework. However, not all those who have done research on the feud have proved themselves as agile as Peters. Whilst the dimension of time has been largely ignored in this context, much effort has been deployed to force the obdurate facts of feud into awkward compliance with the abstractions of the segmentary lineage model. This has led to a muted controversy and a good deal of intellectual hesitation.

The root of the problem lies in certain ambiguities inherent in the Nuer material on feud and the theory of segmentary opposition as originally expounded by Professor Evans-Pritchard. For, in the first place, it is not always clear in Evans-Pritchard's book whether he is writing of empirical realities or whether he is indulging in purely theoretical considerations. The two are often so subtly combined that it is difficult to distinguish one from the other, although on the last page he does honestly recognize these shortcomings and refers to the book as 'a short excursion into sociological theory' which has caused him to 'perceive vaguely how further analysis might be made' (1940:266). So at least part of the controversy as to whether feud is interminable and whether it can be tolerated within a village community is due to the too literal interpretation, at both the theoretical and the ethnographical level, of what Evans-Pritchard has to say in *The Nuer*.

The other part may, I think, be imputed to Evans-Pritchard's firm resolve at the time of writing not to allow himself to be side-tracked into a diachronic perspective when his first intention was to give a synchronic analysis of social structure divorced from history. Thus, on the one hand, it is not always realized that the structure of villages in segmentary societies is not everywhere identical to that described by Evans-Pritchard for Nuerland and, on the other, not enough is made of the occasional references in *The Nuer* to events that occur in an historical sequence implying evolution through time. The remark to the effect that 'a feud goes on for ever' (1940:154) quoted earlier is of this kind.

Elizabeth Colson, who in 1951 read before the Royal Anthropological Institute an important paper on the feud among the Plateau Tonga,[15] was still working within very much the same framework of analysis as that employed by Evans-Pritchard in *The Nuer*. Having identified the Tonga as a matrilineal segmentary lineage society, she then proceeded to examine the manner in which conflicts between individuals involved (as the theory of segmentary opposition predicates) groups of a higher order of segmentation on either side, so that if the two principals are members of different clans, the conflict automatically brings about a hostile confrontation between all members of both clans. She was soon forced to admit that such confrontations never took place in Plateau Tonga society and attributed this apparent failure of the theory of segmentary opposition to the locally mitigating factors of a weak clan organization, oecological constraints forcing tribesmen to farm out their cattle for pasture all over the country, a high incidence of neo-local residence at considerable distance from the family of origin and the 'cross-cutting ties' of kinship, affinity and complementary filiation. From this analysis she derived the opinion that such conflicts of loyalties effectively inhibited the development of feud and that 'Permanent bad relations ... are only possible when the groups involved do not have kinsmen living together in the same local groups, and where they are not tied by the network of kinship and affinal ties to the same matrilineal groups' (1962:119–20).

Gluckman manifested generous enthusiasm for Dr. Colson's treatment of feud in a series of lectures originally delivered to wireless audiences which were later published under the general title of *Custom and conflict in Africa* (1955). Availing himself of an identical method, he re-examined the Nuer material and came

[15] This paper was finally published under the title 'Social control and vengeance in Plateau Tonga society' in Colson 1962.

to the conclusion that although an isolated homicide occasionally marred the turbulent harmony of Nuer village life, the cross-cutting ties of kinship and affinity made a protracted feud an almost impossible occurrence in Nuerland. Gluckman's investigation of the information reported by Evans-Pritchard stressed the fact that almost as many Nuer reside outside their natal villages as remain there throughout their lives. As causes of this dispersion he enumerated the following:

(1) a widowed mother may leave her husband's village taking her infant children to live with her lover elsewhere;

(2) a young man of poor parentage may go to live with a wealthy mother's brother;

(3) a man may leave his natal village as the result of a quarrel and take his wife and children to live at a distance.

According to Gluckman, the scatter of cross-cutting ties created by such spatial mobility would act to strangle a feud before it could develop. It is true that he mentions the technical eventuality of feud with distant sections of the same tribe, but the impression he gives is that only hazardous communications could create conditions of sufficient discreteness for such a feud to be at all possible and that these conditions themselves would make the relations of hostility so intermittent as to be almost negligible.

So, although feud is inhibited at close range by the 'unsegmentary' ties resulting from affinity and residence outside the natal village, Gluckman nevertheless manages to occupy a position from which he is not obliged to challenge the general validity of the principle of segmentary opposition. Although its operation at the lower levels of segmentation may not correspond entirely with the theory, it remains potentially valid at a level where large tribal sections are involved. But since these groups are rarely, if ever, in direct contact due to their spatial distribution and movement dictated by the annual pastoral cycle, little or no opportunity occurs to test the postulate that adjacent local village groups would unite to fight as a large section against a similar grouping at the same level of segmentation. Thus the sociological *Leitmotiv* of Gluckman's previous work was, once more, proved to his own satisfaction: custom was yet again victorious over conflict. For both Gluckman and Colson the contention that feuds are interminable had little sense, because neither of them could seriously entertain the possibility of an armed conflict lasting long enough within the jural community to qualify as a feud in the first place.

Shortly after the publication of Gluckman's essay on 'Peace in the feud' Middleton and Tait were working on their 'Introduction' to *Tribes without rulers* in which they sought to refine and codify the concepts that had been developed in connection with the theory of segmentary lineage systems. The curious contradiction latent in their assumption,[16] on the one hand, that feud bore within it an inherent mechanism for its peaceful conclusion and their refusal, on the other hand, to recognize any distinction between warfare, feud and other forms of violence, led them to avoid any systematic diachronic treatment of the feud, for they had run into a logical *cul-de-sac*: either feud was like warfare, which cannot necessarily be terminated by the offer of compensation and can continue indefinitely; or else feud was by definition endowed with machinery for the achievement of its peaceful conclusion and could consequently not continue indefinitely. Faced with a choice of inconsistencies, they chose the latter.

This disguised hesitancy spelt a new stage in the debate. From Colson's and Gluckman's conviction that feud was in fact almost inexistent among the Plateau Tonga and the Nuer, and, by extension, in segmentary lineage systems as a whole, Middleton and Tait had progressed to an attitude of latent doubt.

The most recent contribution has been made by Stirling in his book on the social structure of a *Turkish village* (1965). Whilst finding incontrovertible evidence to indicate that feuding relations between lineages did endure down the generations, Stirling seems surprised that this should be so. Observing that feuds do oppose lineages for considerable numbers of years, he is even more perplexed by the fact that 'No recognized machinery exists in the village for the settlement of such quarrels,' i.e. quarrels that create a state of *küs*, or 'bad relations', but do not reach the stage of open violence. Third parties on rare occasions offer their services as mediators, but if a dispute involves violence or the honour of a woman, 'then in theory no reconciliation is possible' (1965:248). Stirling proposes that, in these conditions, the hypothesis that feuds cannot subsist within the village community (cf. Evans-Pritchard 1940:159) 'could be saved by arguing that in fact some

[16] Based on Evans-Pritchard's definition of the jural community, cf. pp. 3–4.

efficient means of settling village quarrels existed in the past but has disappeared' since the introduction of a modern police force and a national judiciary (1965:253).

Cohen's material on Israeli Arab villages standing in a similar relationship to the authority of a modern centralized state suggests that this may be partially true: prominent men from outside the community who would previously have agreed to act as mediators no longer do so for fear of their decisions being flouted. Since, in the modern situation, they can no longer command the coercive force necessary to compel respect, they refuse to jeopardize what influence remains to them in the diminished status they now occupy by pronouncing judgements that will not be obeyed (Cohen 1965:142).

In support of his hypothesis that feuds could in the past be concluded Stirling points to the custom of giving a woman in marriage to the aggrieved party once the feud had subsided. He found evidence of this practice in the genealogies he collected from feuding lineages. Yet in an earlier article he states that 'marriage ties do not prevent the development of feuding relationships' (1960:66). Whilst instinctively Stirling feels that there must have been machinery for the conclusion of feud, for 'If every serious quarrel lasted for ever no lineage would be on speaking terms with any other,' (1965:252), he could find absolutely no evidence of this and was energetically contradicted by the villagers.

Stirling's difficulties derive, I believe, from two sources. In the first place, there is a subtle shift of emphasis between his 1960 article and his later book in his attitude to Evans-Pritchard's analysis of the Nuer feud. Whereas he first quoted Evans-Pritchard as writing 'corporate life is incompatible with a state of feud' (1940:156), in his later version of the same argument he takes Evans-Pritchard to task on the basis of another quotation from *The Nuer*: 'feud cannot be tolerated within a village' (1940:159). The first statement is perhaps universally valid. The second was only intended by Evans-Pritchard to apply to the Nuer village in particular. Now, the ethnographic facts that Stirling presents in his article show that corporate life outside the lineage is almost inexistent in the Turkish village and that there are in reality no incentives to encourage co-operation between lineages. The argument in the article is thus more cogent than that to be found in the book, for feuding does indeed *not* occur within the corporate lineage but *is* tolerated within the village. Part of Stirling's confusion is consequently due to his haste to equate the feud in the Nuer context with similar but not identical manifestations of violence in Turkey. In point of fact, the Nuer settlement and the Turkish village have very little in common at all apart from their constitution on a lineage basis.

The second source of uncertainty in Stirling's argument is that he does not seem at all sure of what he means when he uses the word feud. He says of the Turkish situation that when 'compared with many examples of feuding it is highly informal and unsystematic. In practice, not all agnates feel themselves committed; revenge is not necessarily specific or immediate; no system of compensation or reconciliation seems to exist and it is not precisely laid down who is and who is not involved' (1965:251). For Stirling the Turkish feud is little more than a vaguely perceived pattern of sporadic violence between lineages. He refuses to commit himself to a more precise definition than this.

I submit that his perplexity derives from the fact that he is aware that the feud constitutes an historical process, yet he is at the same time unwilling to analyze it within a processual framework. The villagers told him of feuds that were as fresh fifty years later as the day on which the initial outrage was perpetrated (1965:248). But Stirling was unable to reconcile this sort of information with the Nuer model of feud in which Evans-Pritchard deliberately stresses the synchronic and structural aspects of feud in general whilst omitting nearly all reference to the history of individual feuds. Not only does the social structure of Nuer villages differ considerably from that of the Central Anatolian villages studied by Stirling, but it is possible in the latter for whole lineages to avoid each other for years by living in wards located at some distance from one another. A feud can lie dormant for long periods breaking out anew only when it is so desired or if the parties meet by accident. Even when a feud has been compounded the wrongs of past generations, which are not 'normally' spoken of, may, according to Stirling, 'be selectively remembered, that is, they would be remembered if they reinforced existing hostilities, and forgotten if they cut across existing alliances' (1965:252–3). This sounds very like the situation already described for Cyrenaica in the first chapter (cf. p. 19).

Stirling was thus on the brink of adopting an attitude similar to that displayed by Peters in his writings on the feud. He was, however, prevented from pushing his analysis as far as his own data would have permitted by his apparent mistrust of diachronic materials. His doubts are nevertheless symptomatic of the uneasiness felt by a number of British social anthropologists as the historical approach expounded by Leach in *Political systems of Highland Burma* began to gain a wider audience.

None of the writers discussed so far had overtly questioned the theory of balanced segmentary opposition: Stirling's attempt to apply in a peasant lineage society a model of feud developed to deal with conflicts in an exclusively tribal context ran into serious difficulties when he neglected to ascertain in advance whether the model was flexible enough to accommodate two widely divergent social structures. Elizabeth Colson had a moment of remorse when her paper on the Tonga feud was published in 1962. But rather than cast doubt upon the validity of the structural framework within which she undertook her original study, she preferred to take refuge in terminology and added this footnote: 'A talk on the feud among the Bedawin by Dr. E. Peters led me to reconsider my own material. I then realized that I had been using the term to cover isolated acts of vengeance and that the Tonga did not, and could not, have the true feud' (1962:102). This well-meant tribute to Peters distorts in reality what he has written on the terminology of violence, for it implies that 'vengeance' among the Tonga exactly resembles the type of homicide that the Bedouin call *thār*—a term that Peters, it will be recalled (cf. p. 21), has translated by the word vengeance. This is certainly not the case, for *thār* is structurally defined with reference to Cyrenaican Bedouin society alone. Colson's misappropriation of the term to describe another phenomenon in a quite different cultural setting may have prompted a remark at the beginning of Peters' 1967 article where he states that, in his opinion, the Bedouin of Cyrenaica constitute 'one of the few societies in which [feud] occurs' (1967:262). I myself see no reason for accepting this statement unconditionally as the Berber, Somali and Syrian Arab materials with minor variations all corroborate Peters' findings. It does, however, stand as a useful warning to those who might be tempted to apply Peters' terminology uncritically in societies whose structure and oecological environment are not strictly comparable to those of the camel-herding Bedouin of Cyrenaica.

(b) 'Cross-cutting ties'

> Well should I love the day to see,
> When Ruthvin's heir and lovely Kate,
> Were joined in wedlock's holy state,
> And quenched in love this feudal hate.
>
> (Anonymous 1814:25)

If Dr. Colson were to rework her material in the light of the new data on segmentary lineage systems that Lewis and Peters have published since 1960, her view of the feud in Tonga society might be radically changed. It is my conjecture that she would discover a feuding mechanism structurally very similar to those described for Somaliland and Cyrenaica, for the stress recently laid upon choice and contract as factors of great importance in determining how a *particular* segmentary system will function in a *given* set of oecological and political conditions has provided a framework for analysis embodying a degree of flexibility that allows for nuances of interpretation quite inconceivable at the time that Colson wrote her paper.

The crux of the whole peace-in-the-feud controversy is, as Peters has succinctly pointed out, not that Colson's 'cross-cutting ties' should so bind the society in question into a homogeneous whole in which *no* relations of hostility can be tolerated, but that alliances should form in such a manner that it should be in the interests of certain sections only to remain on terms of amity and co-operation, 'leaving others with sufficient discreteness to pursue feuding relationships' (1967:262). These relationships can be 'eternal' between certain groups whilst inexistent between others. Before the imposition of British colonial administration the Tonga, like the Bedouin, may thus have recognized the necessity of maintaining peaceful relations with certain closely linked groups whilst there were less constraints to inhibit fighting with structurally and oecologically more distant ones. Colson seems to think that the complexity of affinal ties and the emotional intensity vested in complementary filiation are both greater in matrilineal than in patrilineal lineage societies and that, therefore, 'In a society of this type it is impossible to have the development and the institutionalization of repeated acts of vengeance, for each act of vengeance, like each original incident, mobilizes different groups whose interests are concerned in the particular case and that alone' (1962:119).

Peters is opposed to this kind of approach and emphatically denies that one type of linkage between groups should take precedence over another. In his view, it is irrelevant to speak of agnation or matrilineal descent 'disturbed' or 'cut across' by affinal ties (1967:272). In a social situation *all* ties must be considered and their potential capacity to modify the situation evaluated. In Cyrenaica, as I have already mentioned (cf. p. 93), to kill the mother's brother is a heinous crime usually treated like an intra-group killing on a par with fratricide. But since marriage with the father's brother's daughter is widely practised, it often happens that the mother's brother is also Ego's father's father's brother's son, that is to say a close agnate and not a member of another lineage:

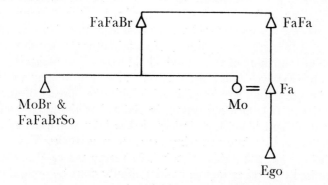

To kill an agnatic mother's brother is regarded as even more iniquitous than the murder of an affinal mother's brother living in another camp. The injection of an affinal quality into an otherwise agnatic relationship both 'transmutes' (Peters 1965: 140) and intensifies the existent tie, thereby leading, in the case of homicide, to differentiation between crimes committed within the tertiary group (1967:274). Peters cites this one example only, but similar instances can be found in all societies to invalidate the folk model and show that each relationship constitutes a unique permutation of an almost unlimited number of potential linkages each having both its own individual significance and a second accrued significance when operative as part of a larger network of ties.

Ties of affinity or cognation certainly help to narrow the field of those with whom a group will entertain relations of hostility. But they will not prevent an outbreak of violence if it is thought that armed force will achieve the desired goal faster than diplomacy. Lewis' statements relative to feuding between affinally linked lineages in Somaliland provide an excellent example of this: the Somali do not trust affines, however they will endure them as long as no direct cause for conflict presents itself. But if affinally linked groups enter into competition over access to land or water, fighting will inevitably result. Or, as Peters has put it, 'Cognation, in short, acts as a check not a preventative' (1951: 366).

Lewis and Peters are in fact not revealing anything new. The Roman episode that tells of the bloody struggle between the Horatii and the Curiatii who were linked by marriage is an ancient example of the inadequacy of affinal ties alone to ensure the maintenance of peace between hostile groups. A much quoted passage from the early history of social anthropology shows that 'the peacemaking of women who hold to one clan as sisters and to another as wives' was not always effective in producing a conflict of loyalties that would of itself inhibit the spread of feuding relations: 'It [exogamy] cannot be claimed as absolutely preventing strife and bloodshed, indeed, it has been remarked of some peoples ... that intermarrying clans do nevertheless marry and fight' (Tylor 1889:268). If this is in reality the case, it may be surmised that other factors besides affinity must be present in an acephalous society if a state of Hobbesian anarchy is not to obtain.

Working on purely theoretical lines, Coser (1965:78) has observed that the coexistence of a multiplicity of conflicts within a society does not necessarily lead to a state of equilibrium in which the forces of violence and self-interest balance each other out: when two stones are thrown into the same millpond the two sets of ripples can either neutralize each other or else combine to make larger waves. Similarly, if social groups have mutually reinforcing interests, they will not fight and will coalesce to further these interests in common against those whose interests are opposed to their own. Thus, if ties of affinity coincide with links created to further interests of, for instance, an economic nature, it might be expected that the lines along which political alliance is contracted in the society in question would closely follow marriage patterns. But if economic interests are restricted to the local or agnatic group, then the possibility of conflict with affinally linked groups should remain untrammelled.

This hypothesis is born out by a comparison of the patterns of alliance and marriage among the Cyrenaican Bedouin and Somali pastoralists. The former, as already described, marry as frequently outside the tertiary section as they do within it. Marriage, however, is not with close collateral tertiary sections occupying an adjacent *watan* or homeland, for it is precisely with these sections that latent conflicts over proprietary rights to land and water are at their most intense. Such conflicts persist but rarely reach the stage of open violence, for it is to the advantage of all concerned to minimize strife between local groups. The impossibility of local territorial expansion makes it expedient for the Bedouin to contract ties with distant tertiary sections. These ties, sanctioned by intermarriage, give access to a greater variety of oecological niches in the event of a local drought or crop failure (1965:135). Affines thus rarely fight among the Cyrenaican Bedouin, as it is to their mutual advantage to help each other in periods of difficulty.

Unlike the Bedouin, the Somali have little or no notion of a 'homeland'. Movement of flocks and access to grazing areas are in general unrestricted, although where water is scarce some proprietary rights are retained over wells. In these circumstances of almost total freedom, few[17] interests of an economic order bind any

[17] It is true that, in a compilation of source materials on the Somali (undertaken before doing his own fieldwork in the Horn of Africa), Lewis quotes one of his predecessors in the area as making exactly the same observations on the oecological advantages to be obtained from a policy of strategic exogamy at a distance as those put forward by Peters in the Cyrenaican context (Lewis 1955:111). However, fieldwork must have convinced Lewis that such exogamous ties were endowed with little or no economic content, since his emphasis in the book he wrote on returning from the field (Lewis 1961) is on the mutually hostile mistrust displayed by affines, whereas a tendency to reciprocal co-operation is hardly mentioned.

group to any other. Alliances occur exclusively for mutual protection against the predatory attack of outsiders and are usually contracted on predominantly agnatic lines, for, in the absence of any other principle, it is clear that a man is liable to trust most those among whom he was born and brought up.

Whereas in Cyrenaica the recognition of territorial discreteness and a considerable degree of oecological variation from one part of the country to another make a spread of ties through women desirable, in Somaliland these variables are apparently not operative to the same extent. Cross-cutting ties of affinity among the Bedouin restrict the number of sections with which it is feasible to maintain feuding relations and militate against the formation of large coalitions based on the single overriding principle of agnation. The Somali, on the other hand, have little reason not to fight against affinally linked groups and do so when involved in large scale conflicts in which their interests—aggression to obtain access to natural resources—are identical with those of agnates. Ties through women thus only inhibit conflict between groups when they coincide with more material goals.[18]

(c) The sins of the fathers ...

> This day's black fate on more days doth depend;
> This but begins the woe others must end.
> *(Romeo and Juliet*, III, 1)

Whatever the precise reasons invoked—affinity, oecology, economic advantage or political alliance to meet a threat from without—the return of peace after an outbreak of hostilities between groups is referred to by the majority of anthropologists cited above (cf. ch. II sect. 3a) as the 'conclusion' of a feud. But this is a very short-sighted view of the phenomenon. The evidence supporting the contention that feud is 'interminable'—that is, survives the death of both principals and continues down the generations until physical distance or extermination bring about a permanent cessation of hostilities—is, as I suggested in the first chapter, overwhelming. For the sake of brevity, I shall give no further examples of actual feuds that have endured in this manner.

---

[18] An interesting perspective for future research would be to find out whether this holds for bilateral feuding societies as well.

Also in the first chapter, I gave a short *résumé* of Peters' analysis of the manner in which the effects of homicide were a function of the passage of time, differential human fertility and oecological pressure combined. It will have now become apparent from the ethnographic facts and the arguments put forward in the second section of the present chapter that, if 'unsegmentary behaviour' provides the means by which feuding societies maintain a measure of equilibrium between the forces engaged or potentially engaged in feud, feud is itself the outward manifestation of the *process* of segmentation that makes this behaviour possible. Feud seen as the history of the consequences of an initial act of violence through time serves as a sliding scale to indicate the quality of relationships. Again, like a slide rule on which information can be read off by first either moving the cursor or else referring to the relative position of figures on the panel at rest, feud can be activated with the express purpose of testing the stability of an existing relationship or, alternatively, its presence or absence between two groups can be alluded to by a speaker to characterize their relationship to one another: the outbreak of feud is engineered as a pretext for fission; its continued existence between two groups of a specific order of segmentation constitutes a description of the type of interaction to which they are party. If a Cyrenaican Bedouin tertiary section enters upon what Peters has called a 'feuding relationship' with another collateral tertiary section, it is clear to the Bedouin concerned that these hostilities are the outward manifestation of fission and that the two sections will henceforth regard each other as belonging to two separate secondary sections.

From this last comparison with the Cyrenaican material it will be evident that I have been using the word feud in the first half of the preceding paragraph in a sense that Peters himself would not allow. He cautiously restricts his own structural definition of the terms feud, vengeance and warfare to Cyrenaica. However, if feud is 'interminable' and intra-group killing, vengeance killing and warfare are also structurally defined and therefore part and parcel of the process of segmentation, there is some justification for regarding each of them as an isolated series of events that together constitute one general historical phenomenon which I have hitherto loosely designated as feud. The definitional distinctions that I made at the end of the first chapter provide useful categories for the rapid identification of individual acts reported in the literature. But they do not, taken together, communicate the idea of process which, with Peters, I consider of paramount importance in segmentary societies to the whole notion of hostilities viewed as a relationship developing and expanding through time to involve increasing numbers of individuals.

An elaboration of the correlation that exists in the Cyrenaican context between different types of hostile relationships and the process of segmentation cannot be made everywhere for the good reason that in a number of lineage societies the oecological constraints are such that frequent segmentation is out of the question. It would appear, for example, from the literature on northern Albania that every square metre of arable land was tilled and every litre of available water used to irrigate the meagre crops. In such conditions it is indeed difficult to imagine where a refractory lineage splinter could have taken up residence to establish its territorial and political discreteness. Lineages did trace their genealogies back to an apical ancestor who was said to have founded the tribe. But as far as the rather inadequate information goes, the Albanian mountaineers did not normally seem to recognize the existence of intermediate levels of segmentation between the local land-owning lineage and the tribe at large. In some cases (cf. Durham 1909:*passim*) the tribe was divided into clans, but tribesmen explained this by reference to the admission of outsiders into the tribe at a time in the dim past when there had been no shortage of land. To account for this absence of segmentary steps it must be surmised therefore that the birth-rate in any one local settlement remained fairly low over very long periods of time or else that a considerable number of adult males were continually sloughed off into the Turkish army, were killed in feud or took up residence outside the tribal system in the wealthy towns of Macedonia or the Dalmatian coast. It seems also that disease took a very heavy toll of life (Albania 1943:3).

At all events, the oecological constraints that prevented segmentation and spatial mobility also inhibited the development in northern Albania of a series of delicately nuanced distinctions between different types of violence that correspond with structural distance as reflected in the genealogies. The distinctions that did occur were instead on the basis of territorial divisions. There were thus four types of killing of different degrees of gravity. The literature does not mention whether they bore different names

The most serious was the killing of a near agnate living under the same roof. Next was the murder of a fellow villager. Beyond this, killings within the tribe were occasionally sanctioned by the tribe at large, whereas those in which the victim was from another tribe were often applauded as acts of bravado. The main criterion for distinction between types of homicide was physical distance which, at the lineage and the tribal levels, corresponded with real or fictitious structural distance, the important factor remaining, however, at all levels that of residence.

Feud in Albania was indeed 'interminable'—that is, sporadically renewed—as is clear from the passages from von Hahn and Tozer that I quoted in the first chapter (cf. pp. 2 and 14). It differs nonetheless from the Cyrenaican version of the same phenomenon in that it remains, at the lowest level of social organization, strictly associated with the direct line of agnatic descent defined by the unit of economic co-operation or *vllazni*. Since segmentation cannot, in principle, occur,[19] feud will be carried on down the generations by those men who succeed each other in the same household. The Albanian feud could not spread to include an ever wider range of individuals, but it could and did frequently survive its 'conclusion' sealed by the payment of compensation to break out anew decades later when a cause of friction arose between old enemies. As the Reverend Tozer remarks, for instance, '. . . the Mirdite [mountaineer from the Mirditë region of Albania] never really forgets blood has been shed' (1869:306).

In another sedentary village-based lineage society where access to arable land in short supply is gained only through agnatic inheritance, an identical situation is to be found: feuding in Stirling's Turkish villages continues down the generations between enemy lineages but never spreads to a wider range of kin, because oecological pressures make segmentation impossible. Although sufficient comparative material is not available, it is not unreasonable to hypothesize that this restriction of feuding to the same agnatic core of relatives from one generation to another constitutes a general pattern in village societies displaying the same genealogical and oecological characteristics as Albania and

---

[19] von Hahn is adamant on this point: 'Der Albanese trennt sich in der Regel nie vom Vaterhause und gehorcht seinem Vater so lange dieser lebt, und nach dessen Tode seinem ältesten Bruder . . .' (1867:338).

Central Anatolia. To judge, on the other hand, by the Bedouin of Cyrenaica and the pastoral Somali, it would seem that the opposite pattern is typical of segmentary lineage societies in which there are few natural obstacles to the segmentation of prolific sections and their subsequent territorial adjustment in relation to available resources. The segmentation of local groups leads in such conditions, in theory, to an extension of hostilities in succeeding generations. But this is off-set by the decreasing physical proximity of those who inherit a feud and the diminishing desire of agnates further and further removed in time and space from the principals to avenge a homicide which was originally no affair of their own. In such societies feud remains dormant over broad structural distances unless it is needed as a pretext to re-engage in hostilities to win advantages of an oecological or political nature.[20]

If feud expresses the varying quality of relationships between groups over interminable periods of time, the events of generations past must be remembered in order that the history of outrage and homicide may serve as a mould in which to cast the pattern of present relations. Largely preliterate feuding societies have consequently created a number of crude devices which serve to record the events of feud and to 'awaken' successive generations to take vengeance for their forbears. In Somaliland,[21] southern Greece,[22] Albania,[23] and Corsica[24] it is customary practice for the women to improvise funerary dirges the principal object of which is to incite the dependants and close kin of the victim to wash the stain of blood from their house by spilling the blood of the killer or his near agnates. These dirges express ferociously blood-thirsty sentiments and are frequently the work of women

[20] The effect of this dichotomy between the radically different sets of oecological variables that characterize sedentary and nomadic societies is not only to be perceived in the structural aspects of the feud. Its importance for the determination of two distinct basic types of feud will be the object of further discussion in chapter IV: the presence or absence of a surplus of natural resources and the factor of spatial mobility combined tend, according to the environment, to alter the emphasis that is placed on the role of honour as a cause of conflict.

[21] Lewis 1961:246.

[22] Andromedas 18–19.

[23] Durham 1909:41, 1928:164; and Hasluck 1954:220.

[24] Busquet 1920:98–102 *et passim*; and Mérimée 1840a:197–8, 1840b:16.

endowed with outstanding poetical gifts. They are remembered
by the kin of the victim over whose bier they were sung and are
repeated by their womenfolk for years after the event to instil
into the male heirs of the deceased, who may have been infants
at the time of the killing, the necessity to bring vengeance when
they grow old enough to bear arms.

Called *voceru, buceratu* or *ballata* in Corsica (Mérimée 1840a:
197), *klama* in southern Greece (Andromedas 19) and *geeraar* or
gabay in Somaliland (Lewis 1961:246), these improvisations are
taken up by the people and occupy a position of importance in
the repertory of local folk poetry. In Corsica they may even be
sung by the menfolk to urge their companions to avenge the
death of a kinsman. When this occurs it is said that the singer has
'dato il rimbecco' or 'levelled a reproach' at the man intended
to hear the song (Mérimée 1840b:16). Busquet reports that the
opprobrium suffered by a man who did not take vengeance after
such powerful provocation was at one period in Corsican history
generally regarded as so unendurable that a jury would acquit
any man charged with murder, if it could be proved that he had
been the object of a *rimbecco* (Busquet 1920:359). Albanian
men also ostracized a fellow tribesman who had not laved his
honour in the blood of the killer of his kinsman. A man was
'reminded' of his duty to bring vengeance by a glass of *rakia*
that was passed to him in public from behind the back of the
giver. If this tacit accusation of cowardice was ignored and no
killing resulted, the man who had not avenged his own kinsman
was shunned by the society at large.

Again in Albania, the idea of vengeance was kept alive in the
regions of Mirditë and Kurbin by the building of a stone cairn
by the victim's kin on the spot where the man fell. On this
cairn 'every passer-by was expected to throw a green leaf, a blade
of grass or a pebble' (Hasluck 1954:231) which constantly reminded the avengers of their duty.

Everywhere in the Mediterranean and the Middle East it was
common also to demand as a supplement to the stipulated sum
of blood money the horse ridden and the dagger or the gun used
in the killing (e.g. Durham 1928:90; Kadhim 1957:70). Kennett
says that this was frequent in cases of abduction and elopement
when the actual camel or the horse on which the couple escaped
was an obligatory part of the compensation due (1925:134). This

ensured that the slur on the family's honour would not be forgotten and would be avenged at a later date. Another custom
shared by all these societies was the preservation of a part or the
whole of the victim's shirt steeped in his blood. This was shown
periodically by the women to his male heirs to keep the idea of
vengeance fresh in their minds (Busquet 1920:101, 339; Durham
1928:164; Hasluck 1954:231; Mérimée 1840a:208).

Dozens of similar customs could be enumerated. Yet there is no
point to such repetition, for, whatever the superficial variations,
their fundamental significance is always the same: they constitute a sort of mnemonic intended to perpetuate feud after the
death of the principals and beyond the acceptance of compensation. They ensure that if the sins of the fathers cannot be visited
upon the fathers themselves, the sons will surely suffer.

(4) DEBT

The mnemonic devices described above do in a general fashion
record feud in order to resuscitate it from generation to generation. But each piece of blood-soaked cloth, each cairn of stones,
each gun received in compensation can only commemorate a
single event. At first sight, it would seem that each killing is little
more than an isolated act perpetrated in revenge for the one that
immediately preceded it. Yet, by Peters' and my own definition,
feuds are interminable, because each homicide inexorably leads
to a *sequence* of hostilities down the course of time.

This apparent contradiction is resolved if it is recalled (cf.
p. 20) that among the Bedouin—and in all other feuding societies
in the Mediterranean and the Middle East—an original homicide
is spoken of as a 'debt' and vengeance as a 'redemption of the
debt': the mnemonics of vengeance may provide a record of individual acts, but are better seen as statements of account, or,
if it is preferred, of the score at a given stage in the game. The
debtor or killer is 'winning', that is, he is in a politically stronger
position than the creditors, once his group has managed to obtain
from the victim's kin recognition and acceptance of the principle
that blood wealth may be substituted for the life taken. For, as
Keynes pointed out, the big man who, by dint of powerful influence, has succeeded in floating a loan of $5,000,000 from the

bank is in a much better position to make the manager and board tremble with apprehension than *vice versa*. The commodity borrowed in the present instance is time—time before vengeance is brought and the honour of the victim's group vindicated. The extension of credit to a killer rather than recourse to physical reprisals is tantamount to acknowledgement of his provisional superiority. The magnitude of the debt owed is exactly proportional to the degree of political ascendancy exercised by the debtor over the creditor. The readiness and haste of the creditor to redeem the debt are likewise a measure of his political independence from the debtor[25] off-set by considerations of an oecological nature, which make it expedient in certain circumstances for the creditor to remain on terms of amity with the debtor without exacting complete payment. Debt constitutes the language and vengeance the executive force of policy.

The idea that 'debt is the lubricant which keeps relationships moving' (Peters 1951:338) is not new to social anthropology. Over thirty years ago Arensberg described the ties between peasant farmers and shopkeepers in rural Ireland as a 'credit system' in which 'the debt the farmer owes, like the fortune he gives in marriage, is a tangible monetary symbol of alliance and mutual obligation' (Arensberg 1937:172). Similarly, in feuding societies, if homicide inaugurates a relationship, debt is the mechanism whereby it is perpetuated (cf. Peters 1951:iii). Debt created by homicide outside the vengeance group but within the jural community provides a symbolic mirror in which are reflected the finest nuances of the changing balance of power between the two groups involved.

This is exemplified by material from Peters' thesis, one section of which is devoted to an extensive study of debt relations among the Bedouin of Cyrenaica. Starting from the loan of goods and animals and working upwards *via* the debts incurred through marriage to those created by homicide, he shows that all social relations are in the last analysis expressed in terms of the bond that ties the debtor to the creditor and *vice versa*. The complexities of the Cyrenaican system defy summary. The basic principle, however, is that the creditor is, with rare exceptions,[26] always in a position of inferiority *vis-à-vis* the debtor, but hesitates

[25] For an ethnographic illustration of this point cf. Lewis 1962:24.
[26] E.g. anti-social killing or homicide within the minimal lineage.

to extract the total sum owed for fear of terminating, in this manner, the relationship of strained amity based on mutual interest. For outside the nexus of relationships based on debt all contact between groups is characterized by potential hostility. The status of neutral is virtually inexistent.[27] Thus, both marriage and homicide compounded by the promised payment of *diya* or compensation are undertakings that make accessible a wide range of different forms of potential interaction between two parties, and as long as the initial debt remains—that is, as long as the agreed sum of bridewealth or blood money is never paid *in toto*—a situation of latent political inequality endures.

Recalcitrance in the payment of bridewealth is normal but is tolerated for two reasons. Firstly, the continued existence of the debt maintains the relationship, which it was the intention of those involved to create. Secondly, affines in other groups are chosen for the role they play as economic partners (cf. ch. II sect. 2 above) and to antagonize them would be equivalent to placing in jeopardy one's access to natural resources in time of need. It may further be assumed that the economically reciprocal function of affinal relations helps to equalize the political ascendancy that is otherwise gained by giving a woman in marriage.

In the case of homicide, however, the position of creditor is not sought after. Compensation is only accepted if very urgent motives militate against the bringing of immediate vengeance. Slowness in the payment of compensation can only be suffered for the same motives. The realization that to bring vengeance would create a state of hostility between territorially adjacent groups making normal life impossible, or the numerical weakness of one of the groups concerned, constitute powerful incentives for the acceptance of a debt relationship attendant upon homicide and the temporary renunciation of the right and duty to exact vengeance.

Debts of blood, as I stated above, therefore provide a mirror in which the changing balance of power between groups is reflected, because groups linked by a homicide will only show themselves amenable to arbitration and the payment or acceptance of compensation if it is to their mutual political and

---

[27] *Marabtin bi'l baraka* or 'clients of goodness' are a notable, though numerically small exception. Their role in arbitration will be discussed in the next chapter.

economic advantage: the killer's group, on the one hand, will offer to submit to arbitration if they feel that they are neither strong enough nor far enough removed in territorial terms to run the risk of reprisals; the victim's group, on the other hand, will only forego vengeance for the same reasons. But the greater the gravity of the homicide for which the victim's group are willing to accept compensation the greater the political victory of the killers, for the acceptance of compensation is only a *pis aller* in lieu of vengeance. The killers have, by definition, achieved a position of superiority by killing.

If, however, willingness to pay a given sum has been expressed by the killer, but the victim's group, in the meantime, have bettered their political situation by contracting a powerful alliance, it is likely that the latter will increase their demands and begin to show impatience at the slow rate at which the compensation is being paid. At this juncture, either the killer's group will make a supreme effort to demonstrate their good will by handing over larger instalments at more regular intervals, or else they will do nothing and the victim's group will in all probability find some pretext to kill the killer or one of his agnates, thereby achieving three goals: reversal of their situation of inferiority *vis-à-vis* the initial killers, precipitation of segmentation[28] and the declaration of an interminable feud.

The example given above is based on an interpretation of Peters' Cyrenaican material and is purely hypothetical. The description of a real situation of this kind among the Bedouin would call for much more detail relative to levels of segmentation and the refinements of different types of compensation.[29] What is important here, however, is that debt is a language that expresses relationships: it is the knot through which pass the strands of oecological necessity, political dominance, alliance and descent. When debt is denied or rapid repayment is demanded, the chances are that the 'debt will be redeemed' and a feud declared. Or, as Peters puts it, 'Debt is the means whereby vengeance [a single isolated killing] is translated into feud' (1951:317). The

[28] —thereby forcing recognition of two distinct secondary sections in a structural context in which, up to this moment, there had existed only two tertiary sections accepting common membership of the same secondary section.

[29] I shall deal with these in the next chapter.

inheritance of debt, and its complement feud, by the new generation from the old endows relationships between descent groups with an element of continuity through time. In an environment and at a level of technology that do not favour the development of an historical perspective, like that fostered by the existence of written records in literate societies, feud and debt constitute the history of the people in question.

This conceptual connection between feud and debt is not restricted to Cyrenaica. In Leach's discussion of the fundamental notion of *hka* or debt in Highland Burma the author shows how the Kachin use the same word for feud: for them feud and debt are synonymous and debts in blood left outstanding are the very stuff of relationships (1954:153). In Albania (Durham 1909:35; von Hahn 1867:47), Egypt (Kennett 1925:52), Eastern Arabia (Lienhardt 1957:128) and in Corsica (Busquet 1920:90) the murder of a kinsman is everywhere said to be a debt that must be redeemed by his agnates. Lienhardt reports that in Eastern Arabia tribal loyalty or *shaff* is described by the phrase 'their blood and our blood are one, their debt and our debt are one' (1957:128). According to Hanoteau and Letourneux, in Kabylia also 'Le premier meutre, le fait qui donne naissance à la dette du sang, s'appelle *ertal*, prêt.' And they remark: 'C'est bien un prêt, en effet, dont la quittance ne se donne que sur un cadavre' (1893:63). The conceptualization of relationships in terms of debt is most clearly demonstrated in the context of the feud by the Corsican dialect phrase 'siamo pace', that is, literally, 'we are [in] peace', but which in reality is normally used to mean 'we are quits' (Busquet 1920:199): the absence or temporary conclusion of conflict in Corsica is conceptually identical to an equilibrium achieved between the accounts of debtor and creditor.

The idea that any value that changes hands should be returned in kind, and usually with increment, is a commonplace in the ethnography of small-scale societies. In feuding societies in the Mediterranean and the Middle East, where the accumulation of great material wealth is oecologically not feasible, the same idea has been translated onto a moral plane and homicide is regarded as a form of prestation in the general context of gift exchange. Transaction by the exchange of goods and services contributes to the cohesion of these societies at the level of subsistence economics. Transactions in homicide and blood supplement the paucity of material wealth and provide a means of differentiating individuals and groups.

Since transaction, as I explained in the last chapter (cf. p. 25), may be thought of as an unending process whereby the satisfaction of debts simultaneously creates new ones, feud is an eternal relationship between groups who by the manipulation of debt constantly endeavour to swing the pendulum of political dominance in their favour.

III

The 'Conclusion' of Feud

And many a direful deed were done
On both sides, yet no victory won.
Till tired at length, they solemn swore
To give this cruel warfare o'er.

(Anonymous 1814:81)

In the first two chapters I have tried to prove the general validity outside the Cyrenaican context of Peters' contention that feud is an interminable process that knows no conclusion. Whilst engaged in this task I also took the opportunity to demonstrate the manner in which previous writers had been prevented by an uncritical acceptance of the postulates of the theory of segmentary opposition from seeing the full implications of feud over long periods of time. The majority of these authors have laid considerable stress on the necessary existence in feuding societies of 'machinery' for the 'conclusion' of individual conflicts, and Stirling, to take but one example, was so thoroughly a prisoner of his expectations in this respect that he was quite perplexed when confronted with the total absence of conciliatory apparatus in a society which by all other standards obviously indulged in feuding.

The arguments of Stirling and those who preceded him are, nonetheless, not entirely unfounded, for feuds can be and are frequently 'concluded'—for the time being. The peace that ensues is, however, never permanent as long as the two parties continue to have male progeny and live within striking distance of each other, but not close enough for uninterrupted hostilities to make the conduct of normal daily life impossible. In the present chapter I shall discuss the nature of these temporary conclusions to feud and attempt to explain how they are engineered, who is involved and what kind of agreements result from them. I shall begin and end the chapter with an investigation of some of the factors which make it desirable to negotiate an occasional truce and act as a deterrent to the renewal of hostilities.

(1) SUBDUED ANARCHY

> The Papuan... would eat everybody, but he
> fears arousing endless vendettas (*The Spectator*
> 7 March 1891).

In his own contribution to the growing body of criticism which
has recently been levelled against the theory of segmentary opposition, Professor Gellner has pointed out that the mechanical
principle of fission and fusion is only conceivable in social conditions approaching anarchy, for as one of the bases of a system
conceived to maintain a measure of order it cannot function
unless disorder threatens: systems can only operate as such if
an alternative to systematic behaviour is logically possible. The
implication is that there would be no need for tribal peoples to
conceptualize their social organization in terms of a 'segmentary
system' unless this were merely an ideal far removed from the
reality of the situation. For perfect balance implies perfect peace,
and if perfect peace prevailed, there would be no necessity for a
system conceived to ensure perfect peace (Gellner 1961:51–80;
1969:53).

A system of alliances—for this is fundamentally what a segmentary system is—can therefore only function if there is some
motive for alliance. In segmentary societies, which are by
Gellner's definition egalitarian and acephalous, since they are
found in areas where oecological and technological circumstances
prevent the accumulation of wealth and consequently inhibit the
development of social stratification based on economic differentiation, this motive is supplied by *fear*. Fear of aggression promotes
egalitarian alliance to create a balance of forces in the face of
potential anarchy. If fear of aggression were removed in societies
of this type, organization into a series of evenly matched 'unsegmentary' coalitions would no longer be necessary and the
system would fall apart. If, on the other hand, aggression knew no
limits and no alliances were formed to check the spread of violence,
total anarchy or, better, Durkheimian *anomie* would reign.

Seen in this light, feud constitutes the main organizational
principle of all the societies in the Mediterranean and the Middle
East that I have mentioned. Feud or the threat of feud, mitigated
by the possibility of recourse to arbitration and, in some societies,

the existence of a number of fierce collective sanctions which are applied when the indiscriminate use of violence by a minority is thought by the majority to be getting out of hand, provide a mechanism whereby some semblance of social structure and legal norms is necessarily maintained. Feud bears the same relationship to social order as blasphemy to the Christian religion: they are both the negation of a specific structural arrangement which would cease to exist were the possibility of negation removed. T. S. Eliot has remarked that 'Genuine blasphemy . . . is the product of partial belief, and it is as impossible to the complete atheist as to the perfect Christian' (1950:373). Similarly, genuine feud is a concomitant of partial order: it occurs in conditions of anarchy—that is, in acephalous societies in which rules of conduct exist but are very frequently not observed—to knit the society into a tissue of relationships based on alliance and balanced opposition. When, on the other hand, there prevails a state of *anomie* or 'social atheism', as it might be called in the present context, that is total disregard for any form of grouping or social rules, vengeance killing, as I defined it at the end of the first chapter (pp. 29–30), is liable to be found as a substitute for feud and as the only means of obtaining redress for wrongs.

Feud itself, then, maintains the social system whilst constituting at the same time a permanent threat to the peace and order of the society in question. Or, as Evans-Pritchard puts it, 'Fear of incurring a blood-feud is . . . the most important legal sanction within a tribe and the main guarantee of an individual's life and property' (1940:150).

The ethnography of feuding societies shows a remarkable consistency on the point. Feud is often simultaneously described as a bane and a blessing. I have already quoted Peters' analysis of the manner in which a social relationship between two groups may be created by a homicide but is then perpetuated through the debt occasioned by this socially disruptive act. Leach has reported from Highland Burma that feuds among the Kachin are likewise 'directed to making life so generally unpleasant for the enemy that he finally agrees to pay compensation' (1954:92). Here too the compensation is rarely paid in full and debts remain outstanding to lend cohesion to relationships. In mid-nineteenth-century Albania a man clearly thought twice before killing another and inaugurating a feud between the victim's lineage and his own, for, as Gopčević observed, in a household at feud 'Man kann weder die Felder bestellen noch das Vieh auf die Weide treiben, ohne plötzliche Angriffe zu riskieren; zudem muss man Tag und Nacht vor Überfallen auf der Hut sein' (1881:73). Fifty years later, Mrs. Hasluck was struck by the same circumstances. With a typically British regard for understatement, she describes how the master of an Albanian household would try to settle a quarrel between his agnates and members of another lineage 'before it reached the shooting stage, which was always a nuisance to everybody concerned' (1954:35). Finally, Burckhardt is of the opinion that among the Arabian Bedouin 'The dreaded effects of "blood revenge" prevent many sanguinary conflicts' (1830:76). Moreover, he declares himself 'inclined to believe that this salutary institution contributed, in a greater degree than any other circumstance, to prevent the warlike tribes of Arabia from exterminating one another' (1830:84).

The very violent and socially debilitating effects of feud themselves thus provide powerful incentives for its rapid 'conclusion' if the parties involved cannot in some way contrive to avoid each other.

(2) UNILATERAL RECONCILIATION

Reconciliation between feuding parties, as I suggested in the last chapter, does occur quite frequently and is sealed by the maintenance of a debt relationship until such time as one of the parties judges it politically expedient and oecologically feasible to redeem or deny the debt. Readiness to pay or accept compensation for an outstanding homicide is expressed in one of two manners. Either the killer's group and public opinion are so outraged by the nature of the crime that the movement is unilateral, that is, the killer is forced to beg for pardon and, in this case, the privilege of paying compensation so as to escape with his life; or else the affair is placed in the hands of a third party who usually belongs to a recognized class of men who regularly serve as go-betweens in this type of circumstance. The latter manner of achieving reconciliation, which covers by far the greater number of cases and is comparatively complex, I shall discuss in the next section.

When the killer himself is obliged by his kinsmen to seek the pardon of the victim's vengeance group, it is usually because he has killed a man who is structurally—that is, genealogically or territorially—very close to him. Alternatively, it can be that he has killed a non-kinsman in a group with which the majority of his own vengeance group are particularly keen to remain on good terms or a man of superior status. The incentives for suing for peace must be very pressing indeed for a man to be willing to submit to the humiliation of this kind of reconciliation, for the ceremony always comprises details calculated to diminish the honour and good repute of the killer. In parts of northern Albania, for instance, the killer had to allow his hands to be tied behind his back by his kinsmen before he could present himself to the victim's kin to ask forgiveness. In Kurbin, Lumë and Krasniqë the killer's wide cloth collar was thrown over his face which he dared not show for shame (Hasluck 1954:257 ff). According to Jennings Bramly (quoted in Murray 1935:209–10) the 'Aliab Bishārīn of the Egyptian desert required that a murderer seeking reconciliation be brought stark naked by 'his friends' to the tents of the victim's group. Among the Bedouin of Cyrenaica the murderer similarly showed his humility by appearing before the victim's kin bound hand and foot and wearing a shroud (Peters 1951:242).

In all such cases of reconciliation unilaterally solicited by the killer and his group it is reported that the killer always offers his life to the victim's agnates. The Awlād 'Alī Bedouin murderer, for example, would say to the 'relations' of the dead man as he introduced himself into their tent 'Here I am, kill me, or accept the ransom' (Burckhardt, in Murray 1935:210). Burckhardt claims that the conciliatory gesture was sometimes refused by the victim's kin and that the murderer was occasionally killed on the spot. The copious evidence that exists on unilateral reconciliation ceremonies would indicate that this is either very exceptional or false, for, as Mrs. Hasluck points out, no man is going to be so foolhardy as to offer his life to the victim's kin unless he is absolutely certain that they are going to refuse it. If his own kinsmen insisted that he ask forgiveness and he felt that his life was in danger, he would most probably circumvent the issue by choosing to go into voluntary exile for some years.

Reconciliation unilaterally sought in the manner described

above was strictly equivalent to the murderer and his kin acknow-ledging that they were in the wrong. It was a procedure resorted to mostly in cases of accidental homicide and the murder of close kinsmen or associates in hot blood. It never followed upon an act of deliberate policy or feud calculated to antagonize a long-standing enemy and thereby gain the politically advantageous status of debtor. Nor was the homicide, for which those seeking unilateral reconciliation desired to atone, intended, like many other acts of violence, to precipitate fission within a group, although it might be used as a pretext to achieve such an end at a later date.

A quite different method of restoring good relations between groups estranged by a killing was recourse to arbitration and the services of a mediator.

(3) ARBITRATION

Recourse to arbitration to put a temporary end to a state of hos-tility between two groups also fell mainly to the initiative of the debtors or the group with 'a man on their backs' (Peters 1967: 276). But it did not have the dishonourable connotations of a craven begging for forgiveness, as did unilateral reconciliation. The killer's group might well make a show of humility and regret, but this was often enhanced and enlarged upon by the mediator whose task it was precisely to emphasize these aspects in the behaviour of the debtors. It was the mediator's duty to convince the creditors of the sincerity of the killer's group in their overtures for peace whilst at the same time endeavouring to cover up any visible signs that might betray the latter's satisfaction at having stolen a political march on their enemies.

Arbitration, as I have already said, never took place unless it was to the advantage of both parties. The desire of neighbours not to live daily in a state of anarchical violence, the unavailability elsewhere of natural resources making it possible to place a certain physical distance between them, the numerical weakness of one of the parties were all factors that might make acceptance of mediation expedient after a homicide or a series of homicides and other outrages. Though the killer's group might initiate the proceedings and might thus appear to be begging that reprisals should not be taken, the dominant role was theirs, for the victim's group, whose sacred duty it was to avenge their kinsman's death at the first opportunity, were, by accepting arbitration, diminishing somewhat their stature in the eyes of public opinion by this readiness to procrastinate for motives of a material nature.

The details of reconciliation ceremonies are everywhere very similar and include a demonstration of mock hostility by the victim's kinsmen when the killer's group arrive at their homestead accompanied by the mediator, eating or drinking—often from one communal vessel—of the same food and beverages usually supplied by the killer's group and prepared by their womenfolk, the communal recitation of a prayer, the handing over of the first instalment of the compensation agreed upon and the exchange of solemn oaths and embraces by the two parties. In literate societies, the reconciliation is sometimes recorded in a document drawn up for this purpose together with the amount of compensation to be paid and the dates on which individual portions are due (e.g. Du Bois-Aymé 1809:586; Durham 1928:88–90; Murray 1935:209; Peters 1951:290–2).

There are many variations on this general theme. In Cyrenaica, for example, the amount of compensation to be paid is decided upon through the mediator a few weeks before the ceremony (Peters 1951: 291). Elsewhere the decision was taken on the spot and after much wrangling between the parties concerned presided over by the mediator. Some societies required that the gun of the killing be handed over as the first instalment of the compensation (Durham 1928:90–1), others did not. In Christian communities—in parts of Montenegro, for instance—the reconciliation was sealed by the creation of links of god-parenthood between infants of the killer's group and agnates of the victim, whereas nearly everywhere else in the Mediterranean and the Middle East the return of peace was sanctioned by a transfer of women from the killer's to the victim's lineage.[1]

---

[1] The woman, who was normally a nubile girl, was given in marriage, in part payment of the compensation due, to a close kinsman of the dead man. It was thought that if she bore a male child to the victim's lineage, this replaced the victim himself and restored the depleted manpower of his group. If the child was a girl, the infant would later be married out to a third lineage. The bridewealth paid for her would in turn permit the marriage of a young man of the victim's group which might be blessed with male offspring. If and when the original girl transferred from the

But there is no point in reproducing here all the details that can be found in the voluminous ethnography that exists on reconciliation ceremonies in the area. As I have already indicated why groups prefer in certain circumstances to submit to arbitration rather than exact vengeance, the topics of importance that remain to be treated in this connection are

(a) the identity and qualifications of those who offer their services as mediators;

(b) their motives for doing so;

(c) the means by which they achieve their ends.

(*a*)

> . . . he quha should be ane Arbitour, sould be of
> gude brute and fame (Skene 1609:20r).

So much attention has been devoted by sociologists to the first of these topics that it is now generally accepted that mediators are always, regardless of the level of civilization or technology, chosen from among those individuals who by virtue of their professional, political, kinship or ideological status stand somewhat outside the system, but not so far outside that they cannot, if necessary, be assimilated into it in the event of confrontation between the system and factors from even further abroad. In the Mediterranean and the Middle East mediators tend to belong to one of two social categories: they are either political or religious leaders. In both cases they stand over and above their fellows, the political leaders by dint of prestige and a reputation for honour and good judgement, the men of religion by virtue of their belonging to another social order at the same time apart from but complementary to the lay community.

Because of their distinctive way of life and their supposed

killer's to the victim's group had produced the required child, she was frequently allowed to return to her paternal kin. In the event of her proving barren, she was repudiated by her husband and another girl was provided by the killer's group to take her place. For customs pertaining to the transfer of women in part settlement of debts created by homicide, elopement or adultery cf. *inter alia*, for the Islamic world, Barth 1965:96, Burckhardt 1830:158, Kadhim 1957:40-1, Kennett 1925:54-5; and, for Christendom, Busquet 1920:224, Durham 1909:30.

proximity to the sources of goodness and 'truth', the role of men
of religion in arbitration is on the whole easier to isolate and
circumscribe than that of their politically defined counterparts
who seldom bear official titles and are usually only loosely alluded
to as grey-beards, elders, 'important men' or chiefs. In the
Mediterranean and the Middle East, men who offer their services
as mediators on the grounds of the prestige and knowledge that
they derive from religious practice are either, in parts of the
Balkans and in Corsica, Catholic priests, or else, in the Islamic
regions, saintly personages who usually belong to specific lineage
clusters or segments, often reckoning specious descent from the
prophet, in which a reputation for saintliness is passed down from
one generation to another. Examples of the latter are the *marabtin bi'l baraka* or 'clients of goodness' referred to in the last chapter (Peters 1967:265), who fulfil the role of mediators among the
Bedouin of Cyrenaica, the *igurramen* (sing. *agurram*) of the
Central High Atlas (Gellner 1969:*passim*).[2]

Gellner, who has made a minute analysis of the constitution of
saintly lineages among the Berbers, discovered that whatever the
number of potential saints living at any one time, many
of these men remain what he calls 'latent' *igurramen* and behave
in almost every respect as if they were laymen. The reason for
this, he thinks, is that the market for saintliness can become
saturated, or, in other words, not all those entitled to do so by
birth can make a living, in conditions of limited demand, out of
arbitration, the sale of protective amulets and other occupations
associated with the saintly calling. A large proportion of the
igurramen continue to live in or around the saintly lodges, but
lead the life of perfectly ordinary tribesmen and even sometimes
indulge in feuds—although the practice of physical violence is in
principle incompatible with their status. Gellner is of the opinion
that achievement of a position of importance as an *agurram*
depends to a very large degree on the success that a beginner
experiences in negotiating a reconciliation between two litigants.
If he is successful at first and continues to be so in subsequent
cases, his prestige and reputation will grow and his services will

---

[2] Saintliness is, however, not always a lineage attribute. The Somali
wadaads, or men of religion, for instance, acquire a reputation for piety
and rectitude as individuals and quite independently of their descent
group affiliations (Lewis 1961: *passim* and 1966:210–11).

be increasingly sought after. If, on the other hand, his first attempts to capitalize on his descent from the prophet and *baraka*, or mystical efficacity, fail and he does not succeed in building a reputation for himself, he will regress to the status of latent *agurram*. It is not enough to be a 'saint' by birth. Diplomatic skill and prestige must enhance this initial qualification. Although Peters has not examined the role of saints in as much detail as Gellner, it is not improbable that the same kind of selective mechanism is at work among Cyrenaican saintly lineages.

Whereas the majority of men of saintly lineage lead an existence very similar to that of ordinary tribesmen, effective saints constantly requested to intervene in disputes stand outside the social system in more than one sense. Not only do they normally not tend their land and flocks like other tribesmen, but they are also physically marginal. In Cyrenaica and the Central High Atlas—the two societies for which there exists sufficient information on this topic—they live in separate communities. The Berber *igurramen* inhabit lodges in the vicinity of shrines which are usually situated in disputed territory between two or more tribes (Gellner 1969:33–4, 134, 144, 154). These lodges serve as places of sanctuary. The *igurramen* consequently experience no difficulty in attracting a constant stream of men willing to work their fields and guard their flocks for the duration of their exile (Gellner 1969:136–7). In Cyrenaica, saints are similarly distinguished by their spatial distribution, for they are not uncommonly the custodians of shrines of which Evans-Pritchard remarked that they were often 'near a tribal boundary or near the boundary between one section and another' (1949:67). Barth has also shown how saints in the Swat valley become territorially marginal by occupying strips of land in the middle of a disputed block: their presence acts as buffer between the former contestants, and the land itself is regarded as the fee paid for their services (Barth 1965:93).[3]

[3] Peters maintains that Evans-Pritchard is mistaken in emphasizing as the main geographical characteristic of Cyrenaican saintly lodges their supposedly interstitial position on the boundaries between tribal territories. On the contrary, it is Peters' contention that Cyrenaican lodges are always to be found *in the middle* of favoured agricultural areas the produce of which serves, in the form of donations by the tribal inhabitants, to

The chiefs, elders and 'important men' referred to by ethnographers and travellers are not physically and morally marginal in the same sense as holy men. Their qualifications to serve as arbitrators derive from the position they occupy as political leaders. Yet, in a way, political office does not exist in these societies. In Albania, for example, the Mirditë region was 'ruled over' by an hereditary 'Prince'. But it will be remembered that this office-holder was quite powerless to prevent the tribesman in the story told by Tozer (cf. p. 14) from making extortionist demands on a descendant of the man who had caused the death of his forbear. 'Elders', according to the literature (e.g. Hasluck 1954: ch. XII), play an important part in the 'administration' of justice, but they are men who accede to these functions only by dint of age, their position at the head of a large and influential family, their wealth, prestige and wisdom, and not as elected representatives of the people. They command no coercive force and can only wield as much authority in any given instance as is conceded them by public opinion in that case and that case alone.

Albania is not atypical in this respect. An eighteenth-century text states that arbitrators in a Corsican feud were expected to be

(1) 'de' persone di probità',
(2) 'de' principali benestanti',
(3) 'di parentela numerosa', and
(4) 'che avessero nome di bravura per il colpo di mano' (Rossi, quoted in Busquet 1920:246).

enrich the lodge and nourish its saintly inmates. According to Peters, Cyrenaican lodges are by no means invariably situated on tribal boundaries, and, if they do happen to be so, the fact is without sociological significance. In view of his own findings in Cyrenaica, Peters argues, moreover, that Gellner is probably equally wrong when he stresses the geographical marginality of Berber saintly lodges (personal communication). I myself feel that, while Peters is in all probability right in stating that lodges inhabited by an economically unproductive saint population must of necessity be situated in the centre of a rich agricultural catchment area, this fact does not obligatorily invalidate the thesis put forward by Gellner and Barth: the political argument is not incompatible with the oecological one; nor is there anything to show that, outside Cyrenaica, the two may not be complementary.

—men of probity, wealth and physical bravery backed by a strong following of kinsmen. With the possible exception of the latter, these are, to say the least, nebulous qualifications that can be variously interpreted. But in egalitarian societies, in which there does not exist a class of hereditary saints, it is men who enjoy a large measure of prestige based on the sort of criteria enumerated by Rossi who are the political leaders and who do in fact at the same time qualify as arbitrators. These same men, as I will show later, are also normally those who have prosecuted successful feuds in their youth.

(*b*)

Whether men of God or laymen, the motives that bring men to accept the role of mediator are normally twofold. The first is the thought of remuneration; the second is linked with the notion of prestige. In nearly all feuding societies the mediator is paid for his pains; and in some the amount of effort the mediator is willing to deploy in favour of the person or persons whose dispute he has been called to settle is directly proportionate to the size of his fee. In Albania and among the Atlas Berbers (Hasluck 1954:139, 228; Gellner 1969:86) the parties to a dispute always paid the elders, priest or saint who offered his services as mediator. The fee paid in Albania was related to the gravity of the case: a murder in Lumë was, for instance, regarded as six times more onerous to judge than a water dispute and was remunerated in consequence (Hasluck 1954:139). The Cyrenaican Bedouin, the Beni Sakhr of southern Jordan and several tribes of the Mosul *liwa* of Iraq (Kadhim 1957:71) all recognize the principle of handing over to the mediator a percentage of the compensation money adjudicated. In Cyrenaica this fee is called a favour, *khatr*, and cannot be refused (Peters 1951:289). Among the Beni Sakhr it is usually an eighth of the *diya*, but 'if the judge is fond of money', it may be as high as a third. Some mediators altruistically ignore the fee altogether (Hardy 1963:83). In both Albania and Cyrenaica the judge must be entertained in fitting style. Mrs. Hasluck believed that the cost of such a feast for which it was usual to cook at least a whole sheep 'sometimes acted as a deterrent to the litigiously minded' (1954:141). Peters remarks, moreover, that the nature of the decision of the mediator tends to be linked to the quality of the entertainment afforded him by the litigants (1951:352).[4]

There were, thus, obvious inducements to accepting an invitation to arbitrate a dispute, especially if the case in question involved murder for which both the compensation and the mediator's fee were the most substantial. A man was also motivated to offer his services by a desire to acquire a greater quantity of one of the very qualities that had made him eligible to adjudicate in the first place. For just as prestige was a necessary prerequisite for becoming an arbitrator, so the fulfilment of such duties and the maintenance of subsequent peace between the two parties constituted one of the simplest manners of, simultaneously, engendering yet more prestige and making a practical demonstration of the prestige a man already possessed. The readiness of a man to preside over the destinies of his fellow tribesmen and to play a role of utmost social importance, whilst nevertheless remaining in his general way of life upon a footing of complete equality with those over whom he was requested to judge, was one of the methods by which a man could overcome the fiercely egalitarian ideals of such societies and gain a position from which he could wield considerable authority. I shall pursue the theme of stratification through prestige in later chapters.

(c)

If arbitrators are regarded as equals by the parties between whom they are called to adjudicate and furthermore have at their disposal no means of enforcing their decisions (e.g. Hasluck 1954: 144), it might be thought that in reality they are little more than the figureheads of a non-existent justice and that they fulfil no useful functions.

This is indeed true of arbitrators without experience and with

---

[4] The Rwala Bedouin of Syria and northern Arabia are the only tribal society in the Mediterranean and the Middle East for which I could find evidence pointing to contrary conclusions. Among the Rwala, 'No chief or surety must ask or accept compensation for aiding those who carry on the blood feud in defence of the culprit, for that would stain his honour. His sole reward is public acknowledgement that he has been instrumental in doing good, *msajjer hsane*, and preventing fresh shedding of blood' (Musil 1928:493).

no talent. The literature is full of instances of arbitration which particularly struck western European observers by the manner in which the arbitrator's decision was flouted as soon as it was made known. Mrs. Hasluck, for example, cites the case of a man from Theth in northern Albania whose house was burgled. Knowing who the thief was, he had him brought before the elders who condemned him to return the equivalent in money of the property stolen. But since the thief had bribed the elders to underevaluate the sum, the victim of the crime shot the burglar as a protest against this unequitable sentence and so began 'a bad blood feud' (Hasluck 1954:144). The weakness of the arbitrator's position as regards the enforcement of his decisions was so notorious in central Albania that arbitrators were wont 'to communicate their findings to the disputants and then add, "Now settle the matter as you like. We have decided that this one of you it right"' (Hasluck 1954:144).

Albania is, however, somewhat atypical in this respect,[5] and up to a certain point the decisions of arbitrators were usually respected throughout the tribal areas of the Mediterranean and the Middle East. There were two reasons for this. Firstly, with the possible exception of unilateral reconciliation described above (ch. III sect. 2) which was a way of forcing the victim's group into a position from which it could hardly do otherwise but conclude a temporary truce or else lose face and honour, arbitration was never resorted to unless both parties agreed to the measure. Secondly, the arbitrator, if he was at all experienced, never attempted to give a decision that would not be palatable to both sides. The first reason is a direct corollary of the social organization of these societies: since no one is explicitly recognized as politically superior to anyone else, no one is in a position to force his adversary to accept arbitration when it is not to his immediate advantage to do so.[6] The second reason touches upon principles that are fundamental to the whole concept of arbitration.

[5] In the next chapter I shall endeavour to provide an explanation of the extremely frequent occurrence of physical violence and lawlessness in Albania.

[6] In some circumstances the mass of public opinion may be so incensed by the disruptive effects of a given act of violence upon the life of the community, that the community may take action as a body. But this is relatively rare. Examples will be given in the last section of the present chapter.

In an early seventeenth-century book of *The auld lawes and constitutions of Scotland faithfullie collected . . .*' in which are tabulated the legal customs of the tribally organized Highlands during the medieval period,[7] there is a series of chapters describing the qualifications that an arbitrator should possess and his responsibilities. Certain passages are extremely revealing in the present context, for the word *compromittis* is constantly used as a synonym for *arbitrie* or arbitration (Skene 1609:20r). An agreement reached through arbitration, it says, can moreover only be terminated by the death of one of the litigants 'Or be paction or mutuall consent of the parties' (1609:21v). A similarly explicit emphasis on the importance of compromise—that is, bilateral concession—is to be found in Corsica, where arbitrators are referred to, among other things, as 'guidici compromessori' (Busquet 1920:248).

Arbitrators in the societies I am dealing with might in fact be described as experts in compromise. Their role is not to impose judgement by reference to objective criteria of justice, but to create a balance between the two parties according to each precisely the amount or value the other is willing to part with, but not more. The arbitrator evalutes the situation as the litigants see it and tries to make each of them perceive the point of view of the other and the advantages that each will derive from a restoration of good relations, even if the party blatantly at fault has to pay for the privilege of renewed peace.

With admirable insight and clarity Coser has made explicit this role of the arbitrator—or mediator—in his analysis of Simmel's essay on *Conflict*:

> '. . . the mediator can achieve reconciliation . . . only if each party believes that the objective situation justifies reconciliation and makes peace advantageous'. The mediator shows 'each party the claims and arguments of the other; they thus lose the tone of subjective passion'. He helps to strip the conflict of its nonrational and aggressive overtones. Yet this will not in itself

---

[7] The author of the article on 'SKENE, Sir John' in the *British National Biography* suggests that the title of the book is misleading and that this compilation 'is now regarded as not properly belonging to Scotland, but based on the legal system of England' (1921:22: vol. XVIII, p. 337). Whether this is true or not is, however, of no importance to my argument.

allow the parties to abandon their conflicting behaviour since, even boiled down to the 'facts of the case', the conflicting claims remain to be dealt with. The mediator's function is primarily to eliminate tension which merely seeks release so that realistic contentions can be dealt with without interference. In addition he may suggest various ways to conduct the conflict, pointing out the relative advantages and costs of each (Coser 1965:59).

To take Coser's enumeration of the functions of the arbitrator a step further, he might be described as a sort of communications engineer whose role is threefold: he selects and establishes a suitable channel of communication between the hostile parties by acting as a go-between and finally arranging for them to meet; he provides a code or language of compromise and peace through which to communicate whilst eliminating the previously existing code of aggressive invective and physical violence; he introduces a considerable volume of (ritual) redundancy—repetitions, stock phrases, formal behaviour, customary gestures—which fosters a feeling in the participants that they are acting out a familiar situation that they recognize as culturally normal and which, by encouraging the expectation of a successful outcome to the negotiations, generally reduces the level of animosity and stimulates a spirit of mutual co-operation.

The arbitrator shows the way, but cannot impose his ideas of what is right or wrong. He is a neutral in the true sense of the word, for he not only stands between two parties but is neither positive nor negative in his attitude to either of them. His task is, by stressing the advantages to be gained from particular concessions, to lead both parties onto a no-man's-land between their respective positions within which agreement is possible.

The arbitrator's role does not, however, finish here. For as I said earlier, a killer is by definition in a potentially stronger position than the creditors to whom he owes blood. If the creditors think it to their advantage to seek composition rather than revenge, they will attempt by every means in their power to pressure the mediator into awarding them the maximum compensation, whilst the killer's group will resist and, by skilful manipulation of the mediator, try to make minimal concessions in conditions least prejudicial to their prestige. For a group earns prestige by killing, but to keep this prestige intact its members should deny responsibility for the murder on the grounds that it was no more than an act of legitimate riposte to insufferable provocation and defend themselves against all efforts by the victim's kin to equalize. To agree to submit to arbitration is for both debtors and creditors slightly inglorious. It does nonetheless permit the creditors, if they are able bargainers and can prevail upon the arbitrator, to recover some of the honour and standing they have lost by imposing upon the killers humiliating stipulations concerning the type of compensation to be paid.[8]

In such circumstances and once his role of communications engineer has been played, it remains for the arbitrator to strike a balance between the opposing forces, for it would be futile for him to make a settlement involving stipulations which one of the parties would find uncongenial, since arbitrators cannot coerce obedience to their decisions.[9] The result of this situation is that the arbitrator develops an acute ear for public opinion and looks for guidance in his assessment, on the one hand, to the relative

[8] For instance, if a killing occurs between two structurally and oecologically distant tertiary sections among the Bedouin of Cyrenaica, the victim's group will attempt to exact from the killers not only the *diya* but an extra amount, or annual 'fee', called *sana'*. It is thought extremely shameful to agree to pay *sana'*, because 'If this condition is accepted it means, in effect, that the offender's group is insufficiently strong to maintain its free status', since the regular payment of an annual fee to a corporation of noble tribesmen is everywhere in Cyrenaica the hallmark of client status (Peters 1968:174). No group will agree, then, to pay *sana'* unless it feels that refusal will precipitate fission and a renewal of hostilities in which they can ill-afford to indulge at that moment. An attempt to exact *sana'* is equivalent to a declaration on the part of the victim's group of willingness to retaliate in spite of the transfer of *diya* if their demands are not met. Its payment by the killers represents a stay of execution, but is a prelude to the declaration of a feud proper when they decide to discontinue payments some thirty or forty years later (Peters 1967:276).

[9] Murray (1935:201) describes the role of the *qadi* or arbitrator in Sinaï in the following terms: 'Parties, that is families not individuals, only had recourse to a qadi, selected by mutual consent from various practitioners, in order to settle disputes generally of long standing, whose continuance had become intolerable. Here was the weakness of the system; for *powerful families, when discontented with a judge's award, were in the habit of ignoring it completely.*' (My italics.) Cf. also Gellner (1969: 129): 'The saints are, ultimately, arbitrators rather than judges: they cannot enforce their verdicts, but depend on the acceptance of that verdict by the tribesmen.'

force, prestige and status of the two hostile parties and, on the other, to public consensus. An ability to perceive the unspoken wishes of the majority constitutes at least half of the arbitrator's skill. Both Gellner and Barth have observed an identical mechanism in the course of arbitration in places as far apart as the Central High Atlas and Swat. Both have shown how the political prestige and authority of arbitrators is diminished if they make the mistake of trying to force the acceptance of decisions which are not ratified by popular assent (Gellner 1961: 211; Barth 1965:98). Among the Berbers this desire for a settlement that will be compatible with the aspirations of all concerned is so strong that parties involved in litigation, if unsatisfied with the verdict of the first arbitrator to whom they submit their case, will go to the expense and trouble of inviting the decision of a second and even a third until total consensus has been achieved (Gellner 1969:129).

The uncertainty in which arbitrators stand as to the outcome of a particular case and its effects upon their reputation as saints or elders makes their behaviour admirably suited to analysis within the framework of entrepreneurial studies. This is not the place to examine all the implications of such a perspective. But I would like to point out that arbitrators, like entrepreneurs, bridge the gap between two value systems—those of the hostile parties to arbitration—and sell risk against remuneration. Their remuneration is in money, kind and accrued prestige. The risk to which they expose themselves is that of being disobeyed, followed by the disintegration of their moral capital and a consequent lowering of their status were this to occur. Like entrepreneurs, they cannot force acceptance of the values they propose, but they can make visible the unseen advantages of a situation the possibilities of which their business acumen and foresight have caused them to perceive before their fellows.

(4) COMPURGATION

Recourse to arbitration is not the only manner in which feud may be temporarily 'concluded'. In all the societies mentioned—with the exception of Central Anatolia, Corsica and Somaliland for which information is not available on this point—there is another method of settling disputes. This is compurgation, or collective oath, a legal procedure which has been known in Europe since at least the times of Gregory of Tours (cf. Galy 1901:204 ff).

Basically, the procedure is very simple: if a body of men—the precise number varies from place to place and according to the gravity of the crime—can be mustered to swear a religious oath attesting the innocence of the accused, the latter is declared blameless and escapes all punishment and opprobrium whatever the crime of which he is suspected and however blatantly obvious his guilt. In theory, the legal efficacy of the procedure is a function of the currency of belief in supernatural sanctions. In practice, however, belief in supernatural sanctions in the marginally Islamic and Christian societies in which the institution of compurgation is or was part of the legal apparatus has always been extremely slight and sporadic. The realization that supernatural sanctions consequently provide a negligible deterrent to perjury led Gellner to examine exactly how the institution worked and to elaborate a theory of compurgation to explain the phenomenon among the Berbers of the Central High Atlas.

Gellner describes Berber compurgation, or *tagellit*, as 'a method for determining the truth or falsity of an accusation and thereby terminating (at any rate in theory) the dispute occasioned by that accusation' (1969:106). Whenever possible, co-jurors are chosen from among the close agnatic kin of the accused and are 'identical with those who must fear or exact vengeance in the case of feud' (1969:107). But, as Gellner observed, perjury is 'quite frequent' (1969:115) and no one worries unduly about supernatural sanctions, although, for the sake of precaution, compurgation ceremonies are nevertheless not held until after the harvest for fear that the ungodly intentions of a few bring disaster upon a whole valley.

The contempt displayed by the Berbers for supernatural sanctions combined with their preference for close agnates as co-jurors convince Gellner that there is more to *tagellit* than a mere legal procedure. He interprets it as a means of making a public assertion of the strength of the agnatic group and its political superiority over its adversaries. For Gellner *tagellit* is an affirmation of the temporary ascendancy gained through feud, a 'continuation of the feud by other means' (1969:122). In his view, this hypothesis is confirmed by a further detail: if agnates asked to take the oath refuse to testify, do not turn up at the appointed time or make an error in their testimony thereby 'proving' the guilt of their party, it is they who usually bear the brunt of the fine imposed as a result of their failing to honour the tenet of agnatic solidarity (1969:113). Participation in *tagellit* with one's agnates is tantamount to a declaration of 'My clan—right or wrong' (1969:114).

Peters, who found the same institution among the Bedouin of Cyrenaica, is also of the opinion that a compurgation ceremony in which fifty-five agnates swear to the innocence of a kinsman accused of murder 'is not so much a verification of the denial as a test of the group's solidarity' (1951:342). Writing of compurgation in the Merovingian period Galy draws similar conclusions:

> On ne se souciait guère de venir attester l'innocence d'un homme, que l'on n'avait pas de raison particulière de défendre. Aussi les conjureurs étaient-ils le plus souvent les parents mêmes des plaideurs . . . l'assistance d'un parent traduit en justice était pour tout parent un devoir impérieux. C'était une des formes de cette solidarité familiale . . . qui est encore le fondement de cette institution des conjureurs (1901:254).

The idea that compurgation can constitute a demonstration of agnatic and sometimes—in village based societies—neighbourhood solidarity does not totally invalidate its traditional explanation in terms of a belief in supernatural sanctions and a disinterested desire that justice be done. In Albania, for instance, provided a man accused of murder could persuade a dozen men of probity and experience to step forward in readiness to ratify the oath taken in his defence by twelve 'murder elders' chosen by the community at large, the esteem in which the honesty and good judgement of the latter were held was so great that it was frequently thought unnecessary to complete the proceedings after they had sworn to the man's innocence, and the former were dismissed before they could discharge their obligation (Hasluck 1954:137). The solidarity of the accused's group was superfluous after the testimony of the 'murder elders' who were thought to be equitable and unbiased. The verdict might be wrong, but there was no question of this outcome being deliberately engineered as seems to be the case among the Berbers.

Whatever the successes of the system and the highly complicated mechanisms that were developed to guard against deceit,[10] there were nonetheless numerous abuses. Mrs. Hasluck tells in great detail the story of a Muslim named Asllan from Labinot in central Albania who stole a plough-ox. When accused of the theft he protested his innocence and agreed to find six co-jurors with whom he would swear on the Kur'ān. The plaintiff also named six compurgators. The oaths were given in good order, and two days later after a banquet to celebrate his acquittal, the ex-accused brought down the ox he had hidden out of a lonely sheep fold and publicly yoked it. The victim of this injustice and the enraged elders could do nothing, for '. . . there was no legal machinery for annulling the verdict. In the opinion of the village, however, Asllan received his punishment when shortly afterwards his son was born lame' (1954:164–5).

Apart from its frequent inefficacy as a means of establishing the truth in cases of murder or merely civil offences, there are three aspects of compurgation that remain puzzling and for which no one has yet supplied a satisfactory explanation. The first of these is the widely attested custom whereby, in cases demanding a number of co-jurors exceeding the number of adult males in the agnatic group of the accused, each co-juror may take the oath more than once until the correct number of oaths required is reached (Kadhim 1961:144; Kennett 1925:42; Peters 1951:242). Kennett believes that this rule was introduced to prevent the establishment of a precedent when in individual cases there were not enough men available to make up the statutory number of co-jurors. This is a weak argument. It does not take into account the fact that a few men swearing the same oath several times are liable to be more consistent than, say, fifty-five—the number required in cases of homicide in certain tribes of the Western Desert—who have a greater chance of contradicting each other, particularly if some of them are only distant agnates and very little concerned with the fate of the murderer.

The second enigma in compurgation is why, when it is not specified that all the co-jurors should be agnates, the community is empowered to elect half their number and the accused the other half. It might be thought that, were the choice placed entirely in the hands of the community, there might be better chances of

[10] Cf. Kennett (1925:41–2) for an account of the intricacies of compurgation among the Bedouin of the Western Desert.

the verdict reflecting the objective truth, though it may be held that this procedure might in the long run prove anti-democratic by providing the community at large with an opportunity of victimizing slightly non-conformist individuals. In view of the strongly egalitarian principles that pertain in all feuding societies in the Mediterranean and the Middle East, I regard this as a feasible interpretation. But it still does not explain why in some areas the co-jurors are ideally only agnates and why in others they may be both agnates and village nominees.

The last problem connected with the institution of compurgation which has so far not been investigated is quite simply why compurgation should in certain circumstances be preferred to arbitration. It may well be that the obvious assumption—that compurgation is, like arbitration, intended to restore peaceful relations between groups—is wrong and that the two institutions, whilst apparently conceived to achieve similar goals, in reality serve quite contrary purposes. The difference between arbitration and compurgation is fundamentally the same as that between acquiescence and denial, between conciliation and defiance. A necessary prerequisite for arbitration to take place is that both parties should recognize the facts of the case, that is, in the event of homicide, that a member of one group has killed a member of the other. The institution of compurgation can only function, on the other hand, if the majority of one party are ready to deny point blank that they are responsible for what has happened. Compurgation, then, involves a denial of the debt, whereas recourse to arbitration implies an *ipso facto* recognition of the debt. Arbitration is the prelude to a relationship; compurgation constitutes a rupture, an unspoken declaration of the intention to continue the hostilities inaugurated through homicide or whatever the initial offence may have been. Compurgation and arbitration are not, then, alternative means of achieving the same ends, but contrary methods of dealing with the same situation to arrive at diametrically opposite goals. Yet even this is not quite true, for, in the feud, the overt aggression of groups up in arms against each other differs little in quality from the tacit mutual hostility expressed by parties to a debt of blood: both are relationships.

But if this analysis is correct, there nevertheless remains one incongruity: compurgation clearly does not always work to the advantage of the majority of those taking the oath, for a single defaulter can 'prove' the accusation to be founded. In societies, like that of the Atlas Berbers, where the group of compurgators comprises only agnates and allies in whose interest it is to eliminate dissident elements within their ranks, compurgation admirably serves this end. But in societies where half the co-jurors are appointed by the community and half by the accused it is difficult to see how such a procedure could be interpreted either as a declaration of hostilities or as a test of group solidarity, since it is the oaths of the community elders and not those of the solidary group that are crucial to the outcome of the affair. Only if the elders sincerely believe the accused is innocent, does the latter's group have an opportunity to prove their solidarity.

Even in cases, as among the Berbers, where those who take the oath are all henchmen of the accused, there is some doubt as to the fate of those who refuse for fear of supernatural sanctions to swear falsely when the accusation is based on irrefutable evidence. Are they automatically ejected from the group? This would seem unlikely in a society in which the ultimate criterion of influence is the number of riflemen a group can command. But if they are not necessarily expelled and have to bear the onus of the fine imposed by the community, it is improbable that one, two or three defaulters will be wealthy enough to do so on their own. In this event, either the group as a whole will have to contribute to the fine, thereby recognizing an obligation of solidarity towards the very defaulters it wished to penalize, or else the fine will be only partially paid. There are obviously very strong incentives, whatever their moral and religious qualms, for individuals to conform with the majority in such a situation. But it is not clear how strong these incentives are, nor are there any available data on who defaults in compurgation and why.[11]

[11] The situation created by a minority of defaulters obliged to pay a fine they cannot afford for a group from which they have marked their defection by refusing to give the oath seems so riddled with internal contradictions that there is cause for serious doubt as to whether such circumstances ever occur. It is not at all clear whether Gellner, the author of a valuable and highly sophisticated, but nonetheless confused, analysis of collective oath among the Berbers (Gellner 1969: ch. 4), himself ever witnessed a compurgation ceremony (cf. 1969:106, note 1). Nor does he give details of a single case in which the defaulting minority were obliged to pay for their indiscipline. Gellner's informants may have been describing in terms of real behaviour a legal dispositon which is and, indeed, can never be put into practice.

Information on the motivation of individuals in compurgation is almost totally lacking for all the societies in which the institution is found. It would, for example, be very interesting to know why a group allows itself to be manoeuvred into a position in which it can be challenged to prove its force and cohesion by submitting to compurgation. But without further fieldwork—and it may already be too late, since customary law rapidly decays when forced to compete with the more sophisticated legal systems imposed by the judicial authorities of modern centralized states— it is impossible to provide answers to such questions. And until they are answered it will remain uncertain whether compurgation does temporarily conclude a feud, or whether it in no way serves to mitigate attitudes of hostility and is, in Gellner's phrase, a 'continuation of the feud by other means'.

(5) COMPENSATION AND DETERRENTS

> Luitur enim etiam homicidium certo armentorum ac pecorum numero recipitque satisfactionem universa domus, utiliter in publicum, quia periculosiores sunt inimicitiae iuxta libertatem (Tacitus: *Germania*, XXI).

In the first and third sections of the present chapter I tried to evaluate the importance of the fear of feud itself and the cost of arbitration as deterrents to the prosecution of conflict by physically violent means. If the mercenary demands of arbitrators upon the killer's group are often thought by observers to act as a powerful deterrent to further outbreaks of feud, the prospect of being obliged to pay compensation is sometimes seen as an even stronger argument in favour of a durable peace.

This is, however, largely erroneous, for, as I took pains to demonstrate in the first chapter (cf. p. 12), compensation is not a substitute for vengeance but a palliative. Compensation is exacted in lieu of the right to exact vengeance only if it is imperative to do so. Its acceptance by the victim's group and the prospect of themselves being eventually obliged to pay back what they have received will in no way deter them from carrying out the duty of vengeance when they feel strong enough and the opportunity presents itself. In one sense, then, the payment of compensation, as long as it remains incompletely paid, itself constitutes one of the mnemonic devices discussed earlier which are designed to perpetuate the memory of feud beyond the conclusion of a provisional truce. Debts in blood translated by compensation into debts of wealth are as much a reminder that enmity has not been forgotten as an indication that peace has been concluded.

Evidence suggesting the validity of this contention is to be found, firstly, in an analysis of the distribution of responsibility for homicide within the compensation-paying group and, secondly, in an examination of the nature of compensation itself.

Although, in Kennett's words, 'The Arab Law concerning the payment of bloodmoney is very elastic' (1925:53)—and this applies to most other feuding societies as well—, there is one point upon which there appears to be little divergence among tribal peoples in the Mediterranean and the Middle East and in medieval northern Europe. The immediate kin of the murdered man always seem to receive a larger portion of the compensation than other members of the same group. But the opposite is by no means always true: a murderer and his closest cognates do not necessarily contribute a greater amount than do their fellow tribesmen. Kennett states that this is the case 'in one or two tribes' in Sinaï and the Western Desert (1925:53). Lewis reports that among the pastoral Somali 'the bereaved family usually receives the largest single portion of the blood wealth', whereas the amount paid by a murderer in a large compensation-paying group may be 'infinitesimal' (1961:174).[12] The existence of similar rules was observed by Peters in Cyrenaica (1967:263). There is also little to indicate that the murderer in Anglo-Saxon England was normally under any obligation to pay more in compensation than other members of his kindred, whereas it is a well attested fact that the victim's close relatives were entitled to the *healsfang* or special supplementary portion of the *wergild*[13] (Maitland and Pollock 1895:241–2).

In all these instances not only does the murderer suffer little or

[12] Cf. Lewis 1962:24 for a circumstantially described case, in which the victim's immediate kin received more than half the *diya*, whilst the remainder was 'shared out amongst other members of the group'.

[13] The *healsfang* was almost identical to the Somali *jiffo*, or situational core of the *diya*, mentioned in the first chapter (cf. p. 15, note 5).

no more from the consequences of his act than do other members
of the same compensation-paying group, but the larger his group
the less he or any other member will have to pay in compensation
for a given homicide. The payment of compensation is thus, in a
number of societies, more an incentive to the formation of large
solidary groups than an effective means of discouraging individuals from killing members of other groups. This makes it abun-
dantly clear that the prospect of paying compensation is
frequently not a deterrent at all. It would, however, be wrong to
say that *all* claims for compensation are met by an equal contribution levied from every member of the killer's group. I shall
return to this point.

The customs concerning the amounts of compensation due and
the apportionment of responsibilities for its payment are indeed
extremely varied. Precedent seems to play very little part in the
conclusion of individual agreements, each case being judged
according to the circumstances and the relative power of the
groups involved. Fixed tariffs of compensation are often reported
(e.g. Lewis 1955:107), but are rarely if ever strictly adhered to in
actual decisions. As a rule though, 'the closer the structural
relationship of the parties involved, the more likely is the wrong to
be rectified, but the smaller is the indemnification required to do
so' (Howell 1954:24).

Du Bois-Aymé (1809:584), Peters (1951:306–8) and Lewis
(1961:164) all confirm the general truth of this assertion as
regards nomadic societies. The situation is not quite the same in
sedentary agricultural communities, as I shall show later. If the
fear of being obliged to pay compensation was in reality a strong
deterrent among pastoral nomads, it might be inferred that homicide in such societies occurs more frequently at close structural
range than at a distance, since homicide is, so to speak, 'cheaper'
between relatives. But this is in fact not the case, and in spite of
the reduction in compensation conceded between structurally
proximate groups in nomadic societies homicide remains relatively
uncommon at this level and is ideally associated with relations
between traditionally hostile sections living at some distance from
one another.

A number of nomadic feuding societies explain the concession
of reduced compensation at close structural range on grounds of
motivation: it is obvious to them that a man and his neighbour

derive mutual advantage from an atmosphere of reciprocal trust and co-operation and that if one kills the other it will have been in a moment of uncontrollable anger, but not with malice afore-thought. Deliberate murder of neighbours and relatives is thus only conceived of with difficulty. The majority of such cases are treated as accidents and the amount of compensation due is reduced accordingly.

In reality, the notion of accidental death among the Bedouin refers not to a lack of intention on the part of the killer but to a common desire to avoid all possible causes for conflict between the groups in question. Criminal intention is not objectively but structurally and oecologically defined. This is borne out by Cyre-naican Bedouin attitudes to the violent death of a woman: since women are of little or no structural importance, their death by violence is unfailingly regarded as 'accidental' and can always be made good by the payment of compensation whatever the struc-tural or oecological distance between the dead woman and her murderer (Peters 1967:270). If, however, friction is already present between structurally proximate groups, even an unmis-takably accidental homicide will tend to be regarded as an excellent pretext for the victim's group to affirm its political independence. The murder is represented as deliberate—whatever the evidence to the contrary may be—and the victim's group sue for an exorbitant amount of compensation.[14] Refusal by the killer's group to pay will provoke fission and eternal feud.

Alternatively, even though it be known that the murderer acted deliberately, his group may decide that it is in their interests to remain on good terms with the victim's section. They will agree to the payment of an abnormally high *diya* for this reason, but they will express their reprobation of the killer's action by obliging him and his immediate kinsmen to shoulder more than their ordinary share of the burden, the rest of the group making only a minimal *per capita* contribution to the total amount. In some nomadic groups, which have been in more or less constant contact with sedentary communities practising a form of customary law based on more objective criteria of penal responsibility or in which oecological conditions and a certain amount of agricultural acti-vity make the maintenance of peace more desirable than in the

[14] E.g. the Somali case of this type quoted in the first chapter (pp. 15–16).

open desert, the murderer is always obliged to contribute more than his fellows. It is reported, for example, of the Terabin of the Gaza Strip that the killer normally pays a full third of the total due whatever the size of the group (Hardy 1963:95). The literature abounds with lists detailing the proportions levied from the killer and other members of his group in varying circumstances (e.g. Kadhim 1961:89).

The statement that the amount of indemnification for homicide varies in nomadic societies with the structural distance between the parties is thus only ideally true. The prior state of relations between the two groups, the degree to which they must compete for the control of inadequate resources within the same area, their relative influence in the political sphere and the personal character and status of the killer and the victim are all factors taken into account. The decision as to whether it is feasible in given circumstances to accept compensation in lieu of vengeance and, if a mediator is requested to intervene, the final reckoning of the actual amount to be paid are determined by a judicious equilibrium struck between expediency and fear. Whether or not a group can *afford* to pay compensation but little influences the outcome of this decision.

In sedentary societies like Albania or Kabylia the situation appears to have been somewhat different to that met with in nomadic societies. Arbitration and blood money were less readily accepted in cases of deliberate homicide. In southern Albania, blood money was scorned as dishonouring and throughout the region 'the formula after a murder was "either pardon or kill"' (Hasluck 1954:239). Hanoteau and Letourneux say the same of Kabylia, where only an unintentional homicide could be pardoned. But no compensation could be accepted and the stain cast upon the honour of a family by the murder of one of its members could only be deleted by vengeance (1893:68). Hanoteau and Letourneux do not specify what they mean by deliberate homicide. But it is reasonable to suppose that the Kabyles, like the Bedouin, acted upon a situational rather than absolute definition of malice aforethought. In northern Albania (e.g. Durham 1909 and 1928:*passim*) compensation was accepted for murder as well as for unintentional homicide, but sufficient information is not available for it to be possible to say whether tariffs of compensation were lower within the village than within the tribe at

large. Outside the tribe it seems doubtful whether compensation
was ever paid.

Although compensation was occasionally accepted in sedentary
agricultural communities, the general attitude in feud was on the
whole more uncompromising than among pastoral nomads. I
shall attempt to explain the reasons for the inflexibility of sedentary communities in this respect and their exacerbated sense of
honour, with which I believe it is connected, in the next chapter.
But for the present moment I shall limit myself to showing how,
whether or not compensation is paid or thought a feasible alternative to vengeance, both nomadic and sedentary feuding societies
have similar manners of registering the gravity of a given homicide. If it can be proved that compensation and killing are merely
two different ways of achieving the same results, that is that they
both represent a form of reprisal directly proportionate to the
gravity of the initial homicide, then it cannot be argued that the
obligation to pay compensation constitutes a deterrent to feud.

When discussing practices connected with compensation
among pastoral nomads I stressed that the primary factor in
determining whether vengeance should be brought or compensation accepted was structural distance. I did, however, also allude
to other factors such as the relative strength of groups and the
identity of the killer and his victim. Structural distance is in reality
only one variable among many. Another of equal importance is
the relative status of killer and victim. Who is killed is just as significant for the nature of subsequent reprisals as the identity of the
group to which the man belongs. All feuding societies recognize
that it is a more serious offence to kill a man of influence and
numerous progeny than to kill a young unmarried man of no
political stature. Although the two men may stand in the same
structural relationship to a potential killer from outside the
community—that is, they belong to the same lineage or village
—the murder of the former may suscitate such a sense of outrage
that three men are killed in retaliation, whereas the death of the
latter could well be discounted as an 'accident' and lead to a
rapid reconciliation between the groups sealed with the promise
of compensation.

Peters says that this was traditionally the rule in Cyrenaica
(1951:294). Among the Shammar of Mosul *liwa* in Iraq the
murder of a tribal *sheikh* by a commoner sometimes led to the

permanent exile of the murderer and his whole lineage whereas less drastic measures were taken in cases of homicide involving men of equal status (Kadhim 1961:101–2). In both Albania and the Iranian province of Fars the murder of a superior was always followed by retaliation in kind, since the honour of the family was at stake. But a simple tribesman of low status in Fars could not satisfy his desire for revenge and was bound to accept blood money if one of his kinsmen were killed by 'un supérieur' (Monteil 1966:121). In Albania, a tribesman might attempt to bring vengeance against a *bajraktar* or chief, but he could be content with compensation of this suited him. The *bajraktar*, on the other hand, had no alternative and was obliged by his position to seek vengeance (Hasluck 1954:125). Similar conditions obtained in eighteenth-century Corsica: 'Si', writes a contemporary, 'ce sont des prêtres ou des chefs qui sont tués, les Corses comptent [ce meutre] pour deux' (Pinello, quoted in Busquet 1920:90). In medieval Scotland and among the Atlas Berbers, the price of blood was also negotiated according to the status of the victim (Skene 1609:73v; Gellner 1961:177); and the same is true in Somali pastoral society (Lewis 1955:107).

Structural distance and the relative status of the killer and his victim are, however, not the only considerations to determine the gravity of the case. Murray, for instance, reports that the Sinaï Bedouin demand fourfold compensation for a killing that occurs between two lineages after *diya* has already been paid for the initial offence (1935:209). Among the Somali a homicide committed in similar conditions calls for double the normal compensation (Lewis 1962:24). In some tribes revenge taken under cover of night is thought to be worse than murder during the day. Each feuding society has its own list of aggravating circumstances.

From the examples given above and what has gone before, it is clear that the acceptance of compensation is at the best optional and that in a number of circumstances it is not even a feasible substitute for vengeance. Both compensation and retaliation are sequels to a killing. The latter may occur before compensation is paid, but even if a feud is provisionally 'concluded' by arbitration, it will in the long run, if it is agreed that feud is eternal, always be followed by retaliation in kind at a later date. The prospect of being obliged to pay large amounts of compensation cannot then act as a deterrent to feud, since feud once begun is interminable. It may not even serve to lengthen the intervals between violent episodes, for, as Professor Whitelock has pointed out, faced with the crippling expense of compensation a poor man may prefer to deny the debt and expose himself and his kin to retaliation rather than suffer economic ruin and the possibility of death by starvation (1952:43).

To return now to the point I made at the beginning of this section: though it may be difficult to prove conclusively whether the payment of compensation does or does not operate as a deterrent—my own feeling is that there is enough evidence to show that it does not—there is no doubt that one object it does secure is, by creating debts in wealth which are gradually reimbursed from year to year and finally allowed to lapse before repayment is complete, to keep the memory of feud alive from one generation to the next. In this respect, compensation differs very little from the mnemonic devices referred to in previous chapters which, like a horse to ride when 'bringing vengeance' (Peters 1951:203) and the gun of the killing (Durham 1928:90; Lewis 1962:24), frequently constitute part of the actual payment stipulated in the agreement to 'conclude' a feud. Moreover, compensation cannot really be said to 'compensate' for very much. Demands are exorbitant, yet the amount awarded is normally but a fraction of the sum originally asked for. Men of eminence present at the reconciliation ceremony employ their credit in favour of the killer's group to obtain a reduction in the amount. This is recognized practice in most negotiations (e.g. Peters 1967:266). Hardy tells how even today in the Gaza Strip the victim's kinsmen 'are prevailed upon for the sake of Allah, President Nasser, Marshal Ameer and others'(1963:95) to make concessions so that the *diya* is pared down to reasonable proportions.

Murray (1935:210) and Burckhardt (1830:88; 1831:318) describe an identical process earlier in the present century and at the beginning of the last. Finally, Peters observed that even though a Bedouin visiting a camp to collect the annual instalment of a blood debt might have seen hundreds of sheep belonging to the debtor on his way to the man's tents, he would accept the debtor's excuse that he was in straightened circumstances that year and unable to pay the full amount due. After drinking coffee with the debtor and attempting unsuccessfully to extort another animal or two, he would leave secure in the knowledge that his debt relationship with the killer's group was progressing satisfactorily (1967: 266–7).

If compensation ever operates as a deterrent, it is clear that this is a secondary function. Fear of feud is its own deterrent and compensation is better seen as a recurrent episode or integral part of feud: it does not inhibit feud but perpetuates it. Feud is nonetheless regulated by the recognition of certain norms. But since feud occurs in conditions of subdued anarchy—that is, the almost total absence of all binding norms outside the feud itself—the infraction of these minimal norms is coterminous with the onset of *anomie*. Such norms as there are are mainly concerned with establishing whom it is licit to kill or outrage without seriously placing in jeopardy the 'feuding relationships' of the group. They constitute a deterrent not to feuding, but to the employment of violence outside the feud. For reasons which appear self-evident, but which are in reality more complex and will be discussed in detail in the last chapter, it is not possible for a man to entertain feuding relations with members of his own group. The norms referred to thus always sanction, among other crimes, intra-group killing[15] and may also, in some societies, as for instance among the Bedouin of Cyrenaica, forbid the murder of certain affines. In Albania and Corsica priests were traditionally protected in the same manner and, in Albania alone, anyone who molested or killed the servant of a priest, if the servant was not a local man, must reckon with the wrath of the whole parish (Hasluck 1954:49). Crimes like sacrilege in Albania and the killing elsewhere of a man seeking sanctuary usually fell into the same category.

In all these cases the sanctions invoked were, in the first instance, exile of the culprit. In sedentary communities this implied loss of all rights of access to land and obligatory recourse,

[15] —with, to my knowledge, only three exceptions: (1) among the Berbers of the Central High Atlas it is permissible, and even laudable, to kill a male sibling who is 'recognised to be a nuisance to his kin and to others' (Gellner 1969:116–17); (2) in Albania, a man who kills a close agnate in defence of a guest or a man with whom he has sworn a *besa* or truce, even though the man be the enemy of his family, is regarded as justified in this act (e.g. Durham 1909:171); (3) when two sons killed their father for staining the family honour by marrying a negress, the Kabyle villagers of Afensou approved their conduct (Hanoteau and Letourneux 1893:101).

if the man and his family were to survive, to the humiliation of taking service in another village or tribe. Among nomadic peoples exile was frequently less severe, since the culprit could take his flocks and tents with him. After a number of years or even generations the killer himself or his descendants could usually return to the section from which they had originally been expelled (e.g. Peters 1951:255). In sedentary societies more rigorous sanctions were commonly wielded by the community at large against men and the families of men who had committed anti-social acts. In Albania and Kabylia it was, for example, customary practice to destroy the houses, food reserves and fruit trees of the culprit and slaughter his flocks and cattle (Hasluck 1954:*passim*; Hanoteau and Letourneux 1893:103). Similar punitive measures seem to have been taken after the flight of the culprit in at least one group of Somali tribesmen, where the elders directed 'the systematic looting of his property' (Lewis 1955:97). The secondary source would appear to suggest that the group in question is at least semi-, if not entirely, sedentary, for the author states that these tribesmen recognize the authority of 'village . . . headmen' (1955:98). This apparently exceptional manner of dealing with anti-social offenders belonging to a sedentary community in an otherwise mainly nomadic pastoral society may be taken as further corroboration of the observation that there exists a qualitative difference between the types of penal sanction operative in sedentary and nomadic societies.

The kind of radical sanction referred to among sedentary tribesmen may indeed qualify as a deterrent. Nevertheless, the deterrent is not intended to inhibit feuding, but rather to discourage any form of violence that is outside the feud and therefore does not foster or contribute to the creation of relationships. Feud is a closed system unmitigated by anything but feud. Fear of feud is the only possible deterrent to feud, since a necessary prerequisite for its existence is the absence of more elaborate types of social control and of all those formal institutions which, under other social conditions, serve to inhibit the unrestricted use of violence by individuals to their own ends. Compensation does not hinder the development of feud, but, on the contrary, is a source of impetus propelling it from one killing to another.

IV
Feud, Stratification and Oecology

My efforts in the preceding chapters have been directed in the main to the achievement of two goals. My first concern was to define the social phenomenon that I have been calling feud. I then turned my attention to describing the visible externals that mark the course of a feud. It may be objected that I have failed to succeed in either of these intentions.

Finding it impracticable to formulate a cut and dried definition that would make is possible to determine whether any given case of conflict might or might not qualify as feud, I have been able to do little more than circumscribe the phenomenon within approximate limits in the wider field of aggressive interaction. My attempt to describe what *happens* in a feud has met with hardly greater success. I have summarized from the literature and discussed numerous instances in which parties are opposed in attitudes of hostility or by acts of physical violence. In both definition and description I have produced little substantial evidence to justify my ascription of all these instances to a single sociological category, thereby postulating that they share a number of common characteristics. The only cogent argument that I have been able to put forward in support of my contention that all the cases I have cited can be subsumed under the general heading of feud is that they all constitute incidents in a chain of such events which may be regarded as an unending process or relationship.

But recognition of the fact that the phenomenon that I have been calling feud implies some sort of permanent relationship between the contestants is on its own insufficient grounds to warrant my placing it in a separate named sociological category in contradistinction to other kinds of conflict. For it is a commonplace among sociologists that *all* conflicts may be seen as a form of communication and, therefore, relationship.[1] Feud is, by this reasoning, merely another more prolonged type of conflict. But it is also something more specific, as I shall show in the present chapter, in which I shall pass from formal description to analysis of the structural and, ultimately, oecological premises which underly the feud seen as a social system *per se*.

Part, at least, of the difficulty I encountered in attempting to describe the course of feud is to be attributed to the absence in most feuding societies of an institutional framework within which feud may be found along with other instruments of social control: without any institutional landmarks outside the feud itself it has been almost impossible to say what is *not* feud in a society which practises it. It is for this reason that I have, on occasion, been reduced to affirming that feud is a 'self-buttressing' or 'closed' system. Unlike most institutions—courts of law or parliamentary government, for instance—which are said not only to provide an objective norm but to control and regulate the conduct of the individual in society, feud controls and regulates nothing but feuding relations themselves and supplies no norms for behaviour outside the feud. Any investigation of the feud is thus handicapped from the start, because it is not at all easy to relate and compare it to any other phenomenon within the same social context. Feud, as Peters has put it, is 'the pulse of society' (1951:239), that is an organ so critical that, were it removed and no substitute provided, the society in question would cease to exist. In other words, in the societies in which it occurs, feud is almost all that *does* occur.[2]

---

[1] Coser cites George A. Lundberg as exceptional in this respect for his view that conflict is characterized by 'a suspension of communication between the opposing parties' (Coser 1965:23).

[2] I am indebted for this formulation to a remark made by Professor Gellner in the course of his critical analysis of the theory of segmentary opposition. Gellner states of segmentary opposition and the state of dynamically balanced social cohesion which supposedly results from it that '*What defines a segmentary society is not that this does occur, but that it is nearly all that occurs*' (1969:42). I think, however, that Gellner's emphasis here on the importance of segmentary opposition as such and its role in maintaining a political balance in certain small scale egalitarian self-subsistence societies somewhat distorts a wider reality. For as he himself says, it is not so much segmentary opposition itself as the notion of fear *behind* segmentary opposition that supplies the ultimate motive for coalition in such conditions (1969:53). It is also fear, as I pointed out at the beginning

Feud, then, like other types of conflict, provides a means of inaugurating and maintaining a network of relationships of both alliance and defiance. But feud is unique in that it provides the *only* channels of communication between groups in the societies in which it is practised, whereas conflict elsewhere constitutes one of a number of such channels. In other words, as a social pheno-menon feud is very nearly synonymous with the social system within which it is found.

In a preliminary working definition of 'social conflict' Coser has said that the phrase may 'be taken to mean a struggle over values and claims to scarce status, power and resources' (1965:8). The feud answers perfectly to this description. The very notion of conflict, as Coser intimates, is a function of the law of supply and demand: conflict arises when two or more parties enter upon a competitive struggle to gain control of a prize or prizes of which there exists an insufficient supply to satisfy the demands of all contestants. The unavailability of a *desideratum* in quantities ample enough to cater for all those who require it, that is the factor of scarcity, is clearly of the utmost importance for the comparative analysis of conflict situations. In my opinion, there-fore, the crucial criterion in a classification of conflicts is not, as Simmel thought (cf. p. 9), their intrinsic accessibility or inaccessibility to compromise, but the precise nature, extent and intensity in any given instance of the scarcity factor.

Now, while most conflicts develop where scarcity is only partial —that is, confined to the objectives of the conflict itself—the characteristic which distinguishes feud, as a type of generalized struggle extending into all spheres of social life at once, from all other forms of conflict is the fact that it can only materialize in conditions of what I shall call '*total scarcity*'.

'Total scarcity' may be summarized as the moral, institutional and material premise of a certain type of society in which *every-thing* felt[3] by the people themselves to be relevant to human life is

of chapter III in my discussion of Gellner's contribution, which is the political motive *par excellence* not only in segmentary lineage societies but in all societies in which the feud is found. Fear, then, is the prime mover in feuding societies; and segmentary opposition may be regarded as merely one among many alternative social forms generated by fear.

[3] A number of commodities like air at low altitude or sunshine in sub-tropical countries are, of course, never scarce and must therefore of necessity escape this definition of 'total' scarcity.

regarded by those people as existing in absolutely inadequate quantities.

'Total scarcity' is the result, in the first instance, of a set of oecological, technological and historical circumstances which cause an endemic insufficiency of material goods and resources and prevent the acquisition and long-term accumulation of wealth by individuals or groups. This in turn inhibits the development of social stratification and an attendant power structure based on economic differentiation. By minimizing opportunities for the transmission from one generation to another of inheritable wealth and its habitual concomitants, status and office, this situation creates conditions generally unconducive to the evolution of efficient judicial and political institutions and tends to give rise to an egalitarian ethos which reflects on the moral plane the material and institutional poverty of such societies.

For the notion of scarcity has such deep roots in the everyday existence of men and women living under these conditions that it extends from the visible external world to include the more intangible sphere of cultural values. Prestige, honour, manliness, fertility and good fortune, or success in the economic field, thus also come to be regarded as commodities which, like land, water or efficient institutions, are in limited supply. The desire of the people at large to ensure that no individual may enjoy more than his 'fair share' of all that is available fosters an egalitarian ideal, which is the source of strong moral sanctions against those who acquire, or may be tempted to acquire, more than a socially approved maximum.

By 'total scarcity' I mean, then, a permanently felt inadequacy of all existing resources and political structure to meet the minimal conscious requirements of the whole population. The most important concomitant of 'total scarcity' is fear (cf. note 2, p. 120)—fear of starvation due to the individual's incapacity to defend his resources against aggression, in the absence of judicial guarantees. Fear, as I have demonstrated, is the ultimate motive for alliance, first between elementary families, then between groups of families. In conditions of 'total scarcity' groups of people form alliances to strike a balance of power, which is maintained through the prosecution of feud, thereby securing an equitable distribution of available resources. The rabidly egalitarian ethos of feuding societies lends moral substance to the overall pattern of political equality that may be observed to characterize the relations between groups by ideally precluding the possibility of inter-personal relations of dominance.

Yet, despite the ideology of equality which is such a pervasive feature of all feuding societies, it is clear that the alliances contracted in response to aggression *cannot* be as uncompromisingly egalitarian in structure and operation as this folk model would suggest. For it is self-evident that a coalition formed to achieve a number of political and economic goals cannot attain its ends unless some sort of leadership emerges to orient the group, win majority support for the implementation of certain key decisions and co-ordinate the efforts of all members in pursuit of a common purpose.

This inevitable tendency to what might be termed tactical stratification, must be accepted as a fundamental postulate in any social situation, as a number of recent experiments by social psychologists on the nature of communication networks in task-oriented groups have suggested (e.g. several articles in Smith 1966). I define a social situation as the interaction of two or more units—individuals or groups. For analytical purposes, interaction can be said to take one of two basic forms: co-operation or conflict. These are, however, not mutually exclusive opposites but the poles of a continuing social process. Co-operation is a necessary prerequisite for the formation of groups. But a group cannot endure unless a leadership or, in more complex structures, a political hierarchy arises to direct the common effort to the accomplishment of pre-established goals. Leadership, while making co-operation possible, nonetheless stimulates an atmosphere of competition which, if it oversteps certain limits, results in conflict within the group. If this internal conflict is allowed to go too far, the group will divide and the social situation of co-operation necessarily mitigated by competition will either be superseded by that of direct conflict between opposed fragments or, through dissociation, cease altogether.

Co-operation and conflict combined thus constitute the irreducible essence of social existence. The predominance of one over the other in any given instance characterizes that particular social situation. Leadership, which develops spontaneously out of co-operation to create conflict, supplies the dynamic factor which transforms static situation into on-going social process. I submit, therefore, that co-operation, conflict and leadership are the three basic components to which even the most complex social structures can in the final analysis be reduced.

If this is so and feud necessarily implies alliance (i.e. co-operation) in the defence of economic interests, as I suggested in chapter II, it might be expected that feud would give rise to some kind of leadership in spite of the inhibitive effects upon stratification of 'total scarcity' and the presence of a strongly egalitarian ideology. Indeed, not only is the existence of some sort of leadership in feuding societies theoretically expedient, but the anthropological and travel literature on the Mediterranean and the Middle East lends ample support to the theory and abounds in well documented accounts of powerful 'sheikhs' and 'princes' who appear to wield considerable authority. The principal problem that it is my intention to discuss in the present chapter is, then, how to resolve the apparent contradiction which opposes the egalitarian folk model and the incontrovertible fact of leadership, or, in more abstract terms, how in feuding societies manipulation of the static premise of equality by self-seeking individuals can generate process, that is social continuity or unceasing structural modification through time, without doing violence to the basic principle of 'fair shares for all'.

A classic anthropological treatment of the problem based on the discovery of a wide discrepancy between the folk model and the objectively reported facts would, in this instance, prove quite inadequate, for the folk model of equality is not only contervened by the anthropologist's observations but also by another folk model which extols virtues quite contrary to those described as meritorious in the first.[4] The problem in the feuding context is not to make a choice between the two models, thereby positing that one is 'right' and discounting the other because it does not correspond to observable reality, but to elucidate the mechanism whereby the two can exist simultaneously and be brought into play on different occasions to justify conceptually distinct types of action, which may on the surface appear very similar.

The second problem I shall explore in this chapter is one to which I have tacitly alluded throughout the first half of this book.

[4] A situation reminiscent of the *gumlao*-Shan dichotomy around which Leach builds the argument central to his book *Political systems of Highland Burma* (e.g. pp. 8–9).

Anyone who has read reasonably widely on the feud in the Mediterranean and the Middle East will have been struck by an at first somewhat unaccountable qualitative difference between the practice of feud in sedentary agricultural societies, on the one hand, and among nomadic pastoralists, on the other. In the former, feud seems on the whole to be more intensive, more frequent, more destructive and less 'rational', that is less bent on the achievement of overtly practical aims. Sedentary societies also appear to be much more prone to intra-group killing, and the penalties incurred by such an act are considerably more severe than among nomadic pastoralists. Feuding relations among the latter, however, tend to oppose groups which, more often than not, have extremely good and perfectly obvious reasons founded in a realistic perception of oecological conditions to distrust each others' territorial ambitions. Nomadic pastoralists also accept compensation to bring about a temporary truce with greater readiness than sedentary populations, whereas the general impression gained from the literature on agricultural village based communities is that feud is often flippantly regarded as a kind of game which it is unsporting to interrupt.

This dichotomy between sedentary agricultural and nomadic pastoral feuding societies closely parallels the geographical distribution of the structural variants I have already analyzed in the constitution of the feuding unit. In both cases the vengeance group comprises in the first instance only agnates. But whereas among nomadic pastoralists the principle for recruitment to the vengeance group beyond the immediate circle of agnates remains agnation but mitigated by contract, sedentary agriculturalists recognize no binding obligations in the feud outside the extended agnatic family and, when they do seek further support, are more liable to ally themselves on the principle of vicinage than on that of kinship. I have already explained this structural disparity between the two main types of feuding society in the Mediterranean and the Middle East in terms of the different set of oecological incentives to economic and military co-operation operative in each (cf. ch. II). The very large number of cases attesting the more 'daemonic' or irrational character of feuding in sedentary agricultural communities would seem therefore, by a process of scientifically legitimate induction, to justify the conjecture that oecological considerations are possibly paramount in determining how the practice of feud will vary from one society to another.

I believe that the explanation of the structural dichotomy between the two types of society, which is reflected in the intensity and quality of feuding relations, is of the same order as the solution of the other problem relative to the nature of leadership in purportedly egalitarian societies. The answers to both problems, that is, are logically germane: both are ultimately to be sought in an examination of the notion of 'total scarcity' which I have as yet only briefly elaborated.

I propose in what follows to construct a minimal model of feud which should be universally valid for any society in which feud occurs. The model is extremely simple. I posit only two interdependent constants: 'total scarcity' and leadership.[5] I postulate that, while the latter is an essential component of all social situations, its occurrence in combination with 'total scarcity' is to be encountered in feuding societies alone. I shall treat all local variations in the practice of feud as evidence that oecological, or possibly historical,[6] variables are operative to modify the constants. The threefold interaction of two constants and a set of variables particular to each individual society and case of

[5] There is a third constant of minor importance which, for the sake of clarity, I shall eliminate from the model: a minimal level of population density below which feud cannot develop as a relationship due to the instability of groups and the rarity of occasions on which they can meet. Although technically possible, it would be extremely difficult to establish an exact figure for this constant and to relate it to the degree of 'total scarcity' in a given case. The available evidence would seem to indicate, however, that low population density and the absence of feud among hunters and gatherers are not unconnected phenomena. Vengeance killing, on the other hand, does occur in such societies. But even this is discouraged, because physical violence can lead to a disastrous reduction in the economic potential of the group. Hence the frequent presence in hunting and gathering societies of institutions, like the Eskimo abusive song contest or the Australian judicial duel, which permit the dispersion of antagonisms in a manner less wasteful of vital manpower.

[6] I shall devote very little attention to historical variables, since they are, in feuding societies possessing few or no written records, quite inconclusive. They cannot consequently be used as a sound basis for argument. This does not mean that they are not potentially of considerable importance. Lack of accurate historical information merely makes the use of historical variables scientifically dubious in an argument which is already perilously near to pure hypothesis.

feud should thus make it feasible to use the same analytical framework to account simultaneously for both the apparent overall unity of the phenomenon and the great range of variety that may be observed in the conduct of feud, not only from one society to another, but even within the limits of a culturally homogeneous tribal group.

As usual in the social, as opposed to the exact, sciences there are two major objections to the utility of such a model: the lack of statistical data on the feud and the extreme multiplicity of pertinent oecological variables (even if they were available in statistical form, which they are not), make the formulation of the model itself little more than an intuitive approximation and preclude any rigorous proof of its relevance through its application on the ground or to the reported facts. I therefore entertain no hope of being able, by manipulating the model, to 'prove' anything with regard to the nature of feud. Instead, I shall use it only to supply the guide lines of a discussion in the course of which I shall bring forward as much evidence as possible to support my view that feud constitutes a mechanism the main function of which is to permit a certain degree of stratification in societies in which conditions would at first sight seem effectively to inhibit it. As the model relies for what cogency it possesses on the extent to which the variables confirm the flexibility of the constants without contradicting them, the investigation of the dichotomy which opposes sedentary and nomadic feuding societies will be closely integrated with the theme of stratification.

I shall prepare the ground for this discussion with two introductory sections. In the first I shall review the ethnography to illustrate the dichotomy in the intensity and nature of feud between the two types of society; in the second, I shall marshall the available evidence to show that, in spite of a situation that I have referred to as subdued anarchy, leaders are everywhere present in feuding societies. I shall also evaluate the extent of their authority. The third section will be devoted to an elaboration of the concept of 'total scarcity' and a critique of an analogous notion—the 'Image of Limited Good'—developed by Foster in the general context of peasant societies. The fourth section will attempt to show how the concept of 'total scarcity' dovetails with the notion of honour in Mediterranean and Middle Eastern feuding societies and how the ambiguity inherent in this notion contributes to an understanding of an apparent incompatibility between the exercise of power and the precepts of the egalitarian ideology. The fifth section will have little apparent connection with those which have gone before. In it I shall present and discuss a number of purely theoretical ideas put forward by Simmel and Coser on the nature of social conflict. These will provide the logical framework for the last section in which I shall bring together the disparate strands of authority, equality, scarcity and diversity to explain, on the one hand, how it is possible to speak of feud as a single phenomenon despite a very wide degree of divergence from place to place and how, on the other hand, as a social system in its own right, feud supplies the matrix in which the fundamental necessity for social stratification is successfully combined with the no less fundamental necessity of preventing the physical disintegration of a society by ensuring that all members can assert their right of access to scarce material resources.

(1) THE DICHOTOMY

> ...und von der Matja [region in northern Albania] meinte der Pfarrer, dass dort die Wochen des Jahres, in welchen dieser Sitte [feud] mehr als ein Opfer falle, häufiger wären, als die blutreinen (von Hahn 1867:28).

> ...their [the Bedouin of northern Arabia] wars are bloodless... The dreaded effects of 'blood-revenge' ... prevent many sanguinary conflicts (Burckhardt 1830:76).

Overall scrutiny of the considerable number of actual cases of feud to which I have referred in preceding chapters would suggest that there exist significant differences in the practice of feud between sedentary agricultural communities and nomadic pastoral societies. This, at all events, is the general impression that may be gained from the ethnographic literature on tribal societies in the Mediterranean and the Middle East. But as soon as an attempt is made to substantiate this impression by identifying

individual features or patterns which may be described as characteristic of the feud in one of these two types of society but not in
the other, and *vice versa*, there suddenly appear to be few or no
factual grounds for the assumption that any dichotomy exists.
There are two reasons for this.

In the first place, comparison of the feud in sedentary and
nomadic societies reveals the presence in the former of all those
elements that may be regarded as typical of the latter, but does
not indicate that the converse is true. In other words, feud among
nomadic pastoralists would appear to represent a minimal development of the phenomenon, whereas feud as practised by
sedentary communities could be seen as an elaboration of this
minimal form.[7] It is thus difficult to account for 'differences'
between the practice of feud in sedentary and nomadic societies,
when what is sought in reality is to explain the presence in one
society of additional features which do not occur in the other.
As I have already given a fairly detailed description of the feud
among nomadic peoples, I shall therefore concentrate in this
section on those features which are peculiar to the feud in
sedentary communities.

The second factor which makes it difficult to be precise when
speaking of the dichotomy which opposes sedentary and nomadic
feuding societies is of a less obviously ethnographic order. It has
to do not with the observable facts themselves but with the relationship between actions and the motives behind them.

I have mentioned the greater 'intensity' of feuding among
sedentary agriculturalists. But it is not at all easy to demonstrate

[7] Feud among nomadic pastoralists may thus be regarded as a kind of
heuristic archetype of the phenomenon. My stipulation that feud occurs
only in conditions of 'total scarcity' places a relatively precise limit on
what can and what cannot be considered as feud in my sense of the word.
But just as feud among sedentary agriculturalists may be viewed as a more
complex version of the feud practised by nomadic pastoralists, so other
types of conflict in other societies unaffected by 'total scarcity' may
exhibit a number of characteristics which cause them to resemble 'feud'.
I must emphasize, therefore, that while feud is a form of conflict and
consequently bears a real resemblance to many other forms of conflict,
the converse is not true: the fact that many forms of conflict have much
in common with the 'feud' does not make them qualify as 'feud' *unless*
their occurrence is associated with conditions of 'total scarcity'. For this
reason, many societies practise 'feud-like' hostilities; but they are not
necessarily feuding societies.

the intensity of a social phenomenon. The sheer number of cases reported from a given society may indicate a high incidence of feud, and I shall presently adduce evidence to demonstrate that the Albanians, for example, *appear* to be more often engaged in hostilities than any other people in the area under consideration. But this kind of ethnographic information should be treated with the utmost caution, since it is quite possible for the conclusions drawn from it to be heavily biased merely because more material and of a better quality has been published on one region than on another. This is in fact the case where Albania is concerned; and I shall consequently be obliged, to illustrate my argument in this chapter, to refer more often to the Albanian material than to the rather inadequate evidence from other sedentary societies. By the mere accumulation of data I may in fact convey the impression that feuding is more prevalent in sedentary societies than among nomadic pastoralists. But I submit that it is only by examining motivation in the feud that it will be possible to establish a satisfactory scale of 'intensity' which will not be skewed by an erroneous interpretation of statistical materials.

For to speak of the intensity of reactions in social situations – and physical violence or homicide in the feud may be seen, as I have said (cf. p. 31), as a penal reaction to the infringement of recognized rights – is in fact to attempt to establish a measure of the relationship of cause to effect. In feuding societies this amounts to assessing the degree of congruence between acts which cause offence and the severity of the sanctions to which the injured party has recourse. If it can be shown that this relationship is more tenuous in some feuding societies than in others, that the actions which justify violent riposte are commonly more trivial in sedentary societies than among nomadic pastoralists, it may be concluded that feud is practised with greater intensity in the former than among the latter.[8]

Before I embark upon a discussion of the manifest dispro-

[8] I am aware that this procedure implies an evaluation of what does or does not constitute triviality and that a given action, which to western European eyes appears trivial, may have far greater significance for an Albanian or Iraqi tribesman for whom it is an incitement to murder. I shall be using the term heuristically in this section from a purely western European viewpoint to emphasize the character of feud in sedentary societies. I shall show later, however, that the seeming triviality of the causes of feud in such societies is in reality not at all trivial but rooted

portion in the relationship of cause to effect which characterizes the conduct of feud among sedentary agriculturalists, I shall state the evidence suggesting that the feud is unusually frequent in Albania. The abundance of individual cases reported from other sedentary societies points to a similar extension of the phenomenon. But while several affirmations of the overall frequency of feud exist for Albania, I have come across none so explicit in the literature on other sedentary societies in the Mediterranean and the Middle East.

Eyewitnesses have never been unduly impressed by the Albanians' propensity to keep the peace and live in amity. I have already cited Gopčević who travelled in the Balkans in the 1870s. It is his opinion that 'in früheren Zeiten'—by which he means the first half of the nineteenth century—'herrschte die Blutrache in Albanien gleich einer bösen Epidemie' (1881:73). Still according to Gopčević, by 1850 'hatte die Blutrache ganz entsetzliche Dimensionen angenommen'. One half of the population stood against the other; for every ten houses there was a death per year. Another visitor to Albania passing through Shkodër in the middle of the last century went to pay his respects to 'the British Council, Mr. Read, who gave [him] a good deal of information about the state of the country . . . He described the continual *vendetta* as being the bane of the whole district. Though the condition of things is not as outrageous as formerly, yet with an average of one murder every week in the city and its neighbourhood, arising from this cause, it can be conceived how little real security there is to human life.' The author goes on to quote M. Hecquard, former French Consul in Shkodër, who 'mentions that in 1857 . . . no less than 500 persons belonging to the city of Scodra alone were wandering about in the neighbouring plain and mountains as being compromised' (Tozer 1869:281). This state of affairs seems to have endured into the present century, for the *Pre-invasion basic handbook* on Albania circulated by the British government in 1943 quotes an unidentified source which estimates 'the average casualties from vendettas' in the country shortly before the First World War 'at 19% of adult males, with occasional local averages as high as 42%.' (Albania

in considerations of a perfectly rational order, which nonetheless differ in quality, if not in kind, from those which give rise to feud among nomadic pastoralists.

1943:9). Even if these figures are not taken too seriously (as the author of the handbook advises) and are regarded as suspect on the grounds that they may only apply to the more accessible areas of the largely detribalized coastal plain, they cannot be dismissed out of hand, for they are corroborated by a considerable amount of more impressionistic information gathered by travellers in the tribally organized regions of the interior. Miss Durham, for instance, who passed through the *bariak* of Dushmani in the tribal north of the country in 1908, writes that it 'consists of a hundred and sixty houses. Of these no fewer than forty were, at the time of my visit, in blood within the tribe. As for external bloods, they were countless . . . one of the tribe bloods has lasted for five generations' (1909:165–6).

These quotations suffice to underline the unmistakable prevalence of feud in Albania. The literature on other sedentary societies – Corsica, Kabylia, parts of rural Iraq and the Berber villages of the Central High Atlas – abounds in accounts of individual cases of feud of which such a large number are reported that it is not unreasonable to surmise that the feud was traditionally no less frequent in these societies than it was in Albania. The most striking aspect of feud in sedentary societies is, however, as I suggested, not so much its frequency as its intensity, which is clearly discernible in the disproportion between manifest cause and violent effect. An apt illustration of this feature is provided by the Albanian case I mentioned earlier (cf. p. 34) in which the refusal of a man to hand over four cartridges to another to whom he owed them precipitated a gun battle and the deaths of twelve men. Nor is this unique in the Albanian material. Mrs. Hasluck cites an almost identical case from Theth:

> About 1890 a man who had lost a lamb promised to give a cartridge to a shepherd if he found it. When the shepherd succeeded, the man went back on his promise saying that he would 'give him five' (*sc.* fingers on the trigger) instead. For the moment the shepherd let the matter drop, but later met the man and asked once more for his promised reward. Again the man refused it, not too curteously, and was immediately killed by the incensed shepherd. Unfortunately, it was Easter Sunday and the murder took place in a meadow where all the men of Theth were gathered for the festival. Immediately

the dead man's *vllazni* (brotherhood), comprising all the males descended from the same ancestor, sought vengeance on the murderer's brotherhood. These were not backward in replying, and within an hour fourteen men lay dead for the sake of one cartridge (Hasluck 1964:225).

In the same book Mrs. Hasluck gives a further example of the manner in which trifling events, which in other societies would have suscitated a much less virulent reaction, are allowed in Albania to develop within minutes into major sources of conflict resulting in numerous deaths: in Lumë

> . . . 'long ago' . . . The sheep belonging to the Onuzi sept were sleeping in a mountain fold near the fold of the Doçi sept. The dogs began to fight among themselves and the Doçi shepherd killed an Onuzi dog. The Onuzi shepherd drew his revolver and shot the Doçi man dead. A general fight then started among the shepherds and in a few minutes six Onuzi and twelve Doçi men lay dead for the sake of a dog. The feud raged on for years, not ceasing until it was at last composed by the direct order of the reigning Sultan (Hasluck 1954:78).

Yet another instance of the same kind of behaviour is cited by Miss Durham who tells of a group of Albanian villagers who began to argue about the relative size of the first stars of evening. The argument degenerated into a brawl and before long there were seventeen dead and eleven wounded in the same village (Durham 1909:131).

In none of the four cases quoted is any information provided to indicate the nature of prior relations between the groups involved in these murderous affrays. On the basis of my analysis of violence in preceding chapters it would seem legitimate to conjecture that there already existed substantial causes for friction between the groups in each of these affairs. Whatever the ultimate roots of the possibly long standing conflict of interests which led to these confrontations, I wish at present to emphasize only the superficial aspect of events, that is the apparent levity with which men kill each other for such trifles as a small debt, a dog or the size of a star. The Albanian attitude to such things is epitomized in the remark that a young man made to Miss Durham in comment upon the violent ways of his countrymen: ' "I often think," he added cheerfully, "we *maltsori* [mountaineers] will really find it very hard to get to heaven. *When the Last Day comes, we shall have a most awful fight with Christ*" ' (1909:169).

The disproportion between the ostensible causes and the observable effects in the Albanian feud is not confined to the type of armed conflict between groups exemplified by the instances quoted above. Quarrels between individuals conform to the same pattern. Miss Durham relates, with a wealth of circumstantial detail, the events which led up to the murder, within earshot of the village in which she was resting, of a defenceless Ghoanni boy by a man from another tribe. The case is interesting not only because it illustrates the extraordinarily violent lengths to which Albanian tribesmen would go to avenge an affront, but also for the light it sheds upon the inexorably logical attitudes adopted by sedentary feuding societies to justify a form of conduct which they recognize as destructive, inhumane and not unconnected with the failure of their efforts to rise above a very precarious level of subsistence. For the Albanians never tired of repeating to Miss Durham and Mrs. Hasluck that what they really needed in order to prosper economically was a strong government with an efficient army to compel them to abandon the feud (e.g. Durham 1909:183, 204–5). Yet feuds continued to rage and were painstakingly defended on the irreproachably logical grounds that, in the absence of government, there existed no logical alternative to feud but anarchy. The arguments produced in connection with the murder of the Ghoanni child provide a particularly good example of this type of logic in which any sense of proportion or relativity is strictly subordinate to a set of rigidly formulated rules which must be obeyed to the letter.

The facts of the case are as follows: two men, one from Shoshi and the other from Ghoanni, were quarrelling when the latter snatched a firebrand from the hearth and flung it at his opponent, whereupon the Ghoanni man fled to avoid immediate reprisals. The Shoshi man crossed the border into Ghoanni territory and, finding neither his enemy nor any of his adult kinsmen as a surrogate, killed the eight-year-old son of the man who had insulted him to wipe out the slur cast upon his honour by the blow he had received.

The reaction to the murder of the child was one of outrage on *both* sides. Ghoanni resented the act for obvious reasons. But although the child seems to have been ritually shaven and was therefore a legitimate victim (e.g. Durham 1909:155), Shoshi were almost unanimous in condemning the act of their fellow tribesman, because, as they readily conceded, 'to kill a child was dishonourable' (1909:112). Nevertheless, when Miss Durham suggested that the man be punished and that Shoshi take the initiative by outlawing the murder of children in vengeance, three points were made. Firstly, said a Shoshi man, who admitted that he did not envy the predicament of a man obliged to bring vengeance upon a mere child, 'if it is the law to kill one of the same house, and the murderer has fled and left no male but a child, then you must. It is a pity, but it is the law' (1909:112). Secondly, it was not possible for the Shoshi tribal assembly to punish the man, because 'The blood had been taken *outside* the tribe, therefore was not a crime against the tribe, and not punishable by it.' Lastly, if the Shoshi tribal assembly had decided to outlaw the killing of children and other tribes had not followed suit, Shoshi would have been at a disadvantage (1909:154).

The most poignant element in these reactions to homicide is the tone of contrite resignation in which the tribesmen communicate their feeling of impotence before the 'law'. They are aware of its failings but unable to modify it. Similar attitudes are typical of all sedentary tribal societies in the Mediterranean and the Middle East. Feuding obligations are felt to be an unwelcome burden which custom nevertheless makes it imperative to bear.

Another case involving the murder of a child shows the presence of analogous attitudes in rural Iraq: as recently as 1955 a two-year-old boy was killed by two old men aged eighty and seventy-five in revenge for the murder of a brother of the former by some cousins of the child (Kadhim 1957:186). The two offenders were arrested and tried. The court could find no evidence to suggest that the defendants were mentally unbalanced and condemned them to penal servitude for life, a sentence which they seem to have borne with fortitude, since it is reported that 'Their conduct inside the prison was good.'

Again, two salient features mark this case: firstly, the disproportion between the cause, murder, and the effect, vengeance

upon a mere child; secondly, the apparently ready and uncom-
plaining acceptance of their punishment by the two men. As in
the Ghoanni case quoted above, it would seem that to bring vengeance constitutes a morally ambiguous act. It is 'right' and
necessary in so far as by the dictates of customary law it is the
only possible course of action open to a man in a given set of
circumstances. But submission to the dictates of the law does not
make the act any less reprehensible on a purely humanitarian
plane; and there is no lack of evidence to show that avengers are
painfully aware of the cruel consequences of their acts both for
themselves and for the families of their victims. The author of
the thesis in which the Iraqi infanticide is reported analyzes, for
instance, a large number of cases of vengeance in which the
culprit was committed to a long term of imprisonment. In none
of these cases does the murderer seem to have regarded the
sentence as unjust, for all those convicted are stated to have
manifested no indignation at their treatment by the authorities
and to have behaved well in prison.

In sedentary societies the bringing of vengeance is rarely
applauded. There is a tendency for the avenger to be pitied as
the victim of ineluctable circumstance. He is admired for his
resoluteness and readiness to fulfil his obligations. But he also
excites compassion, for he may himself die and bring destruction
upon his own family as the result of a chain of events that he
did nothing to inaugurate. He is further condemned as the author
of an act which is socially disruptive. The situation of the
avenger in sedentary societies is thus fraught with ambiguities.
The duty to bring vengeance normally prevails over counter-
motivations, because it is the 'law'. But the law of vengeance is
regarded with very mixed feelings.

This attitude to the feud is well, if a little floridly, summarized
by Miss Durham whose own experience in the Balkans brought
home to her the full extent of the current of pessimistic fatalism
which coloured the sentiments of most tribesmen as regards the
feud. 'The unwritten law of blood,' she writes, 'is to the Albanian
as is the Fury of Greek tragedy. It drives him inexorably to his
doom' (1909:41).

One horrendous story in which vengeance, infanticide and
intra-group killing are combined well illustrates this statement.
At the end of the last century a woman from the tribal regions

of northern Albania married a citizen of Shkodër. Her brother was an outlaw with a price on his head. When he came clandestinely one night to visit his sister, the woman's husband secretly betrayed him to the Turks in exchange for a large reward. On learning of this treachery, the bereaved sister killed, as they slept, not only her husband, but also her two young sons—'seed of a serpent' in the words of the informant—who could not be allowed to live to perpetuate the name and deeds of a traitor (1928:150). Like the others I have mentioned, this case is marked by a brand of 'insane' logic in which human sentiments and a sense of proportion are totally submerged by a strict observance of rigidly defined rules. For it is inconceivable that the woman who committed this multiple murder did not live through a period of great emotional suffering before and after her act; yet, on a purely logical plane, there was no alternative open to her. In a society as strongly patrilineal as her own, her husband's betrayal of her brother automatically brought about the confrontation of two agnatic groups: her brother and herself on the one hand, and her husband and his agnates, her children, on the other. The logic of the situation demanded that she wreak vengeance in the other camp however closely related she might be to the adversary.[9]

The same type of ineluctable logic is characteristic of the whole corpus of Albanian customary law which, for example, enjoins men to walk at a minimum distance of the length of one rifle's barrel from each other lest one should inadvertently jostle his neighbour and thereby cause a feud. For women the distance is measured at the length of a distaff, as they were accustomed to spin as they walked (Durham 1928:25).

This kind of rule is typical not only of the Laws of Lek (cf. p. 13), but also of the customary law of most other sedentary tribal communities in the Mediterranean and the Middle East. A feature shared by all these societies is what might be called the premise of violence: all legislation is calculated in function

[9] Although it is said by Albanians that, in the normal course of events, 'Women don't have blood feuds' (Hasluck 1954:217), they may be forced to countervene the rule if they no longer have any male agnates to vindicate the honour of the patrilineage. Killing by women in these circumstances seems to have been fairly common in the Balkans (cf. *passim* in Durham and Hasluck).

of a recognized innate tendency to violent interaction. The most remarkable aspect of such legislation is, however, not so much the efforts deployed by these societies to restrict recourse to violence, as the fact that the legal sanctions provided for in the code are themselves not only inordinately violent but also conceived in such a manner that their very application can give rise to feud. A notable example is to be seen in the Albanian Law of the Dog (Hasluck 1954: ch. VII). If a dog attacked and killed a man at night, 'the law was entirely on the side of the house dog and its master', and if the man killed the dog in self-defence, 'he must pay blood money or have a feud with its master, exactly as if it was the latter he had killed', for the law states clearly ' "at night a dog is equivalent to a man" ' (Hasluck 1954:75). This sort of ruling is not all that strange if it is remembered that an efficient guard against theft might, in conditions of very low and irregular agricultural or pastoral yield, mean the difference between starvation and survival. Indeed, a very similar set of customs is reported by Burckhardt from among the Bedouin of northern Arabia where the killing of a watch dog was punished by a very heavy fine in bags of wheat (1830:71). The only difference between the Bedouin and the Albanians in this respect is one of degree: it is not at all easy at first sight to understand why the Albanians regard the life of a dog killed at night as on a par with that of its master, although it may be thought that recourse to feud by the master, if blood money is not paid for the dog, constitutes a perfectly logical act of self-help in the absence of judicial authority and government.

Nor is it that the nocturnal killing of a dog is merely 'likened' to the killing of its master or a member of his household, as is shown by the converse case. For if a dog attacked and killed a man in daylight, it was usually 'as if its master had killed him and a blood feud sprang up between the two families'. There is here little or no possibility of substituting an indemnity for the life of the victim. It is therefore no distortion of the facts to say that the life of a dog and a man were seen as strictly equivalent. Again, if it is accepted that the form of most legal sanctions is everywhere but tenuously related to the type of crime they are conceived to punish, this equation of the life of a dog with that of a man is not strictly speaking illogical. But there is an evident lack of proportion between the offence and the sanction which is not to be found in the Bedouin version of the same custom. Moreover, the sanction itself is ultimately the declaration of a feud—an eventuality which a large number of other legal dispositions in the same society are intended to prevent. The law itself incites to the very violence it is conceived to quell. Violence, instead of acting as a deterrent to violence, actually gives rise to more violence.

This vicious circle is particularly noticeable in the laws relating to asylum and the conclusion of temporary truces between feuding groups. In all Mediterranean and Middle Eastern tribal societies there exists a highly developed code stipulating the conditions under which asylum may be sought, protection guaranteed and cease fire agreements made. The extreme elaboration of such codes reflects the general state of insecurity which reigns as soon as a man travels beyond his home territory. But whereas breaches of the code of asylum and protection are everywhere comparatively rare, the Albanians appear to derive a perverse pleasure from testing the rules to the limit and creating situations which are quite ludicrously tragic.

Miss Durham relates how she one day hired a young Kastrati man to guide her on a visit to Hoti, another tribe. They crossed the frontier together and were invited to sup in the house of a tribesman:

> The Kastrati man was specially pressed to drink; his presence caused great mirth. The 'joke' was a particularly Albanian one. Not only was Kastrati at blood with Hoti, but Kastrati had blackened the honour of the very house in which they were sitting, so bitterly, that the whole of both tribes was involved. Except with safe-conduct of a Hoti man—or under the protection of a stranger,[10] as was the case—my gay young Kastrati could not have crossed the border-line save at the peril of his life. But he had chosen to come right into the lion's jaws, and the 'cheek' of him pleased everyone immensely. All drank healths with him, he was the honoured guest, and

[10] The fact that Miss Durham was a woman also doubtlessly helped, since the laws of asylum forbid the taking of vengeance when women are present (Durham 1909:32). The same custom occurs in Kabylia (Hanoteau and Letourneux 1893:65).

they discussed pleasantly how many bloods would be required before peace was made . . .' (1909:61).

For Miss Durham such episodes are proof that the Albanians regard the feud as a noble 'sport' (1909:170). Absolutely literal observance of the rules of asylum and hospitality can, however, veer rapidly from sport to dead earnest and result in intra-group killing. 'Children in Shalë', for instance, 'were taught with great pride that once a tribesman killed his brother for killing a guest, for an Albanian's duty to his guest transcends the claims of blood relationship' (Hasluck 1954:211). A similar story is reported from another region:

> A certain family was at blood with a man, but one member of the family made it up with the enemy—temporarily, at any rate—and swore *besa* [a truce] with him. This included a vow to protect each other. His own brother then shot the family foe dead; by the terms of his *besa*, he who had sworn it was bound to avenge the slain, or be for ever dishonoured. He shot his own brother and cleaned his honour, and came to confess wild with grief, weeping bitterly and lamenting the deed which a cruel fate had forced upon him . . .' (Durham 1909:171).

'. . . nor is this an isolated case', adds Miss Durham. In both instances, as also in the case of the Shkodër woman who killed her husband and sons, the inexorable logic of the law prevails over sentiment.

Now, the law of asylum as such differs very little throughout the Mediterranean and the Middle East. But while an Albanian, a Corsican or a Kabyle will allow himself to become involved in a situation in which he is forced to kill against his own better judgement, a Bedouin anticipating similar circumstances will normally flee or give his adversary a chance to take flight, making it impossible for the traditional sanction to be applied. Sedentary agriculturalists seem to practise a blind obedience to the letter of a highly dysfunctional law and revel in the 'grudging respect' (Campbell 1964:200) which is accorded to them by the community for the accomplishment of acts which most nomads would look upon with unmitigated horror. Sedentary agriculturalists might be described as the prisoners of their own legal conventions, while nomadic pastoralists possess a less elaborate body of customary law which they apply literally, modify or circumvent entirely according to the necessities of the case in hand.

Whilst deliberately avoiding for the present moment any precise comparison of the legal norms operative in sedentary and nomadic tribal societies, I should like to suggest that the peculiar brand of 'logical' thinking combined with an almost total disregard for personal sentiment and a lack of any sense of proportion, which characterizes the numerous instances of violence I have reported from sedentary communities, has little connection with the stated objectives of the contestants in a feud or even with an exaggerated respect for the law, but proceeds rather out of a desire to acquire and safeguard a reputation for honour.

Some of the cases I have quoted are quite unambiguously concerned with honour, notably that in which a man kills his brother for breaking the *besa* he had sworn. In others, such as the killing of the Ghoanni child and the multiple murder committed by the Shkodër woman, the reason invoked is the 'law' of blood. In yet others, it is a small debt, an unfortunate moment of anger or a mere argument over the size of a star which precipitates an armed confrontation and the beginning of a feud. It is my opinion that this variety of motivations is only apparent and that, in the final analysis, all conflicts in sedentary societies which reach a stage marked by the outbreak of physical violence are conflicts in which the most important prize is honour, all other considerations having lost by this time much of their initial significance.

If this is true, it would explain why the Albanians and the Kabyles, for instance, can be described as 'really peaceful and law-abiding' (Albania 1943:52) peoples, who live 'under the tyranny of laws' (Durham 1909:41), and yet be observed simultaneously to practise one of the most developed and destructive forms of feud known. For I submit that sedentary tribal societies in the Mediterranean and the Middle East possess not one but two codes of law which complement each other. One is the customary 'canon' to which most ethnographers refer when discussing tribal law in the area. The second is a quite separate law of honour which parallels the 'canon', must constantly be taken into consideration when efforts are made to interpret the 'canon' and, finally, supersedes it in certain situations when the 'canon' proves inadequate to resolve conflicts. Recourse to the law of honour when the 'canon' fails to function efficiently translates the conflict into different terms and permits an escalation of hostilities far above the level beyond which the 'canon' becomes impotent to ensure that a certain measure of justice is done.

In all sedentary tribal communities in the Mediterranean and the Middle East litigants are expected to resort to arbitration or compurgation to settle their differences. Killing is nowhere in these societies a prescribed manner of obtaining redress for material wrongs. The ideal primacy of customary law is made explicit in the (lamely translated) Albanian adage 'Killing for a fault is not permissible' (Hasluck 1954:139). The *only* legitimate motive for murder is slighted honour.[11] Nonetheless, despite this ideal and as I have already had frequent occasion to show, by no means all litigants in disputes over rights and property agree to submit to the vagaries and expense of arbitration, preferring to entrust the outcome to a more conclusive test of strength. On the one hand, the law forbids killing except where honour is at stake; but the inefficacy of legal institutions is, on the other hand, such that force of arms and killing are the only sure means of getting the better of an opponent. If, then, one or both the parties to a dispute concerning property or access to natural resources believe that they will not obtain satisfaction from the 'canon', the whole tenor of the conflict is changed by introducing the motive of honour: if a man can envisage the claims of his adversary *vis-à-vis* himself as incompatible with his status as a man of honour, he may with impunity overstep the limits imposed by the 'canon' and resort to murder in order to regain 'face'.

The process whereby conflict over a material prize is converted into conflict on an ideological plane to justify 'illegal' recourse to arms is nicely illustrated by a case from Shalë which occurred in about 1932 even after the establishment of a relatively strong central government backed by an efficient police force:

While two families were quarrelling about a piece of land, the wife of Grimës one day voiced her opinions so volubly in Gjelosh's house that he lost his temper and pushed her out. She fell down some steps by the door and bruised her hip. She showed the bruise to the gendarmerie, who were sympathetic

---

[11] —or, of course, riposte for a death inflicted by the other party.

enough to arrest Gjelosh and to imprison him for three months. The woman, who cared more for the violation of her honour by the push than for the bruise, was not satisfied and instigated her son, a boy of twelve or thirteen, to vindicate her honour by killing Gjelosh's son, who was of the same age. Since the boys habitually herded their goats together, her son found the opportunity of pushing the other boy over a rock and as he lay there helpless he stoned him till he died. Then Gjelosh, still in prison, paid a man to kill the little murderer. Grimës retorted by killing Gjelosh's remaining son and dooming Gjelosh's family to extinction (Hasluck 1954:236–7).

The gendarmerie and a national legal code have here taken the place of the elders and the 'canon'. But the process remains the same: honour serves to raise the conflict from the domain of civil law onto another plane on which there are less inhibiting rules. The fact that the concept of honour is ill-defined and consequently liable to any number of interpretations by the contestants themselves and the society at large makes it possible for the conflict to continue indefinitely, since as long as one of the parties is 'losing' they can always make out that their honour has not yet been satisfied and claim another life to 'equalize', whereupon their opponents will seek to do likewise and there will develop a self-perpetuating eternal feud.

The intensity and prevalence of violence in sedentary societies is thus not unconnected with the manner in which individuals manipulate to their own ends the ambiguities and lack of precision inherent in the concept of honour: as the notion of honour itself is unbounded by definitional limits, conflicts purportedly over points of honour are equally unrestricted in scope and virulence.

In nomadic societies in the Mediterranean and the Middle East, the concept of honour, though far from absent, plays a very different role. Nomadic pastoralists would on the whole appear to be more sober and less foolhardy in picking quarrels than sedentary agriculturalists. The Bedouin of Cyrenaica, for example, seem to feud for more practical reasons than their sedentary counterparts. 'The origin of the feud is wealth', say the Bedouin (Peters 1951:393), by which they mean that competition between sons of co-wives to gain control of a larger part of the paternal heritage is frequently the cause of fission leading to the inauguration of feuding relations between the descendants of half-siblings. Elsewhere, Peters defines the feud in Cyrenaica as 'a violent form of hostility between corporations which has its source in the competition for proprietary rights in land and water' (1967:279). A similar view emerges from Lewis' study of the pastoral Somali among whom a typical cause of armed conflict is a dispute over access to a well (1961:46). Indeed, the Somali pastoralists even 'equate war and drought' (1961:45). In other words—and this applies not only to the Somali but to all pastoral societies in the Mediterranean and the Middle East—conflict is in the main directly associated with the struggle for survival and is explicitly recognized as such.

It is true that an occasional reference can be found in the literature on nomadic pastoralists to acts of revenge that bear the same stamp of inexorable logic and disproportion as those which occur with such frequency in sedentary communities. Burckhardt, for instance, tells of 'a skirmish between Maazy [Ma'aza] Arabs and those of Sinai, in 1813', in which the former accidentally wounded a woman of the latter. When the Sinaï Arabs retaliated in the following year, they had killed eight or ten men, when one of them remembered the previous year's injury to one of their women and therefore inflicted a sabre wound upon one of the helpless Ma'aza women. Of this act Burckhardt comments: 'His companions, although they applauded what he had done, acknowledged that they should not like to imitate his example' (1830: 173). This sentiment very closely resembles that of 'grudging respect' (cf. p. 140) which is so characteristic of the manner in which sedentary communities regard similar atrocities performed in the name of honour.

But the instance cited by Burckhardt is somewhat exceptional. For although, according to the same author, 'The Arab regards this blood-revenge as one of his most sacred rights, as well as duties, [which] no earthly consideration would induce him to relinquish', Burckhardt is careful to add that vengeance is only brought 'whenever the security of the whole is not affected' (1831:313). The bringing of vengeance among nomadic pastoralists is thus subordinate to considerations of an economic and political nature. An offence or killing will not be avenged unless it is expedient to do so. This is in sharp contrast with the practice of sedentary agriculturalists who appear to feel themselves obliged to bring vengeance whatever the cost to themselves or the group as a whole. Nomadic pastoralists engage in violent conflict to accomplish specific material objectives, such as seasonal access to land and water, which are clearly defined in time and space. Because the objectives are limited, the intensity and scope of the conflict are also limited.

The notion of honour may be invoked among nomadic pastoralists to justify a given conflict, but, like criminal responsibility (cf. pp. 111–12), it tends to operate as a function of oecological and structural distance. The motive of wounded honour becomes increasingly effective as a pretext for violence the greater the physical and genealogical distance which separates the parties concerned. Honour does not always, as in sedentary societies, supply an unimpeachable justification for recourse to violence, but is regarded as a useful adjunct to support certain types of claim the very assertion of which implies prior physical alienation between the parties. Sedentary argriculturalists, on the other hand, ignore the oecological or structural distance which separates them from the adversary and deliberately exploit the ambiguities inherent in the notion of honour to circumvent the dictates of a narrowly conceived and ineffectual code of customary law which provides inadequate guarantees for the preservation of rights and property.

I shall attempt later in the present chapter to relate these two forms of conflict to oecological variables in conformity with the model of feud which I postulated in the introductory section. But before I do this, I shall examine in the light of the ethnographic evidence the validity, in the context of feuding societies, of my hypothesis that leadership is a basic component of any social situation and that leaders must therefore emerge even where their presence is in theory precluded by a fiercely egalitarian ideology.

(2) THE EXTENT OF LEADERSHIP

> Where there is no proper Government, the bad rule (an Albanian Muslim, in Durham 1909: 140).

John Locke was of the opinion that 'civil government is the

proper remedy for the inconveniences of the state of nature', which he depicts as a social situation in which 'self-love will make men partial to themselves and their friends, and . . . ill-nature, passion and revenge will carry them too far in punishing others, and hence nothing but confusion and disorder will follow' (1690: II, 13). Now, while it is perhaps questionable, as I have shown, whether feuding societies can be described as 'nothing but confusion and disorder', it is certain that, with rare exceptions to which I shall return later, the practice of feud—or, in Locke's terms, the punishment of the offender by the offended party—is confined to societies in which there is little or no instituted 'civil government'. I shall not quibble about the precise definition of this phrase. For my present purpose it is sufficient to state that the main characteristic of government is the possibility of employing physical force to coerce conformity to any decisions that may emanate from those who ultimately control the destinies of the majority. In this sense government is absent from most feuding societies.

This fact is so generally acknowledged that it might be said to constitute a commonplace of the literature on feud. Thurnwald, for instance, writes that 'In many small politically independent communities where there is no fixed authority, bloody reprisals follow the infliction or the supposed infliction of an injury' (1930:598). So insistent is he upon this point that he repeats it twice more, asserting that 'Blood vengeance cannot be eliminated by composition but only by strong political authority' and that it is 'through a lack of political authority' that it has persisted in 'parts of Europe such as Corsica and the Balkans', where it 'has undergone the most bizarre exaggerations' (1930: 599).

Middleton and Tait who, it will be remembered (cf. p. 4), indiscriminately label all forms of violent interaction as 'self-help' and consequently include feud under this heading, add precision to Thurnwald's original statement by postulating that 'It occurs in those societies which lack centralized political authority that can provide sanctions to regulate relations between constituent units, and where commonly accepted values which prohibit the use of armed force are not recognized' (1958:19). Similarly for Robiquet, 'La vengeance est la justice des temps barbares', in which society has not yet come into being or, having ceased to exist, has been superseded by anarchy (1835?:394). In the same vein, Busquet affirms of Corsica that

> Les hostilités en effet sont continuelles avec les groupes étrangers. Un pareil état de choses est réalisé quand la nature et l'organisation d'Etat sont encore absentes. Il se prolonge après leur apparition tout en reculant et retrécissant de plus en plus ses limites, au fur et à mesure que l'Etat accroît sa force et son prestige et remplit davantage ses fonctions essentielles de défense et de justice. Jusque là ces fonctions primordiales, c'est la famille qui doit s'efforcer d'y pourvoir (1920: 24).

The absence of centralized government in feuding societies may be associated with two main factors. From a comparison of those societies throughout the world in which the feud is practised it would seem that its principal concomitants are, firstly, as I have already suggested, material poverty which inhibits the spontaneous development of an internal power hierarchy based on the control of economic resources, and, secondly, lack of an adequate system of communications: where rapid means of conveying men and materials, coercive force and wealth, from one place to another are lacking, a centralized government cannot impose itself from without, because the administrative centre can neither militarily control, nor economically exploit the periphery to make the expenditure incurred by this control worthwhile.[12]

It is obviously impossible to specify with any precision an economic threshold below which—given topographical and technological conditions unconducive to easy communications—centralized government cannot develop and feud will invariably be found. However, as a rough indication it may be said that feuding societies live so close to a minimum subsistence level that a bad year can be fatal to part of the population. But precarious conditions such as these do not make it impossible for some degree of economic differentiation to arise within the existing oecological limits. Some families or groups of families

---

[12] Amery, for instance, writing of attempts made by the authorities to eradicate feud in Albania, remarks that 'Bad communications made coërcion difficult' (1938:9).

are always a little more fortunate than others and there develops a minimal form of stratification. Although this tendency is largely neutralized at an inter-group level by the formation of strategic alliances grouping families of disparate means in mutual defence, in circumstances in which alliance is not feasible feud is an obvious surrogate for government—or bad government—by a slightly privileged minority, as was the case in Corsica when, under Genoese rule, 'la vengeance fut autrefois une nécessité . . . [parce que] le pauvre ne pouvait obtenir justice des torts qu'on lui faisait' (Mérimée 1840a:41–2).

Feud is thus not confined, as the majority of authors seem to think, to totally unstratified societies (if such a phenomenon can ever in reality be held to exist) and is not infrequently found in conjunction with some degree of 'civil government'. It can, as Mérimée intimates, provide a means of equalizing opportunity and surmounting the barriers created by economic differentiation even when these barriers are theoretically sanctioned and re-inforced by an inefficient totalitarian government which has sought to overcome the communications problem by instituting, as in Corsica, a system of indirect rule in which authority is wielded locally by those who are economically more favoured than others. Where local office-holders acting on behalf of a central government are unsupported by effective coercive force, feud will function as an instrument of 'democratization' to main-tain a tradition of political equality in the face of efforts from above to impose a pyramid of executive authority. The situation in Albania since the Turkish conquest is comparable to that of Corsica in this respect. Commenting on the relations between tribesmen and the Turkish government in the last quarter of the nineteenth century, Gopčević notes, for instance, that

Die türkische Regierung ist ohnmächtig, denn in den Bergen der Maljsoren und Mirediten war sie niemals Herrin. Diese Gebirgsvölker, eben jene, bei welchen die Blutrache am meisten in Schwung ist, sind Leute vollständig unabhängig von der Pforte und der Pascha von Scutari würde ausgelacht werden, wenn er ihnen befehlen wollte, der Blutrache bei Todesstrafe zu entsagen (1881:71).

The Corsican and Albanian examples show that the practice

of feud is not restricted to societies totally unendowed with an instituted power hierarchy. They are typical of societies in which the feud persists as a means of 'punishing others' where a colonial government is unable to employ coercive force to implement its policy in the conquered territory.

Yet there exists another type of society possessing instituted centralized government in which the feud occurs, not merely as a legal sub-system which comes into operation where the official system is impotent to ensure the administration of justice, but in effect with the assent of the state as a prescribed sanction to certain categories of injurious behaviour. Middleton and Tait recognize this possibility in the discussion of self-help I have already quoted, where they concede that self-help does not necessarily run counter to the principle of authority: 'it is found in many centralized states. But it is there under the control of the chief, who makes use of it as a means to enforce his judgement' (1958:19). This is the case in Buganda, where a feud can be declared to redeem a debt of blood only if the chief first gives his explicit permission and it is understood that he will benefit from a fixed proportion of any sum of compensation which may be agreed upon to close hostilities (Beattie 1966:174–5).

Nor does this indicate that the authority of the state is so weak that it prefers a compromise solution to the eventuality of being placed in a situation in which its authority can be put to the test. For Gregory of Tours reports an episode from Merovingian France which dispels any idea that feud is only ever countenanced by the state if it cannot prevent it. Two families 'of high birth and among the first of the court of Chilperic' linked by marriage entered into conflict over the alleged infidelity of the daughter of one of the families to her husband, who belonged to the other. Hostilities were discontinued and composition was finally achieved with the help of the bishop of Paris, but only after some delay, because the king himself, when solicited, had already refused to act as mediator (1927:203).

This and the Buganda examples make it clear that, in spite of my initial strictures, feud can occur in comparatively efficient centralized states provided that the authorities decline all responsibility for the consequences. In the Merovingian episode the parties involved are of equal status. I would conjecture that the same is true of all similar occurrences of feud in centralized states: as long as feuding is restricted to conflicts between fairly small groups of equal status and does not upset the traditionally defined relations between the different strata of the society by mobilizing support on vertical lines of interdependence, the feud is perfectly consonant with the existence of centralized government. Though even in these conditions the basic postulate of equality in feuding societies remains. For if the simple transactional model of feud I put forward in the first chapter (cf. p. 25) is accepted as valid, feud can only function as a means of obtaining redress and prosecuting a relationship if the belligerents subscribe to the same egalitarian ethos positing that, whatever the 'state of play' at any given moment, neither of the two parties can ever gain a position of intrinsic superiority over the other.

Whatever the observed state of internal political relations in feuding societies at any particular moment in time, there is a convincing amount of evidence pointing to the long term prevalence of this egalitarian ethos. From his own experience in the Near East one hundred and fifty years ago Burckhardt writes, for instance, that 'the Bedouin truly says, that he acknowledges no master but the Lord of the Universe' (1830:67). A similar sentiment was expressed, though in a more pejorative vein, by the Buganda companion of a British traveller entering Somaliland at the turn of the present century: when happening for the first time in the journey upon a Somali caravan, the African turned to the whiteman and contemptuously remarked, 'Somalis, they no good: each man his own Sultan' (Drake–Brockman 1912, quoted in Lewis 1955:130). In a quite different area, where violence of the feuding type was prevalent despite a fairly marked degree of economic differentiation, Mérimée was able to declare of Corsica in the 1830s that

le riche n'est point séparé du pauvre par une haute barrière comme en France. Nulle part peut-être on ne rencontrera moins de préjugés aristocratiques, et nulle part les différentes classes de la société ne se trouvent en relation plus fréquente et je dirai plus intime . . . Souvent on voit le maître assis à table avec ses ouvriers qui l'appellent par son nom de baptême et se considèrent comme membres de la famille. Cet amour de l'égalité . . . produit ce résultat que riche et pauvre ont les mêmes idées, parce qu'ils les échangent sans cesse (1840a:41–42).

Robiquet corroborates this view when describing the island, which he visited a few years before Mérimée, as 'un pays où personne ne vent servir et où les hommes veulent vivre noblement' (1835?: 398).
The same theme emphasizing the intrinsic equality of servant and master recurs frequently in much of the literature on Albania. For although a man would normally resort to taking service only if he were in the direst straights, he was, according to von Hahn, treated exactly like any other son of the house (1867:340), 'ate out of the same dish as his master and slept in the sitting-room or elsewhere in the same conditions as the young unmarried men of the family' (Hasluck 1954:43). Indeed, so closely was he identified as a member of the family in which he served that any insult to him must be avenged by his master, and in the region of Martanesh, if he seduced a woman of his master's house, he was sentenced to death by the community for com-mitting incest, since as a son of the house he was considered to have lain with his sister (Hasluck 1954:43).
This acceptance of every man by every other as his equal is best expressed in the Albanian dictum that all men are equal before the law (Hasluck 1954:159). This is a principle upheld by all feuding societies and amounts to giving each man the opportunity to have his say in the tribal or clan assemblies sum-moned to decide upon matters of importance such as external political relations, the annual division of pasturage and water supplies and the administration of justice in cases of crime both against the community and other individuals. Miss Durham says of the assembly called in Shoshi to deal with the murder of the Ghoanni child that 'The proceedings . . . were very orderly, save for the great noise; usually a man was heard out with few in-terruptions' (1909:154).
Mrs. Hasluck takes pains on several occasions to emphasize that 'Tribal government was entirely democratic—of the people, by the people and for the people,' (e.g. 1954:11, 163). A similar insistence upon the participation of all male members of any constituted group in the decision-making process marks Lewis' book on the Somali. Although for some purposes only the elders

may confer together, it is not unusual for a Somali *shir*, or lineage council, to unite in one place at the same time several thousand members who stand in a rough circle sending representatives into the centre to thrash out the matters on hand, while the majority stand by to listen and see that fair play is observed (Lewis 1961: 198; cf. also Lewis 1955:97). Though less precise information is available, the Kabyle *djemâa*, or village assembly, seems to have operated before the French conquest in much the same manner, working on the principle of total consensus among adult males of the community (cf. Hanoteau and Letourneux 1893: *passim*; Larousse 1873: vol. 9, p. 1142).[13]

Like the *djemâa*, the Albanian and Somali village and lineage councils also administer justice. One of the main objects of mass consultation of all adult male members of the community in these societies is to reach decisions concerning the collective punishment by the community of an individual who by his actions has jeopardized the good reputation or the social cohesion of the community as a whole. I have already mentioned the Albanian custom of collectively sentencing to death and killing persons accused of incest. Albanian tribesmen sometimes go so far as to collectively exterminate whole families. Miss Durham relates what she calls 'an amazing case of wholesale justice' (1928:75) which occurred in 1912, when 'a gathering of the whole tribe' condemned to death and ambushed all the male members of a family which had made itself notorious in the district for robbery, shooting and general misconduct. The Kabyle *djemâa* acting with the support of all members of the community would similarly cause a woman to be stoned to death for killing her husband (Hanoteau and Letourneux 1893:71) or exhort a husband whose wife had been unfaithful to avenge this stain upon his honour and, by extension, that of the village as well (1893:75).

Although tribal assemblies among nomadic pastoralists are on the whole more often called with a view to the formulation of a policy to be approved by all, collective justice is not unknown and the Somali have an institution known as *yakays* whereby 'A recalcitrant member of the group is bound to a tree and several of his best sheep or a coveted camel slaughtered before

[13] For a brief and incomplete account of the functioning of the Berber *jema'a* in the Central High Atlas cf. Gellner 1969:89–90.

him until he agrees to the judgement of the elders' (Lewis 1961: 232–3). This method seems to be used to enforce compliance to group policy and not to punish individual acts of 'illegal behaviour'. *Yakays* is employed when the culprit is thought worth saving for the sake of group unity. It implies that the victim of such coercion has not yet committed an irreparable act of a gravity sufficient to alienate his birthright, which may be summarized as the prerogative to be regarded as an equal and thereby to enjoy an equal portion of the natural resources to which he and his fellow lineage members have access. A man who has gone beyond the limit of what can be rectified by judicious application of *yakays* is irredeemable and is subject to the only remaining sanction short of execution, that of expulsion from the group (Lewis 1961:168). Indeed, it would appear that it is only among sedentary agriculturalists, like the Albanians and Kabyles, that the group ever takes collective justice to the point of killing the offender. The levying of fines and the punitive destruction of property—fruit trees, grain reserves, houses, animals (e.g. Durham 1909:33–4; Hasluck 1954:38, 135; Hanoteau and Letourneux 1893:103)—by the community appear to be far less frequent among nomadic pastoralists for whom the most common collective sanction is the sending into exile of the offender and his family.

Whatever the matter on hand in both sedentary and nomadic societies, whether it be the misdeeds of a fellow tribesman, the conclusion of an alliance or the formulation of more general policies, it is noteworthy that in each case the participation of *all* adult males is ideally required for the assembly to be able to vote measures affecting the whole group. Sheer numbers may sometimes make it expedient for only one man from each household to represent the opinions of his kinsmen. The representative is nevertheless well briefed and it is probably not inaccurate to say that, whatever the system of representation adopted, the view of all those eligible to air them are ultimately heard and taken into consideration. In conformity with the principles inherent in the egalitarian ethos every male adult has the right to a voice in the 'government' of the tribe.

Yet no assembly can operate efficiently unless one or a number of individuals take upon themselves to organize the proceedings, count the votes and orient the discussion by mooting tentative solutions to problems of which most of those present have possibly very little experience, either because they are too young or because a particular type of issue has not occurred for many years and the solution previously implemented has been forgotten by the majority. It is in response to this need for leadership by persons of pre-eminent ability possessing a long standing memory of precedent that there emerges in feuding societies a category of individuals whose activities are in apparently blatant contradiction with the folk model of equality. The Somali, for instance, in no way hide their allegiance to 'clan heads' (Lewis 1961:205); the Albanian mountaineers not only allow their opinions to be swayed, as do the Kabyles, by a variety of 'elders' each passing judgement in his own specialized field of arbitration, but also recognize a class of tribal headmen or *bajraktars* (Turkish: standard bearer) (e.g. Hasluck 1954: ch. XI); the Bedouin tribes of northern Arabia and the Syrian desert are endowed with both chiefs or *sheikhs* (Burckhardt 1830:168; Musil 1928:493) and judges (Murray 1935:228); finally, the Berbers of the Central High Atlas (Gellner 1969: ch. 4) and the Kabyles (Larousse 1873: vol. 9, p. 1142) acknowledge the offices of an elective tribal chief and other administrators, but, in common with all the other societies mentioned, do not allow the presence of authority to stand in their way when prosecuting feuds with one another.

The existence of leaders is an incontrovertible fact. Their function is to co-ordinate collective action and to act as a focus for group loyalties. But before I attempt to explain who attains a position of leadership and the means employed to achieve this end without doing violence to the premise of equality, I shall try to demonstrate the exact nature and extent of the power entrusted to such men by their fellow tribesmen.

For Lewis the clan head is no more than '*primus inter pares*' (1961:205). Murray asserts of the Sinaï *sheikhs*, with whom as a colonial administrator he was well acquainted, that their power is often 'exaggerated . . . to strangers' (1935:41), though he does little to enlarge upon this statement. Nevertheless, he is obviously not referring to a local anomaly in the position of the *sheikh*, for the same pattern is repeated in Islamic tribal societies throughout the Mediterranean and the Middle East. In Cyrenaica, for instance, Evans-Pritchard was able to observe at first hand that the *sheikh*'s 'social position is unformalized . . . he must in no sense be regarded as a ruler or administrator. Bedouin respect their shaikhs but do not regard them as superiors' (1949:59).

In these nomadic societies living in an extremely inhospitable environment there is no means at the disposal of the chief whereby he may acquire and store substantial amounts of wealth permitting him to lead a life of leisure and luxury and to build up a body of armed retainers whose services he can recompense in money and kind. Du Bois-Aymé, an early anthropologist who accompanied Napoleon's oriental venture in the years 1789 to 1801, has left a remarkable description of tribal life among the Terabin of Sinaï in which he depicts with exceptional subtlety the exact position of the *sheikh vis-à-vis* his subjects in these unfavoured regions:

Quand la famille n'est pas assez nombreuse pour se défendre seule, elle se joint à d'autres familles: le plus puissant des cheykhs donne son nom à la tribu que forment ces familles réunies, et il exerce sur toutes le pouvoir qu'il n'avait d'abord que sur ses parents. Son autorité est fort bornée quant aux individus; mais il a une assez grande influence sur les affaires d'intérêt général: il ordonne les déplacemens de la horde et désigne les campemens; il fait même la guerre ou la paix; droit dangereux, si son propre intérêt, lié intimement à celui de la tribu, ne l'empêchoit d'en abuser. . . Son pouvoir se règle sur l'usage; il n'y a point de lois qui le déterminent de manière fixe; et si ses richesses, si le nombre de ses amis, de ses domestiques, le portoient à en abuser et pouvoient le garantir de la vengeance que la vie du désert rend facile aux opprimés, on verroit bientôt une foule de familles se détacher de lui et s'incorporer dans d'autres tribus. C'est ainsi que des tribus nombreuses ont fini quelquefois par disparoître totalement, tandis que d'autres, à peine connues, s'accroissoient avec rapidité.

Plus on y réfléchit, moins on voit de moyens d'oppression dans le gouvernement des cheykhs . . . le cheykh Arabe, sans gardes, sans cortège, passe sa vie en plein air; ses actions, ses discours, ont pour témoins tous les hommes de la tribu; il ne peut rien dérober à la censure de l'opinion, il ne peut pas couvrir un abus du pouvoir du masque de l'intérêt public, et ses sujets ne sont pas assez nombreux pour qu'il puisse, en les divisant d'intérêts, les subjuguer les uns par les autres...

La vie privée du cheykh ne diffère de celle des autres Arabes que par une nourriture un peu plus abondante, des vêtemens meilleurs, des armes plus choisies (Du Bois-Aymé 1809:581– 582).

The Terabin inhabit an area which is more inimicable to human life than most in the Middle East. It is thus not surprising that the Bedouin tribes, which occupy the vast tract of land in northern Arabia between Palestine and Mesopotamia in which the prevailing oecological conditions are less severe than in Sinaï, are endowed with a more highly developed power structure than that of the Terabin. For in addition to a *sheikh* many of these tribes boast an *agyd* or hereditary military chief, whose duty it is 'in time of war' to supersede the authority of the *sheikh* and to direct all operations against the enemy.[14] Whereas the status of *sheikh* is largely achieved, that of *agyd* is ascribed by birth. The former is a political officer, the latter a charismatic figure, 'a kind of heaven inspired leader', says Burckhardt (1830:171), who may be craven and lacking in judgement, only acting upon the counsel of dreams and of those more experienced in the art of war, but nonetheless remains in sole command for the duration of a warlike expedition. Burckhardt speaks of the *agyd* as an 'institution' conceived

to check any increase of power in the person of the chief of the tribe. By preventing him [the *sheikh*] from commanding his Arabs in time of war, he rendered it difficult for him to engage in feuds merely from private motives, and effectually hindered him from exercizing any undue influence in the division of the plunder, which would most probably have been the case, had he, as military chief, the opportunity of augmenting his own wealth in a degree disproportionate to that of his Arabs; and this wealth might, in process of time, induce and enable him to assume arbitrary power . . . [The *agyd* is] a salutary balance to the sheikh's power (1830:171).

There is a quite striking degree of congruence between this

[14] An analogous office exists among the Somali (Lewis 1955:89).

analysis of a mechanism deliberately designed to restrict the effective political influence of individual leaders and Du Bois-Aymé's description of the extent of sheikhly power among the Terabin. Such mechanisms are, however, not only found in nomadic pastoral feuding societies. Analogous checks upon authority have developed in sedentary communities. The Berbers studied by Gellner have, for example, a system whereby a 'chief', or administrative official, is elected annually by the adult male members of all clans but one.[15] The clan which is not eligible to vote in a given year provides the candidates for office, and each year eligibility for office falls to another clan in strict rotation (1969:81-8).[16] Election to office can only be achieved on the basis of a unanimous vote (1969:84). This system ensures that the chief is impartially elected for his qualities as an administrator, and not for his ability to mobilize ties of kinship or amity; the brevity of his period of office prevents him from accumulating a following from outside his own clan by the distribution of favours; and, finally, he commands no constituted military force to further his own political ends, since it is the tribal assembly, and not the chief, which is responsible for all decisions relative to military and 'external' affairs and the election in time of danger from without of a 'chief-of-the-war' (1969:91) who entirely supersedes the administrative chief for the duration of hostilities.

A similar pattern may be observed in Albania, where each tribe was headed by a family which traditionally provided incumbents for the hereditary post of *bajraktar*. But although the members of this family generally enjoyed a large measure of dynastic prestige, it was recognized that the eldest son of a ruling *bajraktar* was not necessarily a fit person to succeed his father. 'Succession from father to son', writes Mrs. Hasluck, 'depended on merit' (1954:117). Descent had to be confirmed by the unanimous acclaim of the tribe, for if the tribe was of the opinion that the reigning *bajraktar*'s first born son was unsuitable to succeed to the post, he 'was passed over in favour of his younger brother. Both, if unfit, might be superseded by their paternal

[15] A similar system seems to have operated among the Kabyles (cf. Larousse 1873: vol. 9, p. 1142).
[16] A system of rotational eligibility to the chieftaincy likewise obtains among the Somali (Lewis 1955:99).

uncle or cousin in the male line' (1954:117).[17] Descent was thus mitigated by considerations of a more practical nature which no doubt hinged upon the character and experience of the candidates. The *bajraktar* was not only carefully selected by those he was to rule over, but, once installed, had almost no liberty of political or judicial action at all:

> In all areas the jurisdiction of the bajraktar was subject to certain limitations. If the commoners did not like one of his decisions, even if made in concert with the headmen and elders, they were not bound to abide by it and could compel him to re-examine the case. Neither he nor a headman could, singly or in combination, fine a tribesman without first securing authority from the tribe (1954:122).

He was, in time of peace, less an independent ruler than the mere spokesman or chairman of the elders, who themselves, with prior consent of the General Assembly, were only able to 'impose, but . . . not collect fines . . . They could not pass heavy sentences like banishment or death unless a General Assembly demanded them, and if it did, they could not resist its will' (1954:10).

The activities of both the *bajraktar* and other administrative officers, like headmen and elders, were thus narrowly controlled by the tribe at large. As is also the case among the Berbers, they were furthermore subjected to yet another check at the highest level: in many tribes there existed one or more 'good families' who by nobility of descent were regarded as superior to the lineage of the *bajraktars* and whose veto, particularly in time of war, could effectively prevent the *bajraktar* from undertaking almost any action in the name of the tribe (Hasluck 1954: 123–126).

The material I have quoted proves without any possible doubt that, despite a fiercely egalitarian ideology common to all feuding societies in the Mediterranean and the Middle East, the phenomenon of leadership is widespread. Following my own postulate that a social situation, to persist through time, must necessarily be based on co-operation and that co-operation cannot occur without the emergence of leaders to co-ordinate the efforts of

---

[17] For a not dissimilar situation among the Somali cf. Lewis 1955:97, 99.

those who have agreed to co-operate, I have tried to show from the ethnography how the notion of equality is not incompatible with that of leadership and how the two concepts can, and indeed must, operate in feuding societies to complement each other.

I have in this section deliberately refrained from *analyzing* leadership in feuding societies. I have sought only to extract from the literature a static picture of what in other societies might be termed the 'institution' of leadership. Institutions, to qualify for identification as such, are, however, usually regarded as enjoying a certain measure of both permanence and public recognition of their utility[18] to the societies in which they are found. But in feuding societies neither of these conditions are met by what I have provisionally called the 'institution' of leadership. For, firstly, there is little or no continuity or permanence in leadership, the status of leader being, as Du Bois-Aymé pointed out, extremely precarious and dependent, if the incumbent is to maintain his position for any length of time, more often upon a sense of tact and diplomacy than on hereditary or elective office; and, secondly, where the 'office' of chief, *sheikh* or *bajraktar* does occur in feuding societies, the executive power wielded by the office-holder is so tenuous and so frequently both disregarded by individuals and overruled by the majority, that it is difficult to argue that the members of these societies recognize much intrinsic utility in the office. So, though it would perhaps be a questionable and foolhardy statement to say that leadership in feuding societies definitely does not constitute an institution, it is nonetheless evident that, if it is thought to qualify as an institution, it is at the most a very weak and sporadic one.

Now I suggested earlier that the presence of feud in a society was in some way connected with a phenomenon to which I have given the name of 'total scarcity' and that one of the characteristic features of 'total scarcity' was the absence or minimal development of any institutions outside the feud itself. The weakness of instituted leadership in feuding societies would seem to support this view. In the next section I shall, by elaborating the concept of 'total scarcity', expand the argument that material and institutional poverty are closely related. Then, passing from description to analysis of social process, I shall show, in the remainder

[18] I define social utility as congruence with the long term interests of the majority.

of the chapter, how feud arises in response to conditions of 'total scarcity' and produces, or *is*, a surrogate social system of its own conceived to make good a variety of institutional deficiencies which are determined by a constellation of oecological and historical variables. Employing violence or the threat of violence as a catalyst, feud survives as a social system, despite a strong in-built tendency to self-destruction, by fostering the dynamic interplay of the three basic social components—co-operation, conflict and leadership (cf. p. 123)—which, taken individually, neutralize each other's potentially deleterious effects and, together, constitute the unique premise of ongoing social process.

(3) 'TOTAL SCARCITY'

I have said (cf. pp. 121–2) that 'total scarcity', 'may be summarized as the moral, institutional and material premise of a certain type of society in which *everything* felt by the people themselves to be relevant to human life is regarded by those people as existing in absolutely inadequate quantities'.

'Total scarcity' constitutes a 'folk' or conscious model. Analytically speaking it may be broken down into two distinct spheres of scarcity. The first of these comprises all those manifestations of scarcity which ultimately create an observable insufficiency of material goods to meet demands. The second cannot be empirically observed and comprises a series of commodities the scarcity of which cannot be 'proven' by scientific means. The first is objective and is perceived by both the outside observer and the people under observation. The second is subjective and of palpable significance only to these people, although the observer may also apprehend it through the behaviour and statements of those who believe in its existence. The first I shall call material or oecological scarcity;[19] the second, moral scarcity.

[19] The term oecology is normally used to describe the nature of symbiotic relations between living organisms and their environment such that the former contrive to subsist by adapting themselves to and exploiting the possibilities offered by the latter. In what follows I shall be using the phrase 'oecological scarcity' to isolate a specific aspect of what I have more generally termed 'material scarcity': if material scarcity implies a shortage of material goods to meet consumer demands, oecological scarcity refers to a limited availability of the environmental and human factors

Material scarcity may further be said to be 'realistic', while moral scarcity is 'nonrealistic'.[20] The first can occur in any society at any time in connection with any human activity touching upon the production or exploitation of material goods and resources. The second, moral scarcity, is only found in oecological conditions in which material scarcity has reached such a high pitch of intensity that it affects nearly every aspect of a precarious subsistence economy and has a decisive influence upon patterns of social organization designed to facilitate group survival.

Material or oecological scarcity is, then, directly observable, objective and realistic; moral scarcity is only indirectly perceptible, subjective and nonrealistic. Where the former is extreme, the latter also occurs. Where this happens, they together constitute a situation characterized here as 'total scarcity', in which oecological and moral scarcity are paralleled by a paucity of autonomous institutions and a minimally developed form of social structure. 'Total scarcity' is a folk model in which an objective and a subjective apprehension of the same basic reality —oecological scarcity—are mingled and confused.

I will not pretend that the model is, on the basis of existing data, demonstrably present in the collective conscience of those tribal societies in the Mediterranean and the Middle East which practise the feud. Since no fieldwork has been done on these lines, it is extremely difficult to know precisely how the members of feuding societies envisage scarcity. The small amount of tangible evidence available to indicate that the model is not a pure figment of the writer's imagination will be produced as the occasion presents itself in the course of this and following sections. The notion of 'total scarcity' is, as it stands, an heuristic device designed to explain certain aspects of the feud. Its heuristic purpose and hypothetical character in the present context do not,

required to produce such goods. In other words and in the present instance of an oecosystem centred on the human exploitation of agricultural or pastoral resources, by oecological scarcity I understand the restrictions placed on the overall yield in farm or animal products by a chronic inadequacy of the means of production. These include, for example, water, land, manpower, and, in any given case, an historically determined level of technology.

[20] The importance of this distinction will become apparent in sections 5 and 6 of this chapter.

however, preclude the possibility of its corroboration by future field studies.

In this section I shall be using the notion of 'total scarcity' to achieve two aims. The first of these ((b) below) is to demonstrate in theoretical terms what I mean when I speak of feud as 'a social system in its own right' (cf. p. 128). The second ((c) below) is to prepare the ground for the next section, entitled 'Honour', in which I bring forward evidence in support of my contention that, in conditions of 'total scarcity', material (or realistic) scarcity has a number of important concomitants on a moral (nonrealistic) plane, which are of crucial significance for an understanding of what feuding is all about. I shall try to show that, to a greater or lesser degree, these 'moral' concomitants all impinge upon the struggle to acquire and retain power, wealth and status. But before I fulfil either of these intentions, I shall examine the realistic bases of material, or oecological, scarcity in feuding societies in the Mediterranean and the Middle East ((a) below).

(a) *Oecological scarcity*

In self-subsistence societies in which scarcity of material goods is endemic it could be said that the most important single factor in determining this scarcity is historical coincidence. For it is only by an examination of history and the operation of political pressures on a very wide scale in both space and time that it is possible to appreciate why a given population came to inhabit a given tract of land, what were the technological limitations that it brought with it and what elements of other cultures it was able or unable to borrow and employ to exploit its environment with maximal efficiency. Were it known in detail, the history of feuding societies would doubtless go far towards providing the answers to many questions concerning their level of technological development and the provenance of agricultural and herding techniques which by their inefficiency give rise to shortages of a kind which do not occur in more sophisticated societies. An almost total lack of relevant data makes the explanation in historical terms of material scarcity in feuding societies unfortunately quite impracticable. It is thus necessary to fall back on the only other field in which adequate information exists, that of oecology.[21]

As I have frequently pointed out, the most obvious manner of beginning a classification of tribal societies which practise feud in the Mediterranean and the Middle East is to separate those which are predominantly agricultural from those in which herding is the principal means of subsistence. Material scarcity in both types of society is a function of the interaction of three factors: access to land, availability of water and the density of population in relation to the first two factors. Given a roughly comparable level of technological development, the reactions in both types of society to the same set of oecological factors are remarkably similar: they all practise the feud, they all suffer from a lack of strong instituted leadership and all share the same egalitarian ideology. But the two types of society differ radically in one essential: the nature of the end product of the economic cycle in each case. This difference is obvious, but its importance cannot be overstressed, as it is crucial to an explanation of how the same combination of the basic factors of land, water and population density can, given a different productive cycle, create two very distinct types of oecological scarcity.

As it is a less complex phenomenon, I shall first enumerate the elements which in agricultural societies make for a situation in which there are never enough material goods to satisfy the minimal requirements of all tribesmen simultaneously.

A shortage of fertile land is a common feature of all the sedentary tribal societies I have mentioned. The habitat of most of these societies is mountainous and rocky. The only good land is to be found on the narrow valley bottoms and in the occasional depressions left by dried up lakes where rich alluvial deposits ensure a plentiful crop. In some regions a certain amount of hill farming is also carried on by those who find themselves with insufficient valley lands to feed a large family. But, unless copiously irrigated, hill land in the Mediterranean, when planted with cereals or other subsistence crops, usually produces a very unreliable yield which fluctuates greatly from year to year. Valley

[21] For my present purposes I intend the term to include those aspects of technology which are directly related to the sphere of subsistence economics and permit a more or less efficient utilization by man of his environment. Cf. note 19 above.

land is thus incomparably easier and more fruitful to work and is consequently the most sought after commodity in these societies.

Secure possession of sufficient fertile land does not necessarily guarantee, however, that the owner will enjoy a harvest plentiful enough to meet his needs and those of his family. As valley land is normally irrigated, it is planted with a crop which requires constant watering if it is not to wither and die before the harvest which coincides with the height of the prolonged acute summer drought. But if there is insufficient good land to go round, there is usually even less water, and even those who are fortunate enough to possess land in the more favoured spots must constantly guard against any infringement upon their water rights.

Thus at the best of times there is no surplus of land and water in sedentary tribal societies in the Mediterranean and the Middle East. The situation is further aggravated by a generally elevated birth rate which is by no means entirely compensated for by a high rate of mortality (e.g. Albania 1943:9).

To cite but one example, Kabylia, in the nineteenth and early twentieth centuries, was notoriously overpopulated with an average overall density of 250 inhabitants to the square mile in the Djurdjura region. Of this last figure the author of the article on Kabylia in the *Encyclopaedia of Islam* pertinently remarks that it indicates a population density comparable with that of Holland, which was at the time and still is the most heavily populated country in Europe (Encyclopaedia of Islam 1927: vol. II, p. 597). In spite of the safety valve provided by a tradition of seasonal and permanent labour migration to other parts of Algeria and advanced techniques for commercial fig and olive farming on mountainous terraces at relatively high altitudes, the available agricultural resources in Kabylia proved chronically insufficient for the number of people forced to compete for access to them.

Oecological scarcity in these sedentary societies is, then, in the final analysis, clearly associated with the ratio of resources to population density. Land and water are in fact in short supply; but this shortage itself is a function of heavy population pressures which, combined with the technological requirements of an agricultural existence, inhibit spatial mobility and induce a rigid and relatively stable pattern of settlement.

The nature of oecological scarcity among nomadic pastoralists is determined, as in sedentary societies, by the same basic factors of land, water and population density. But whereas agriculturalists are usually confined by spatial imperatives to exploiting the resources of a single locality, the mobility of pastoral productive capital in the form of flocks and herds adds a dimension to the concept of oecological scarcity which is lacking in sedentary societies. While the water factor remains of paramount importance to nomadic herdsmen, the factors of land and population density tend to take on a fundamentally different significance in the pastoral environment.

In both types of society the presence of water supplies, whether for irrigation purposes or to water flocks, constitutes the *sine qua non* of existence. But while in sedentary societies land is normally in acutely short supply, this is quite untrue of the majority of pastoral societies in the Mediterranean and the Middle East. Evans-Pritchard asserts, for example, that there is no land shortage among the Cyrenaican Bedouin (1949:45)—an opinion which is corroborated by Peters, who remarks that 'Pressure on land for growing a crop of barley is never very great in Cyrenaica. Shortage of territory is not a problem, since the population density is very low' (1968:175). A similar situation would seem to be implied by Lewis' statement that Somali pastoralists enjoy total liberty of movement (1961: ch. 3). With regard to pasturage it appears that the Somali are inclined, with certain reservations, to recognize the principle of 'first come first served'.

However, although in most pastoral societies there is more land available than can be used, not all land always provides grazing of equal quality. Some areas may have a rich coverage of fodder at certain periods of the year but not at others, and some may offer grazing only after a freak and unforeseeable downfall of rain. But most important of all, not all relatively good pastures are provided with adequate facilities for watering the herds. This fact rules out vast tracts of land which, without wells, remain useless. The more wealthy Somali have in modern times solved this problem by bringing water by motor transport to otherwise barren but potentially rich pastures (Lewis 1961:35). But where it has not been possible to introduce such technological innovations, the availability of pasture land has been linked to the spatial distribution of watering points.

Nevertheless, although water is an undeniably scarce commodity in the semi-desert environment of many pastoral societies in the Mediterranean and the Middle East, it is not the only or even the most vital factor determining land use patterns among nomadic herdsmen. Nor is population pressure an element of cardinal importance,[22] as it is among sedentary agriculturalists, for it would seem that the desert fringes of North Africa, the Sinaï peninsula and northern Arabia support a population which is far from maximal for the potential overall carrying capacity of the land.

On the contrary, it can be argued that the scarcity which prevails in many nomadic pastoral societies in the Mediterranean and the Middle East is due, in part at least, to a lack of manpower. For flocks and herds have to be shepherded, watered, milked and generally attended to. Where sheep and goats are concerned and individual herds are numerically much larger than those comprising only camels the labour involved is considerable. I submit that the ratio of animal to human population is thus to a large extent conditioned by the birth and mortality rates of the latter and not *vice versa*.[23] Where neither pasturage nor water are in permanent and absolutely short supply, the animal population should increase to a level at which it is in equilibrium with the natural environment.[24] As this does not appear to

---

[22] —though Lewis seems to think that a recent increase in population among the pastoral Somali is in the process of significantly altering their oecology. He is, however, unable to produce conclusive evidence in support of this hypothesis (Lewis 1961:88).

[23] This is an hypothesis which I do not attempt to prove here. Only intensive fieldwork could ever substantiate it. It should be borne in mind, moreover, that the hypothesis is not intended to be valid outside certain tribally organized nomadic herding societies in the Mediterranean and the Middle East, the pertinent characteristics of which are, in the present context (a) a primarily self-subsistence economy, (b) reliance on an entirely traditional pastoral technology, (c) the unavailability of manpower from outside the society itself.

[24] The slaughter of livestock, although frequent in most pastoral societies, does not necessarily affect this equilibrium, since normally only male animals, and never females until they are past their reproductive prime, are in fact killed for meat: since a single male can serve a relatively large number of females annually, the elimination by slaughter of a significant proportion of the male stock in no way diminishes the overall fertility of the herd or flock. These remarks clearly do not apply to those

happen, the only possible explanation of the phenomenon is that the human factor intervenes to check this increase.

As in sedentary agricultural societies, so for nomadic pastoralists too the availability of usable land and water is of considerable significance for the creation of a situation of oecological scarcity. But these two factors are less compelling in herding societies, because the mobility of pastoral groups enables them to exploit a wide range of oecologically distinct areas and thereby escape the consequences of local drought or overgrazing. The only commodity in actual permanent and absolutely scarce supply among the nomadic pastoralists referred to in this book is animals, the number of which can never be increased beyond a certain maximal figure which is related to the level of human population.

The nature of oecological scarcity in sedentary agricultural and nomadic pastoral societies in the Mediterranean and the Middle East thus differs considerably as regards the extent and force of individual pertinent factors. Nonetheless, the result of oecological scarcity in both types of society may be summarized as an endemic insufficiency of food products to meet the conscious requirements of all members of these societies. My hypothesis is that whereas in sedentary societies this insufficiency is largely due to the presence of an excessive number of competitors striving for the control of limited resources, quite the reverse is true in nomadic pastoral societies where the amount of food available may be seen as a constant and invariable function of the number of producers. In other words, while it is obvious that a fall in population density in a sedentary agricultural society, if it were not too drastic, would alleviate conditions of oecological scarcity, I suggest that a similar reduction in numbers among nomadic pastoralists would bring about little or no change in the ratio of men to animals, or, therefore, of population to food resources. I will show later that this has a direct bearing upon the nature of hostile relations in many nomadic pastoral societies.

Even on the rare occasions, in both types of society, when there is a glut, yet another kind of scarcity—a lack of advanced techniques for preserving foodstuffs and converting them by

nomadic pastoral societies in which livestock production is primarily market-oriented and where it is therefore often a paying proposition to indulge in the premature culling of numerous females for sale outside the tribal context.

marketing facilities into a durable form of wealth—intervenes to inhibit the accumulation of inordinate riches by individuals and groups and the opening up of a wide gap between rich and poor. This is the point at which oecological scarcity shades off into the sphere of institutional scarcity to which I have already referred, for the absence of striking economic differentiation and the impossibility of maintaining a stable control of wealth over a number of generations in the same group hinder the development of a pronounced class structure simultaneously shored up by and giving rise to a proliferation of institutional guarantees conceived to protect the exercise of privilege.

(b) *Models: feud and society*

In the preceding treatment of oecological scarcity as it affects feuding societies in the Mediterranean and the Middle East, I have investigated the nature of the variables which impinge upon the two constants inherent in the model of feud I postulated in the introduction to the present chapter (cf. pp. 126–7). These constants, I said, are 'total scarcity' and leadership. I shall now make a shift of emphasis from the examination of oecological variables to an analysis, in purely theoretical terms, of the structural implications of 'total scarcity' and leadership in feuding societies.

If it is conceded in the abstract that co-operation, conflict and leadership are the irreducible components of all forms of prolonged social contact, it is necessary to posit the existence of a set of variables, which, in combination with these constants, generate empirically observable social situations. The three constants combined with historical and oecological variables constitute a model of society.

At the outset (cf. p. 123) I isolated the factor of leadership as the component which mediates the dyad co-operation-conflict and transforms situation into process. Advancing from the general to the particular in an attempt to differentiate feuding societies from other types of society, I constructed a universal model of the feud in which I proposed leadership and the existence of a situation to which I gave the name 'total scarcity' as the constants, and oecology and history as the variables. It will be immediately apparent that my model of feud differs very little from my model of society as a whole. I intend to show that the reason for this is not that one or both of the models is defective, but that they are in fact coextensive, for feud, as I suggested at the end of the last section (ch. IV sect. 2), is a social system *per se*.

My model of feud differs from my model of society in one detail: I have replaced the basic components of co-operation and conflict by a single constant, 'total scarcity'. This is, however, not so much a substitution of one element for another, as an elaboration and refinement of the model of society to lend it greater analytical potency in the context of feud, for the concept of 'total scarcity' may be taken to subsume under a single heading a unique form of interaction between the two components, co-operation and conflict, which is only found in societies which practise the feud. If, therefore, I can demonstrate that 'total scarcity' necessarily implies both co-operation and conflict, I will have established—providing my initial model of society is valid—that feud is in fact a complete social system in its own right, because I will have shown that my model of feud is no more than an extension of that which I have constructed for society.

I have quoted Coser to the effect that conflict may be taken to mean a struggle over a prize or prizes which are in scarce supply (cf. p. 121) and put forward the view that different types of scarcity give rise to different types of conflict. Now, for heuristic reasons, I have postulated a concept of 'total scarcity'. But if scarcity can be 'total', there must also exist a type of scarcity which is less than total. This is partial scarcity. I submit that a comparison of the patterns generated when my model of society is applied in hypothetical conditions of partial scarcity, on the one hand, and 'total scarcity', on the other, might suggest some interesting conclusions as to the nature of conflict and its structural significance for societies subsisting at different levels of scarcity.

For clarity I shall again repeat my summary definition of 'total scarcity': 'the moral, institutional and material premise of a certain type of society in which *everything* felt by the people themselves to be relevant to human life is regarded by those people as existing in absolutely inadequate quantities' (cf. pp.

121–2). In contrast to this, partial scarcity obviously connotes an insufficiency of certain *desiderata* in some spheres but not in others.

I shall first analyze the relationship between social structure and scarcity in conditions where the latter is only partial. According to my model of society the three components—co-operation, conflict and leadership—must be present simultaneously for the situation to be identified as social. Co-operation occurs to exploit those resources which are in scarce supply. Leadership arises to co-ordinate co-operation; and leadership itself, which is by definition a scarce commodity, excites conflict. Conflict will, however, be confined to those spheres in which scarcity is seen to prevail, that is those areas in which co-operation and leadership are essential. But since scarcity is only partial, there are a number of spheres in which there exist surpluses. If, therefore, some individuals or groups, who are less ambitious or aggressive than others, are willing to opt out of the competition for maximal gains in some spheres and to rest content in the main[25] with what they can procure in those spheres in which scarcity and, consequently, conflict are absent, conflict will remain focused on a limited number of issues involving part only of the total membership of the society at any given moment.

The model of society I have proposed yields very different structural results when applied in conditions of what I am calling 'total scarcity'. For if scarcity characterizes every sphere of human life, it is clear that co-operation and leadership which arise in response to scarcity, and conflict consequent upon the appearance of leadership, will be as pervasive as scarcity itself. In conditions of 'total scarcity' no one can opt out of the system at any level or any time, because co-operation to exploit insufficient resources is the *sine qua non* of existence in *all* spheres. As leadership and conflict are the ineluctable concomitants of co-operation, they both constitute as strong and ubiquitous an obligation as co-operation itself. 'Total scarcity' makes it imperative for *every* individual and group of individuals to do their utmost to co-operate, lead and conflict if they are to survive. Where there is only partial scarcity this is not so, because sur-

---

[25] If such individuals and groups were to content themselves *exclusively* with what they can glean in spheres where no scarcity prevails, they would, of course, cease to form a part of the society.

pluses provide a means of subsistence for those who wish to reduce their co-operative obligations to the minimum consonant with continued membership of the society and refuse to engage upon the struggle for leadership.

This comparison of the structural consequences that derive from an application of my model of society in conditions of both partial and 'total' scarcity shows that, whereas the component of leadership stands unaltered in both situations, the nature and structural scope of the remaining components—co-operation and conflict—fluctuate according to the type of scarcity involved. Partial scarcity promotes the fragmentation of society into a number of interlocking sub-groups whose interests may overlap at certain points but not at others: the interests of all members of the society will not be identical, because the presence of felt surpluses provides the option of retreat into spheres of activity in which conflict and the necessity for co-operation are absent. Where 'total scarcity' prevails, however, no such retreat is possible and co-operation and conflict permeate all spheres of human action.

Since 'total scarcity' leads to an ubiquitous extension of co-operation, conflict and leadership throughout the social fabric and since feud always, and indeed only,[26] occurs in conditions of 'total scarcity', it may be said that my model of feud is identical with my model of society, albeit trimmed and improved for the analysis of a specific conjuncture of oecological and historical circumstances. As my model of feud coincides with my model of society, feud can be regarded as a social system *per se*.

I tried to show in previous chapters that feud is a means of establishing relationships between hostile groups, of binding together a number of loosely connected parts into a coherent whole. This is achieved, in the absence of conditions conducive to the development of a power hierarchy and centralized authority, by the use or threatened use of violence which serves to create a balance of power and an attendant state of subdued anarchy.

---

[26] —with the exception of borderline cases such as the Buganda 'feud' (cf. p. 149), which may legitimately be seen as the survival from an era before the introduction of a centralized monarchy of violent interaction between groups very similar to those met with in the acephalous societies I have described.

As a social system in its own right feud can thus operate success-fully to control the relations between groups and coerce con-formity to social norms. Violence, wielded by both groups and individuals, constitutes an integral part of the system. It is at one and the same time an instrument of social control, a means of communication and a language for the expression of temporary relations of dominance and submission. Where scarcity is 'total', feud and violence become synonymous with society and institu-tions.

The absence or weak development of institutions in feuding societies can therefore, in part at least, be attributed to the nature of feud itself. The very occurrence of feud is linked to a dearth of institutions. Feud may be said to act as a substitute for political and juridicial institutions where these are wanting in feuding societies for the oecological and structural reasons outlined above.

(c) *Moral scarcity*

The institutional poverty of feuding societies is a result of the combination of inherent structural features and oecological con-straints. Both the lack of strongly developed institutions and the precarious nature of an existence on the margins of subsistence find expression in the egalitarian ideology. The implications of this ideology are, however, not confined to the field of inter-personal or inter-group relations. They extend, as I have intima-ted, to nearly every aspect of human life to inhibit any acquisition of any commodity which places the acquirer in a situation of superiority *vis-à-vis* other members of the community. For in-stance, the Somali believe that a lineage which expands owing to an accelerated birth rate is doing so at the expense of other lineages (Lewis 1961:144). A sudden increase of male births in one lineage is seen as adversely affecting the fertility of others. Similarly, it is widely held in Mediterranean and Middle Eastern societies that 'the success and prosperity of other families is necessarily a threat to the very existence of one's own' (Campbell 1964:204). Such attitudes are typical of oecologically unfavoured societies in which there obtains a belief in the existence of what I have called nonrealistic or moral scarcity. Belief in moral scarcity and the sanctions which sustain this belief help to ensure that the principle of 'fair shares for all' is respected despite the absence of institutions conceived to enforce adherence to this norm.

This mentality whereby any achievement or betterment of his lot on the part of another is automatically interpreted by the individual as potentially deleterious to his own interests is the subject of an interesting chapter in Foster's book on the Mexican peasant village of Tzintzuntzan. Foster has coined the phrase 'The Image of Limited Good' to describe the complex of social and psychological attitudes which express the notion that success attendant upon the actions of individuals necessarily diminishes the total fund of 'success' at the disposition of all other members of the community. Foster claims that the Image of Limited Good, which in a piece of unnecessary jargon he calls a 'model of cognitive orientation', applies to every sphere of Tzintzunteño culture in which he stresses for particular attention the fields of politics, law, religion, economics, medicine and folklore. 'By the Image of Limited Good', he writes,

> I mean that behavior in these and other broad areas is patterned in such a fashion as to suggest that Tzintzunteños see their social, economic, and natural universes—their total environment—as one in which almost all desired things in life such as land, other forms of wealth, health, friendship, love, manliness, honor, respect, power, influence, security, and safety exist in absolute quantities insufficient to fill even minimal needs of villagers. Not only do 'good' things exist in strictly limited quantities, but in addition there is no way directly within the Tzintzunteño's power to increase the available supplies . . . 'Good', like land, is seen as something inherent in nature, there to be divided and redivided if necessary, to be passed around, but not to be augmented (1967: 123–4).

In Foster's opinion the logical consequence of such a 'view' is 'That someone's advantage implies someone else's disadvantage.' This he says is 'the key to understanding the Image of Limited Good', which to him appears 'to characterize peasants in general, and is found in other societies as well' (1967:124).

For Foster 'Two theoretical avenues of action are open to

people who see themselves in the threatened circumstances which the Image of Limited Good implies': they may either co-operate to better their communal lot or else 'follow the opposite road of unbridled individualism' (1967:133). Foster believes that societies in a Limited Good situation always prefer individualism to co-operation, because, in the first place, toleration of the leadership required to make co-operation viable is tantamount to the admission that some individuals have a right to a larger portion of the Limited Good than others, and, in the second place, co-operation is regarded as pointless, since it is believed that no human efforts can possibly increase the supply of 'Good'.

Foster is obviously describing a phenomenon which is very closely related to that to which I have given the name of 'total scarcity'. Although the two concepts are not identical, I shall, in furtherance of my own argument, draw some parallels between the Image of Limited Good and the notion of 'total scarcity' and formulate some strictures as regards the shortcomings of Foster's analysis.

The principal criticism that can be levelled at Foster's Image of Limited Good is that, although he claims that the model is valid for 'peasants in general' and a number of other types of society, as an analytical tool it is of scant use outside the immediate social context of Tzintzuntzan village. Foster devotes thirty pages to developing his Image of Limited Good and illustrates its existence in the mind of the villagers with examples such as the Tzintzuntzeño peasant's desire to be as unostentatious as possible and to hide his wealth from his co-villagers in order that they will not be motivated to take reprisals against his inequitable appropriation of inordinate quantities of 'Good'. Having shown that the Limited Good mentality exists and used it to interpret a number of such traits, Foster passes blithely on to the next chapter without attempting to apply his concept at a deeper, more significant level of analysis. Apart from his statement to the effect that Tzintzuntzeño villagers 'see' a large number of *desiderata* as available in inadequate quantities, he appears to be at a loss to explain why this is so and, consequently, why other societies should share this conviction.

It is true that he puts forward the hypothesis that the absence of a co-operative spirit from what he calls 'peasant' societies may be imputed to a process of reasoning upon which the Limited

Good mentality has a powerful influence. But the absence of a will to co-operate in Tzintzuntzan may just as easily be ascribed to a feeling that co-operation and leadership are no longer necessary now that the modern national state has theoretically replaced traditional patterns of mutual aid and collective action and has made it possible for individuals to proceed legally against their adversaries, whereas formerly recourse to alliance and the menace of collective physical violence were very nearly the only means of obtaining redress. But even then, whatever the explanation of this particular case, the absence of a will to participate in co-operative action is not, as Foster suggests, characteristic of *all* peasant or other societies in which the Image of Limited Good may be encountered. The Image of Limited Good is in fact powerless to offer an adequate explanation of anything as it stands.

Whatever Foster's methodological failings (and there are others I have not mentioned), they do not necessarily invalidate his general insight, for his development of a concept of Limited Good is clearly not totally unfounded. But they have caused him to approximate in matters where more precision would have been helpful. He affirms, for instance, that Tzintzuntzeños regard 'their total environment' as subject to the principle of Limited Good. Yet later in the same sentence he exhibits more caution and states that the Limited Good is seen as effecting *'almost* all desired things in life'. He then gives a list of 'desired things', which includes 'land, other forms of wealth, health, friendship, love, manliness, honor, respect, power, influence, security and safety'. From the context it would appear that Foster sees in these items no common denominator and that he has chosen them at random from among a large number of similar *desiderata*.

Now, it is my contention that the 'desired things in life' quoted by Foster were not selected as random examples, as he seems to imply, but are all related as factors which impinge to a greater or lesser extent upon the struggle for one of them: power. With the possible exception of love—and I doubt whether Foster is correct in his supposition that love, whatever that may be, is a Limited Good—Foster's 'desired things' may be divided into three categories. Firstly, in small-scale agricultural societies land and wealth are at one and the same time a necessary prerequisite for the exercise of power, an indication of status achieved in the power hierarchy and the material reward which accrues from the continued skilful manipulation of this hierarchy once the individual has managed to climb the first rungs of the ladder. Secondly, friendship, influence, security and safety constitute both the minimal preconditions without which no man can begin to acquire power, and also, like land and wealth, the objects of the power struggle itself. Finally, manliness, honour and respect (together possibly with good health, upon which these are to a large extent dependent) are likewise, but on the less tangible plane of moral values, the initial qualifications which enable a man to offer himself as a candidate in the competition for power; like land, wealth and the other factors mentioned they are also diacritical marks of success in this competition.

While I deny, therefore, that in largely self-subsistence societies the total environment is necessarily seen as subject to the principle of Limited Good, I nonetheless agree with Foster that a substantial part of this environment is conceptualized as 'limited' or inadequate to meet the conscious needs of the population. And I would broadly circumscribe this part of the total environment as comprising all those aspects of social existence—both realistic and nonrealistic, material and moral—which relate to the acquisition of power by competing individuals and groups. But since political[27] power in small-scale societies ultimately relates to the control of material resources, and to exercise power is consequently strictly equivalent to 'having more' of those material goods which are in short supply than those who wield less power, it is possible to hold that the Limited Good is not only an image but a reality: in as far as those moral commodities which are seen as limited are the concomitants of power and a thirst for material gain they are *in reality* in scarce supply.

Interpreted in this manner, the Image of Limited Good is clearly germane to my remarks on the nature of the egalitarian ideology which characterizes feuding societies and could be said to constitute a feature of all societies in which 'total scarcity' prevails. However, my criticism of Foster's Image of Limited Good was not intended to be exclusively destructive. Nor do I wish to imply that Foster's ideas are entirely eclipsed by my own

---

[27] Nowhere in this discussion of the relationship between power and the feud shall I be referring to either charismatic or religious power not based on or conditioned by the acquisition and possession of material wealth.

analysis. For I do believe that he has something interesting to say when he includes in his list of commodities which are limited such moral concepts as manliness, respect and honour. But he unfortunately fails to follow up the clue he himself supplies.

I think that Foster's juxtaposition within the Image of Limited Good of notions belonging to the same conceptual gamut as honour and prestige with other concepts like land and wealth, which are apparently of a quite different order, is of fundamental importance for an understanding of the political mechanisms of feuding societies, and indeed of feud itself. For if honour and similar 'nonrealistic' attributes are regarded both as prerequisites for political achievement and as the insignia of success, then the struggle to acquire and retain them will be identical with the struggle for the acquisition and retention of material advantage. On the assumption that this equation is valid, honour and cognate values are nonrealistic commodities the scarcity of which is commensurate with the scarcity of material goods and resources.

Bearing in mind Coser's dictum that the initial causes of conflict are to be sought in an insufficiency of supply to meet demand, it is thus not surprising that feuds are frequently declared to vindicate a 'point of honour'. As the scarce concomitant of an extremely scarce commodity, power—that is, the ability to acquire and control wealth or the means of subsistence—honour may be seen as the cause of feud *par excellence*. As an allegory of power it permits the escalation of conflict outside and above the sphere of oecological friction, in a domain in which there are no material limits to restrict the magnitude of the prize.

Feud operates on two levels at once. Like all social systems it is primarily concerned with regulating relations of subordination and superordination between individuals and groups. But in conditions of 'total scarcity' where the control by one individual or group of more than a certain proportion of all available resources would place in jeopardy the continued existence of the society as a whole, the inevitable conflict for power and leadership cannot be allowed to get out of hand and must therefore be prosecuted on another less inhibiting plane. Honour, I have said, may serve as a *pretext* for conflict in the competition for control of natural resources. In Albania it is sometimes used in this manner to circumvent the dictates of an inadequate legislation and judiciary (cf. pp. 142–3). But it is more frequently invoked as a cause of hostilities in order to provide a symbolic representation of the struggle for political dominance in those situations in which people recognize that conflicts for a material prize would imperil the very fabric of society. A high evaluation of honour and its acceptance as a permissible excuse for armed confrontation create a symbolic arena for political strife in which prestige accruing from the successful outcome of a series of individual encounters can be accumulated to supply the bases of moral stratification despite a relatively close adherence in the economic field to the principle of 'fair shares for all'.

In feuding societies honour and power are synonymous. The one implies the other. A group's defence of its honour is thus in a very real sense the defence of its right to live in a given area and to exploit its birthright of natural resources. Through the exercise of physical violence, which causes fear and leads to the construction of a network of alliances, each group ensures respect of its rights to an equal place for itself in the social system which is feud. For the individual, on the other hand, defence of his own honour and that of his group provides an opportunity for self-aggrandizement and the acquisition of prestige. In an economically very homogeneous society a man's prestige ultimately summarizes all those qualities which differentiate him from other members of the same society and together constitute his qualifications for success in the competition for leadership. Feud is then, simultaneously, a violent affirmation of the rights of all to treatment on a footing of equality and a means of selecting those most qualified to orient the co-operative efforts of the majority.

In conditions of 'total scarcity' the translation of conflicts over materially limited goods into conflicts in which the prize at stake is said to be honour smooths away the potential incompatibility between equality and leadership and prevents extreme material scarcity from resulting in wide scale destruction and survival of only the fittest.

(4) HONOUR

It may be objected to this analysis that it is all very well to speak of honour in the feud, but that the word 'honour' is liable to a very large number of interpretations and that this fact makes it quite impossible to generalize. I counter this objection with two quite opposite arguments.

In the first place, I believe that, whatever the outward appearances in any given case, *all* conflicts over honour or acts of violence are designed to show that the protagonists react 'honourably' in all circumstances. Such conflicts may in the long run all be attributed to the *same* desire to acquire and demonstrate the possession of prestige, thereby reaffirming political status and reinforcing claims to leadership.

In the second place, the very versatility of the notion of honour is intrinsic to its function, which is to provide a zone of ambiguity creating room for political manoeuvre. In feuding societies there are few hard and fast rules as to which actions are honourable and which are not. Individuals interpret the notion very much as they please and as circumstances permit, manipulating it in furtherance of their own political ends.

Like so many aspects of the feud, honour is therefore at once an extremely simple and an extremely complex phenomenon. Acts of violence carried out in the name of honour may always ultimately be seen as moves in the struggle for power and dominance. But the almost total lack of uniformity which characterizes reactions in numerous cases, in which an apparently similar point of honour is at stake, bears witness to the flexibility of a notion which defies summary in terms of a limited number of well attested ethnographic facts.

There is no lack of documentary evidence to support the first of these contentions. In his essay on 'Honour and social status' in Mediterranean society Pitt-Rivers is quite explicit in stating that honour belongs to those who can both morally and physically command it (1965:24). Successful defence of honour by force of arms safeguards the prestige of the defender.[28] Honour has

[28] Pitt-Rivers also nicely confirms my own view that honour is a Limited Good by pointing out that it is the object of bitter competition: 'the victor in a competition for honour finds his reputation enhanced by the humiliation of the vanquished' (1965:24). It is as if he who gains honour from victory actually depletes the store of honour possessed by his opponent. This seems to have always been an attitude widespread in Mediterranean society, for Pitt-Rivers quotes a study of *The point of honour in sixteenth-century Italy* in which the author asserts, for instance, that the

little to do with intrinsic virtue and everything to do with force
of arms and a readiness to employ them, although a man known
for his wisdom and equity gained, for example, by offering to
arbitrate disputes can, by selfless conduct at the service of the
community, add substance to a reputation for honour acquired
in other fields.

But this 'selflessness' is only relative, for the arbitrator, it will
be remembered, is paid for his efforts (cf. p. 97) and even the
act of arbitration itself can be regarded as a test of the arbitrator's
strength and ability to constrain the litigants to abide by his
judgement, for he will refuse to intervene in a dispute if he is
not confident that he has reputation and force enough behind
him to coerce conformity to his decisions (cf. p. 67). The prestige
associated with the office of arbitrator is thus but little derived
from the exercise of this function. Rather, it is a prerequisite
without which a man will not be asked to become an arbitrator
and it is not unconnected, as I have already mentioned, with the
reputation that older men acquire from the successful pursuit of
honour in feuds in which they participated in their youth (cf.
p. 97). In such feuds they would normally play the minor
rôle to which their junior status in a large kin group assigned
them. Though they might perform unusual acts of individual
valour, the prestige, which remained with them throughout their
lives and which formed the basis of any personal reputation
which they might subsequently make for themselves, was closely
connected with the physical force of the vengeance group to
which they belonged. Hence the Corsican stipulation referred
to earlier that arbitrators must be 'di parentela numerosa' (cf.
p. 96).

That the notion of honour is narrowly associated with force
and sheer numbers is well illustrated by the statement, reported
by Campbell from a Greek transhumant pastoral society, to the
effect that 'Nobody takes account of a man without kinsmen'
(1963:78). Other societies are similarly insistent upon the importance for the honour of the group of large numbers of male
kinsmen. Somali pastoralists, for instance, speak of lineages not
only as *ḍeer* (long) and *gaab* (short) (cf. p. 59), but also as *gob*

common people believed that 'one who gave an insult thereby took to
himself the good reputation of which he deprived the other party' (Bryson
1935:84).

and *gun*. 'Long branches' are described as *gob*, that is strong, prolific and honourable in upholding the values of pastoral society. 'Short branches' are *gun*, a word in which dishonour and non-adherence to these values are associated with military vulnerability and numerical weakness. 'He who is weak in numbers', say the Somali, 'is the son of lowliness' (Lewis 1961:192).

Honour is thus to a large extent a function of force, and if it is frequently held that bastards are without honour (e.g. Campbell 1964:187), it is primarily because a bastard has no kinsmen upon whom he can rely to defend him and help him to attain a position of political importance, and not merely because of the stigma of sexual shame attendant upon the mother's fornication, though the latter is not entirely without significance.

Julian Amery, who, as leader of a wartime military mission to Albania, was probably one of the last western Europeans to observe feuding in conditions where political constraint and centralized government were totally lacking, likewise stresses that honour is almost identical with the ability to defend it: 'The same considerations of prestige which lay at the roots of the blood feuds', he writes, 'were the cause of their persistence. The rights and wrongs of a particular vendetta might arouse little interest, but the manner of its prosecution was the public test of the power of the clans concerned' (1948:8).

Observations from other areas confirm this analysis (e.g. Barth 1965:82). Personal honour and collective force are the principal ingredients of prestige; prestige is the summary or outward manifestation of those qualities required of pretenders to leadership.

Honour, is, then, in one sense a simple phenomenon, because it may be seen as a synonym for effective political power. But it becomes infinitely complex when the ethnography is examined to ascertain what constitutes behaviour *normally* regarded as honourable in a given society. The task is in fact impossible, because, with a few notable exceptions such as the almost invariably violent reactions to offences involving the sexual honour of women, a prescribed norm rarely exists and each case must be taken on its merits.

In Albania, for example, it was usual for the family of a man killed in daylight by a watch dog to take vengeance, presumably in order to show that they possessed strength and honour enough to defend themselves against the assault of a mere dog. But if they felt themselves to be in a position of considerable political and military inferiority *vis-à-vis* the owners of the dog and did not think it to their immediate advantage to embark upon a feud, it was just possible for them to accept compensation (cf. p. 138). Similarly, it was considered dishonouring when meeting a traveller on a narrow road to allow him priority and let him pass (Hasluck 1954:85). Yet this rule can rarely have been observed to the letter or the population would have been decimated daily.

Just as the amount of compensation paid for a homicide or the number of victims required to avenge the death of a particular individual varied with the relative status of killer and initial victim (cf. pp. 114–15), so the concept of what constituted honourable or dishonourable conduct fluctuated considerably according to the circumstances; and a slight of minor importance, such as a word of irritation or some unintentional jostling at a crowded gathering, might furnish the pretext for murder, if the offended party were of great numerical strength and political power, just as the theft of an animal might go unpunished if the owners were too weak to run the risk of a feud. Riposte in the first case might cost the death of a man or two, but the gain in prestige would more than outbalance the loss. Riposte in the second case would merely reduce an already feeble group to totally unviable proportions.

It is this kind of calculation which determines the manner in which individuals or groups will envisage their obligation to act honourably. By manipulating the notion of honour and by offsetting the risk of numerical depletion against that of political gain, groups and individuals within groups can acquire prestige and rise to a position of authority over their fellow tribesmen which the folk model of equality would seem to proscribe.

The sole desire of individuals to attain a position from which they can exercise authority is, however, insufficient to explain why men are willing to risk death in the pursuit of honour in order to qualify as leaders. There are obviously more tangible benefits attached to leadership than the gratification of purely personal pride. Now, I intimated earlier that, in feuding societies, political and material success were commensurate. Indeed, whilst leading a life in most external details identical with that of the majority of those over whose destinies they preside, tribal leaders nonetheless usually appear wealthier than the average tribesman. They possess larger houses or tents, more fields or greater flocks, better horses and more costly arms than most other members of the tribe. These are so much regarded as the prerogative of a leader, who must of necessity be a man of honour, that poverty is in places seen as quite incompatible with honour (e.g. Campbell 1964:300). Wealth is nearliy always cited by observers as the *sine qua non* of power in Mediterranean and Middle Eastern tribal societies (e.g. Evans-Pritchard 1949:59). Yet, the possession of wealth, like that of power, is also in absolute contradiction to the folk model of equality.

But here again the contradiction is only apparent, for although the chief, *bajraktar* or *sheikh* is undeniably better off than those enjoying a lesser status, to maintain his prestige and, consequently, his position he is obliged to act with the utmost generosity dispersing a large proportion of the income from his land or flocks in gifts and hospitality to ensure the continued allegiance and respect of those who tolerate his leadership. Evans-Pritchard writes, for instance, of the Cyrenaican Bedouin *sheikh* that he 'ought to be rich because the demands of hospitality are considerable' (1949:60).

In the literature on Mediterranean and Middle Eastern tribal societies the obligation to offer hospitality, even in certain circumstances to an enemy (cf. pp. 139–40), is continually emphasized. Unfailing hospitality and the presentation of generous gifts are two manners in which honour and prestige may be enhanced once a measure of power and wealth has been achieved. It is, however, interesting to note that generosity and hospitality cause honour to accrue at a rate inversely proportionate to that at which wealth is expended. Thus, although the honour of an individual is in the first instance a function of his own prowess and the military force of the group which helped him to attain a position of dominance and wealth, his maintenance of this position depends to no mean extent upon his readiness to surrender a large amount of the benefits to which the status of leader gives him access.

Just as leadership is only effective if the incumbent can obtain consensus, so also wealth can only be enjoyed by the leader if it is in greater part recirculated among those who support him. Both leadership and wealth are conditional. Neither are inalienable rights. Both are prerogatives dependent upon popular consent. Excess in either may upset the delicate balance which obtains between the premise of equality and the necessity of hierarchy. If a leader loses the respect of the majority by becoming a despot, by monopolizing resources and discontinuing the tradition of lavish hospitality expected of him, in short, by acting in a fashion incompatible with a whole series of values going under the general heading of honour, all confidence will be withdrawn from him and group loyalties will be transferred to another more 'honourable' man.

Honour, then, is a blanket term which subsumes all the qualities required of a leader. Honour is acquired in the successful prosecution of feud, that is 'a struggle', in conditions of 'total scarcity', 'over values and claims to scarce status, power and resources'. By analyzing the manners in which different tribal societies in the Mediterranean and the Middle East envisage the acquisition of honour and by relating the findings to a number of oecological variables which characterize some of these societies but not others, it should thus be possible to detect certain oecologically determined patterns of behaviour in the feud which will contribute to an understanding of the mechanisms which underly the dichotomy to which I drew attention at the beginning of this chapter.

Before I attempt this undertaking, however, it is necessary to make a short digression in order to set out a few ideas of a purely theoretical order taken from Simmel's and Coser's work on social conflict. I shall later elaborate these in support of my own argument concerning conflict in the specific context of feud.

(5) REALISTIC AND NONREALISTIC CONFLICT

Unlike Coser, his exegete, Simmel takes it for granted that his readers know what conflict is. He never defines the phenomenon as such, but gradually builds up a picture of conflict by analyzing its causes and results and demonstrating how they are related. He succeeds in further clarifying the meaning he attaches to the word conflict by contrasting it with competition, 'the foremost sociological characteristic' of which is, for Simmel, 'the fact that conflict in it is indirect'; and in illustration of this remark he adds: 'In so far as one gets rid of an adversary or damages him directly, one does not compete with him' (1966:57).

Competition differs from conflict in two important details: the nature of the prize and the attitude to one another of the protagonists. As regards the first of these details, in 'the pure form of the competitive struggle' two parties compete for the acquisition of a prize which neither of them controls at the outset. Conflict, on the other hand, postulates the possession of the prize by one of the contestants who tries to defend it against the rapacity of others.

Simmel distinguishes two types of competition. The first is

(1) a form of interaction in which 'victory over the competitor is the chronologically first necessity, it itself means nothing. The goal of the whole action is attained only with the availability of a value which does not depend on that competitive fight at all' (1966:57–8).

As an example of this type of competition in which one of the parties must worst the other(s) but access to the prize depends upon circumstances beyond this victory, Simmel gives that of 'The lover who eliminates or shames his rival [but] is not a step ahead if the lady does not bestow her favors on him' (1966:58).

Simmel's second type of competition is

(2) a struggle in which no direct collision of interests occurs and the goal is achieved by the triumphant competitor 'without using his strength on the adversary' (1966:58).

In a competition of this sort each competitor acts more or less in isolation, and overall victory is gauged independently by a comparison of the efforts and not the material gains of the adversaries. Examples are a running race or the undercutting of prices in business circles where competitors cannot truly be said to interact: 'Each party fights its adversary without turning against him, without touching him, so to speak' (1966:59). Moreover, the prize is identical with successful prosecution of the fight itself. Each competitor strives to win without directly damaging his opponent or altering the intrinsic situation of his opponent prior to the beginning of the competition. In Simmel's opinion this second type of competition 'differs even more greatly from other kinds of conflict' than the first; and it is upon this second type that he concentrates his attention.

In this type of competition interaction between participants is minimal. In contrast to conflict, in which the prize is at the outset in the possession of one of the protagonists and it is the purpose of the adversary to wrest the prize from its possessor, pure competition remains uniquely concerned with the acquisition of immaterial values of which a certain amount accrue to the victor. The loser, however, is usually not denied a share in the 'winnings'. For instance, if two men run a race, the victor will gain acclaim for this feat. But if the loser runs well, he will not be entirely ignored and will have increased his reputation. By vying for the same immaterial goal both competitors will have gained something, but one will have gained more than the other. It is for this reason that Simmel asserts that the goals of competition are largely subjective: they are more in the nature of values relating to the moral sphere than the goals of conflict, which may be objectively defined in terms of material gain. While the goals of conflict are thus objective, tangible and definite, those of competition are relativistic, unmeasurable and unlimited. The goals of conflict cannot be increased beyond their initial dimensions. But competition, as Simmel remarks, tends to promote and intensify subjective values; the act of competing itelf effectively modifies the prize and enhances its desirability.

Simmel must have already had in mind this analysis of the nature of competition when in an earlier passage of the same essay he distinguishes between conflict as a means to the attainment of an objectively definable end and conflict as an end in itself.

> 'Where conflict', he writes, 'is merely a means determined by a superior purpose, there is no reason not to restrict or even avoid it, provided it can be replaced by other measures which have the same promise of success. Where, on the other hand, it is exclusively determined by subjective feelings, where there are inner energies which *can* be satisfied only through fight, its substitution by other means is impossible; it is its own purpose and content. . .' (1966:27–8).

Now it is tempting to associate conflict as an end in itself with the phenomenon which Simmel later calls competition. But competition, even as Simmel defines it in the second of his two types, does not necessarily arise out of a need to dispel 'inner energies which *can* be satisfied only through fight'. There obviously exists some relationship between Simmel's two notions of competition and conflict as an end in itself, but it is not quite clear what this relationship is.

Without explicitly referring to the connection between this passage and that on competition, Coser suggests that Simmel's efforts to descriminate between conflict as a means and conflict as an end might gain in intelligibility by the introduction of a new distinction of his own invention between *realistic* and *nonrealistic* conflict:[29]

> Conflicts which arise from frustration of specific demands within the relationship and from estimates of gains of the participants, and which are directed at the presumed frustrating object, can be called *realistic conflicts*, insofar as they are means toward a specific result. *Nonrealistic conflicts*, on the other hand, although still involving interaction between two or more persons, are not occasioned by the rival ends of the antagonists, but the need for tension release of at least one of them. In this case the choice of antagonists depends on determinants not directly related to a contentious issue and is not oriented toward the attainment of specific results (1965:49).

Coser's reformulation of Simmel's original proposition has the advantage of making it possible to avoid Simmel's rigid and somewhat uneasy distinction between conflict and competition by subsuming both under the single heading of conflict and introducing a scale of 'realism' which can be employed to characterize any combination of the two.[30] For Coser readily concedes that realistic and nonrealistic elements may be found side by side and in unequal proportions in one and the same conflict. Seen in this manner, Simmel's perception of two quite different types of competition ((1) and (2)) appears less incongruous than before. Whereas, as the passage stands, Simmel seems to be collating in the same category two phenomena which have very little in

---

[29] —the word 'conflict' being here understood to include under a single heading the *two* categories which Simmel elsewhere distinguishes as 'conflict' and 'competition'.

[30] At this point, my reasons for qualifying moral (or subjective) scarcity as 'nonrealistic' should begin to emerge (cf. p. 161).

common, viewed as two forms of predominantly nonrealistic conflict the first (1) can be said to include a number of realistic factors which are almost totally absent in the second (2). Pure competition can thus be regarded as an extreme type of non-realistic conflict. An extreme instance of realistic conflict, on the other hand, would be the assault of a footpad with the intent to rob and kill his victim.

One of the elements which Simmel leaves out of his description of the second type of competition (2), which, since he does not again mention the first type (1), he seems to consider the 'purer' of the two, is the necessity to give vent to 'inner energies which *can* be satisfied only through fight'. Yet he includes it in the passage on conflict as a means and an end. If competition can, as I maintain, be described as a type of conflict in which nonrealistic elements predominate over realistic ones and if it is agreed that the ideas expounded in both passages are demonstrably related, then competition—or conflict for what Simmel calls 'subjective' goals—should be associated with a need to express pent up energies which can find no other channel for release.

To return for a moment to Simmel's examples of 'pure' com-petition, it is possible that races are run to dissipate surplus energies in a harmless fashion, but this is certainly not true of the undercutting of prices in business, where the results can spell material ruin for the unsuccessful competitor and the business community at large. The long term effects of athletic competition and business competition are very different indeed. Simmel either glosses over this fact or fails to appreciate it, while Coser provides a satisfactory solution in the form of his realistic-nonrealistic scaling of conflicts.

In Coser's terms, the running race is almost totally non-realistic,[31] while the conflict between business competitors is largely realistic. Coser's approach to the classification of different types of conflict is thus far more useful than Simmel's. It is not 'pure' competition which enhances values and intensifies conflict, but the preponderance in a given conflict of nonrealistic factors over material goals (Coser 1965:68).

Despite these strictures, Coser's criticism of Simmel is in no way destructive. He constantly relies upon the insights of his in-

[31] —unless, of course, the competitors are striving for a material or money prize such as is often the case in 'professional' sports today.

tellectual precursor to lend substance to his own intuitions. In this manner he develops Simmel's idea that the goals of competition are unlimited and incommensurable and incorporates these characteristics into his notion of nonrealistic conflict, which, like Simmel's 'pure' competition, is subject to unrestricted spontaneous intensification through emulation suscitated by equally unrestricted goals. Realistic conflict, however, remains stable at a constant level of intensity as long as the goal remains the same. Coser endorses Simmel's view that some forms of 'pure' competition—or entirely nonrealistic conflict, as he calls it—act as a safety valve to 'clear the air' (Coser 1965:39). But he is not in agreement with Simmel's contention that such a clearing of the air necessarily provides permanent release of tension; and he quotes Kluckhohn's work on *Navaho witchcraft* to the effect that conflict is never without a 'cost' which someone or other must finally bear (1965:46). Conflict may canalize tensions in a social environment, but by the very nature of the phenomenon one of the parties inevitably loses in comparison with the gains of the winner.

On this basis Coser argues that the admixture of nonrealistic elements in conflict will increase in direct proportion to the structural proximity of the conflicting parties. For the closer the structural and physical distance between the contestants and the more materially destructive a conflict consequently threatens to become for the community at large, the greater will be the tendency to translate realistic goals of a finite and material nature into nonrealistic terms, in order that conflict may not result in the destruction (or monopolization) by one party of the material premises of subsistence and, thereby, the community itself. The transformation of realistic conflict into a struggle in which the values at stake are nonrealistic does not cancel out the cost which must still be paid. But since nonrealistic goals are, as it were, nonexistent, conflict for their attainment in no way jeopardizes the material security of the community as a whole and is therefore not liable to spread and involve other parties against their will in a struggle for survival. Nonrealistic conflict is optional in so far as it is not suffused with realistic factors. Realistic conflict is more compelling and tends to be contagious once it has begun.

Nonrealistic elements in conflict thus increase with what Coser rather vaguely calls 'the rigidity of the social structure' (1965:

156). They are a concomitant of the need for 'safety-valve institutions' in situations where realistic conflict might annihilate
the fabric of society. They are a means of ensuring that someone
but not everybody pays the cost. Not only are they, for the
reasons given, more frequent in conditions of social confinement,
but the inherent tendency of nonrealistic elements to spontaneous
intensification in combination with this frequency naturally
causes conflicts to be more intense, where the 'social structure' is
rigidly defined, than in societies where the structure is somewhat
looser.

(6) HONOUR, LEADERSHIP AND OECOLOGY

The first conclusion I wish to draw from the preceding theoretical
discussion of conflict is that honour, the principal qualification
for leadership in feuding societies in the Mediterranean and the
Middle East, may be regarded, in Coser's terms, as the largely
nonrealistic prize of aggressive interaction. If it is agreed that
this constitutes an acceptable interpretation of the phenomenon,
then an attempt to elucidate other aspects of the feud in the light
of Coser's theory might prove rewarding.

I have cursorily described how honour is acquired in the feud.
But since my own perception of feud as a social system *per se*
has of necessity remained on the level of generality, I have so
far had but little opportunity to give a detailed account of how
the principle of honour operates 'on the ground'.

On the assumption that honour, in its most unadulterated
form,[32] may be interpreted as the nonrealistic prize of a certain
type of conflict called feud and bearing in mind Coser's hypothesis that the intensity of nonrealistic conflicts 'increases with
the rigidity of the social structure' (Coser 1965:156), I shall try
to relate the frequency and intensity of feuding for honour to
the relative flexibility of different types of 'social structure'. An
analysis on these lines of honour and physical violence, or the
threat of violence, in feuding societies will, it is intended, provide
solutions to the two problems I mentioned at the beginning of
this chapter, namely

[32] I.e. in which it is associated as a goal of conflict with few or no
realistic factors.

(1) how leaders arise to fulfil indispensable functions despite a fiercely egalitarian ideology, and

(2) why there exists a very marked difference between the frequency and intensity of feud in sedentary agricultural societies, on the one hand, and nomadic pastoral groups, on the other.

There is one major difficulty attendant upon such an approach: Coser does not adequately explain what he means by rigidity of the social structure. He does nonetheless enlarge somewhat upon his original statement relative to the increase of nonrealistic elements in proportion to the rigidity of the social structure by qualifying the latter as 'the degree to which it disallows direct expression of antagonistic claims' (1965:156). This rider admittedly helps to divest the words 'social structure' of any of a number of more precise meanings current in anthropological circles. Coser seems to be using the term in a deliberately imprecise manner in order that his hypothesis may enjoy the widest possible validity.

If this is the case, it is legitimate for those seeking to apply the theory to concrete facts to interpret the phrase 'rigidity of the social structure' very much as it suits them, as long as their interpretation does not countervene the rider.

Now, in my model of feud as a social system I postulated the interaction of two constants—'total scarcity' and leadership— and of an indefinite number of variables. I also demonstrated in my discussion of 'total scarcity' that the variables, which may in the main be reduced to constraints of an almost exclusively oecological order, were crucial in determining a state of 'total scarcity'. Moreover, I have shown that these same oecological variables are not without considerable influence upon the nature of leadership itself. Since the oecology of feuding societies has such undeniable relevance for all major aspects of their social existence, I believe that in the feuding context it is not unreasonable to equate Coser's 'rigidity of the social structure' with the degree to which *oecology* 'disallows direct expression of antagonistic claims'.

If honour is a nonrealistic prize of conflict, then conflicts in which the prize is control of material resources—i.e. land, water and flocks—are clearly primarily realistic in character. To paraphrase Coser, where scarcity prevails, the less it is possible, for reasons connected with the survival of the community at large, to indulge in aggressive interaction for the control of material resources, the more honour will be invoked as a pretext for conflict. I shall endeavour to prove this hypothesis by relating the premises of material scarcity in sedentary agricultural and nomadic pastoral feuding societies to the extent to which the defence and acquisition of honour are recognized as permissible and even laudable grounds for physical aggression.

I have already pointed out a number of major differences between sedentary agricultural and nomadic pastoral feuding societies in the Mediterranean and the Middle East. These, I said, were most evident in the organization of labour in each (ch. II sect. 1). Sedentary agriculturalists rarely enter into relations of sustained economic co-operation outside the extended family. Nomadic pastoralists, on the other hand, are obliged to in order that they may form herding units of an optimal size and that they may, for instance, guard against the eventuality of a bad drought in their own territory by being able to avail themselves of the surplus grazing and water of their allies elsewhere. Agriculture and pastoralism as means of subsistence thus engender different types of basic economic interest group, which in turn elicit similarly divergent types of defensive alliance in the feud. In sedentary societies alliance tends to be sporadic and is dictated by vicinage, whereas among nomadic pastoralists it is a permanent necessity and is more frequently based on a combination of kinship and contract.

Such differences are, however, the end result of two major disparities. The first is obvious: nomadic societies enjoy an infinitely greater degree of physical mobility than do their sedentary counterparts. The second I have already discussed and concerns the nature of oecological scarcity in the two types of society. While sedentary agricultural feuding societies in the Mediterranean and the Middle East are all overpopulated in relation to the availability of resources and the level of technology on hand to exploit them, nomadic pastoral societies are subject to only one constant restriction on their wealth: that of the animal: human population ratio (cf. p. 166). Material scarcity in nomadic pastoral societies is thus truly endemic, whereas a decrease in population density would do much among sedentary agriculturalists to alleviate the scarcity of resources. But in the nomadic pastoral situation, although scarcity is 'total' and therefore conducive to conflict, the mitigating factor of mobility makes it possible to avoid a headlong clash of real interests, if one of the parties involved feels that it is insufficiently strong to have a reasonable chance of winning the contest. For land as such is rarely in scarce supply, and when a nomadic group feels itself outclassed it merely removes itself, together with its flocks, herds and tents, to another area.

In sedentary societies land is, together with water, a supremely scarce commodity (cf. p. 164). Without it a family has no means of survival unless it accepts the inferior status of servants.

This disparity between the relationship of nomadic and sedentary feuding societies to actually scarce resources goes a long way to explaining why feud is more frequent and intense in the latter: the oecological constraints attendant upon a sedentary agricultural means of subsistence are manifestly unfavourable to the 'direct expression of antagonistic claims' over land and water which, if allowed, would lead to the appropriation of the best and the most by the strongest, and the complete disintegration of the community as such. Oecological scarcity nonetheless causes antagonisms to arise among sedentary agriculturalists. But these are controlled and prevented from spreading throughout the social structure by the existence of the concept of honour which makes it possible to avoid a conflict over real goals by interpreting it in nonrealistic terms.

A conflict in which the stated goal is the defence or acquisition of honour may well be and usually is related to some material cause of friction—such as the disputed possession of a field—between the parties. The end result of such a conflict for honour may even be the illegitimate acquisition of the field, as well as honour, by one of the parties if they succeed in exterminating the other. The Albanian episode I referred to earlier is a case in point (cf. pp. 142–3). But *in the eyes of the community* the material realistic prize will be a mere concomitant of the nonrealistic prize and no one will feel obliged to jeopardize the unity of the community by proceeding to collective sanctions against the victors, who, it will be said, were after all only acting in defence of their reputation even if they did obtain a field at the same time. Moreover, their material and immaterial victories taken together, by increasing both their wealth and their prestige, will have demonstrated that they possess cunning, physical strength and political ability, in short, all those qualities which are demanded of the leader and his group. Finally, the fact that conflicts over honour are strictly the concern of those whose honour is at stake inhibits their spreading to involve other members of the community. Unlike conflicts for realistic goals which may be interpreted by those not directly implicated as a menace to their own future security, conflicts purportedly over honour make it possible for hostile groups to expend their aggressive energies upon each other without drawing in the society as a whole.

Honour in this case, where customary legislation and public opinion forbid territorial encroachment, serves four different purposes simultaneously. It is

(1) a licit means of achieving an 'illegal' material end;
(2) an affirmation of aptitude for leadership;
(3) a medium for the escalation of conflict for material ends beyond a level at which hostilities of this type are no longer normally tolerated by the society at large and would in principle (were the pretext of honour not invoked) be liable to legal sanctions;
(4) a means of ensuring the non-proliferation of such conflicts throughout the social structure.

I believe that this kind of analysis can be used in Mediterranean and Middle Eastern sedentary tribal societies to explain most if not all instances of physical aggression in which the original cause of hostilities is said to be a disputed point of honour. Conflicts over honour are the enactment of another plane of aggression stimulated by a combination of scarce resources and an insufficiently developed agricultural technology. The frequency of feuding for honour is a function of oecological scarcity unalleviated by mobility.

In contrast with sedentary agricultural societies nomadic pastoralists can move from place to place and are indeed obliged by the search for grazing and water to do so. In all but exceptional circumstances—a particularly severe drought, for example— enemy groups can avoid each other if they feel that it is expedient to do so. Although it is inevitable on occasion that conflict should occur over access to water, and this may happen at any time of the year, pastoralists seem to prefer to concentrate hostilities with enemy groups in a particular period of the pastoral cycle. The period chosen is without exception always the spring, at which time the flocks and herds are in milk, there is an abundance of food, pastures are greener and water is usually more readily available than in other seasons.

Peters, for instance, states that this is true of the Bedouin of Cyrenaica (1951:241). According to Musil, the Bedouin of northern Arabia are also inclined to regard the spring as the most favourable time for warlike enterprises (1928:10); and Lewis reports that the Somali pastoralists recognize a season they call *gu*, in which food is plentiful and '. . . old injuries remembered and feuds revived' (1961:44). None of these authors deny the fact that hostilities continue throughout the year. But the general impression is that whereas conflict in the dry season results from dire necessity (cf. p. 144) and is averted whenever possible, hostilities occurring in the season of plenty are in a way looked forward to and are vested with a gratuitousness which is totally lacking at other times of the year.

It may be concluded from this evidence that the pattern of hostilities common among nomadic pastoralists is, in a way, quite the opposite to that found among sedentary agriculturalists. Whereas sedentary agriculturalists constantly engage in hostilities for the control of perennially scarce resources without regard for a particular season of the year, nomadic pastoralists appear to fight mainly at moments when there is no immediate scarcity of food and resources such as grazing and water. The explanation of this contrast is to be sought, as are most other divergences between sedentary and nomadic feuding societies in the Mediterranean and the Middle East, in the significance of oecological scarcity, which affects the pastoral cycle in a quite different manner from that in which it impinges upon the existence of agriculturalists.

Oecological scarcity in the form of thin grazing and lack of water forces pastoral groups to split up into smaller herding camps at periods of the year when the carrying capacity of the land is considerably less than just after the rains. This dispersion of groups, which tend to congregate in the breeding season in larger camps spread over a relatively restricted area, reduces opportunities for contact at the most difficult times of the year.

So when scarcity is most intense, contact is least. Although fighting may break out when two groups accidentally or by *force majeure* find themselves competing for the same resources, such conflicts are on the whole deliberately avoided, because at the height of the dry season both men and beasts are weak and the mere effort of staying alive is sufficiently engrossing for there to be little surplus energy and time to devote to hostilities which are not vital for survival.

When surpluses are at hand, however, fighting is rife, raids are organized (Musil 1928:10) and old debts of blood redeemed. Whereas fighting at other times of the year arises in direct response to oecological scarcity and is undertaken with strictly realistic goals in view, the objectives of the hostilities which mark the season of plenty are less overtly material in character. Lewis writes of *gu* fighting that it 'tends to result from the desire, often long matured, to revenge previous wrongs and to satisfy honour and "name"' (1961:45). These are obviously more in the way of pretexts than actual causes of conflict and they resemble similarly nonrealistic features, such as 'face', which I have described as characteristic of the feud in sedentary societies. Yet this intensification of hostilities and these nonrealistic elements occur in conditions of material abundance in which, according to my own and Coser's analysis, aggressive interaction should diminish and conflicting claims should grow more realistic.

I propose that the only manner in which it is possible to solve this apparent contradiction of the theory by the facts is to add a further dimension to the notion of oecological scarcity in the pastoral context. I have already said that the most important limitation on the wealth of pastoralists is perhaps not so much the absolute amount of land and water available as the constant maximal ratio of men to animals which engenders an endemic scarcity of food over long periods of the year. There is, however, another factor present in the pastoral cycle which aggravates this fundamental scarcity: the factor of herding luck.

For, like nearly everything else in societies living on the margins of subsistence in conditions of 'total scarcity', luck is, to use Foster's term, an aspect of the Limited Good. It is thought to exist in finite quantities insufficient to satisfy the needs of all. It is thus not surprising if in the season of *gu* Somali herdsmen 'hesitate to say too much of their good fortune'. They feel that 'It is beyond speaking of: to express too much delight is inadvisable lest God replace good fortune by disaster' (Lewis 1961: 43). Such sentiments, like all others ultimately associated with power and wealth in conditions of 'total scarcity', are, however, not entirely subjective. They do reflect, albeit somewhat distantly, elements of empirical reality. The pastoral way of life in a semi-desert environment is extremely precarious. A chance rainstorm at an opportune moment over a very small area in a period of widespread hard drought may enable the animals belonging to the groups occupying that area to survive the season, when the flocks of groups not ten kilometres away may suffer a mortality of up to 80 per cent. Epidemics can likewise decimate several adjacent flocks almost overnight, while a nearby camp, remaining in isolation, may escape unscathed. This kind of hazard striking indiscriminately gives substance to the pastoralists' belief that herding luck is, like water and manpower, a scarce commodity.

I suggest, therefore, that while fighting among pastoralists is on the whole less intensive in the dry seasons of the year, because they are fully occupied by the struggle for subsistence, non-realistic goals of conflict come to the fore in the season of plenty to provide an opportunity for spreading the burden of misfortune. Nonrealistic conflicts for 'name' and revenge permit the appropriation of animals to make good losses incurred in the past. The successful prosecution of such conflicts further enables the victorious group to build up a reputation for superior force, which will help them in the coming year to remain unmolested in their pursuit of good pasturage and water. Individuals, moreover, use such confrontations to demonstrate their personal valour and cunning. In this manner they attract public attention, inspire respect and ultimately reinforce their claims to leadership within the group and prominence in the context of wider alliances. Conflicts of this kind among nomadic pastoralists are nonrealistic in character, that is predominantly concerned with honour and other subjective values, because the scarcity to which they constitute a reaction—the scarcity of good herding luck—though believed in, is not real and present, but intangible and always either past or potential.

Although pastoralists do tend to indulge at certain times of the year in intensive hostilities at fairly short range for largely non-realistic prizes, conflict in nomadic societies generally has the outward appearance of a highly realistic struggle for gains of a purely material order. It is true that some writers occasionally have doubts as to the authenticity of Bedouin claims that they are fighting for access to resources. Peters, for example, is convinced that disputes over land and water are, in Cyrenaica at least, more in the nature of pretexts than causes (1951:354). This, of course, nicely confirms his notion of feud as a structural relationship between groups living within particular territorial limits: groups entertain feuding relations 'because they happen to live at a certain distance' (1951:371). But then Peters seems to believe that the Cyrenaican Bedouin constitute 'one of the few societies in which [feud] occurs' (1967:265).

Now, although I am largely in agreement with Peters with regard to his interpretation of feud as a relationship, I cannot, as I have said before (cf. p. 69), endorse his strictures concerning the distribution of the phenomenon. Nearly all nomadic pastoral societies maintain traditional inter-group relations of hostility which vary in intensity and character with the oecological distance and the nature of the terrain which separate the groups and determine the frequency and persistence of communication between them.

Such hostilities may occur between adjacent groups. Their goals may also be largely nonrealistic. But this type of hostile relationship does not preclude the existence of others of a more realistic nature. Peters does not mention whether the Cyrenaican Bedouin are addicted to raiding for flocks and herds. But among the pastoral nomads of northern Arabia and the Syrian desert raiding is a serious business carried out with great regularity and on a very large scale. It continues throughout the year. In winter only small parties band together for this activity; but in spring, when there is no lack of food, the noble[33] tribes launch an annual raid characterized by a great amount of ceremonial and led by the paramount chief (cf. Musil 1928:10; and for a full description of such a raid, 507–12). These raids are always against traditional enemies and are reciprocal. Their object is

---

[33] There are also a number of client tribes regarded as of humbler origin who are raided by their more powerful neighbours, but who do not themselves indulge in organized pillage.

quite unambiguously to obtain a maximum of booty, mainly in
the form of camels, and to return safely to base (Palgrave 1868:
23). They are called *ghazw* and as such are distinguished from
ḥarb, war, in which the goals are territorial gains and the political
subjection of other groups (Sweet 1965:1139).

In a recent article, the American anthropologist Louise Sweet
has minutely analyzed the numerous descriptions which exist of
these raids and has come to the conclusion, similar to my own,
that they constitute a mechanism for the equalizing of opportunities in hazardous conditions of breeding and pasturage (1965:
1139). In her opinion, they result from an endemic scarcity of
camels in the area and a need to ensure the circulation of wealth.
Unfortunately, she does not press her analysis any further.

My own hypothesis that pastoral wealth can never grow beyond
a certain ceiling imposed by the ratio of labour force to the
number of animals supplements Sweet's argument and suggests
an oecological reason for the scarcity which she postulates but
does not seek to explain.

The fact that raiding among the Bedouin tribes of northern
Arabia and the Syrian desert is for mainly realistic goals is born
out by a mass of detail, which may be summarized in the
Shammar saying 'Raids are our agriculture' (Musil 1928:10).
Unlike feuds of the Cyrenaican type (which are not absent among
the tribes further east, but are of minor significance in comparison
with raiding), these collective forays for booty are hedged around
with innumerable rules to regulate the manner in which they
are carried out, the aim of which is to minimize the destruction
of life and property. Dickson (1949:341), Palgrave and Burckhardt (1830:76, 84) concur in their opinion that 'the Bedouin,
though a terrible braggart, has at heart little inclination for
killing or being killed . . .' (Palgrave 1868:23). Firearms are
rarely used. Women in the attacked camp who remain when
their menfolk have been routed can obtain concessions in animals
and property from the victors if they have the courage to run
after them and shout the appropriate precisely stipulated formula
(Musil 1928). The object of this rule is that innocent women
and children shall not be left to perish without means of sus-
tenance.

Sweet gives a long list of points of raiding étiquette all designed
to reduce the risk of permanent loss to the society at large through

200   *Feud, Stratification and Oecology*

aimless destruction (1965:1143). And although men are occasionally killed in these encounters, this only occurs when the victims
put up a particularly stubborn resistance to the attackers. Burckhardt, for instance, stresses the Bedouin preference for submission
rather than a fight to the death (1830:76). It is even possible for
a man pursued until his mare is no longer able to bear him to
throw himself to the ground and cry *howel*. In return for the
loss of his clothes and his horse his life will be spared. But the
'disgrace' incurred is so great that this would seem to have been
a rare occurrence (1830:81).[34]

The Bedouin obviously do everything in their power to make
raiding for realistic goals as little destructive as possible. But
though Bedouin raiding may in the main be interpreted as a
mechanism for the maintenance of an oecological balance between
groups in conditions in which there must always subsist an endemic scarcity of flocks and herds, it is not entirely devoid of
nonrealistic elements. Indeed so conscious are the Bedouin of
the possible danger to human life which they associate with the
spontaneous intensification which Coser has identified as characteristic of nonrealistic conflict, that they have formulated certain
rules the main purpose of which may be seen analytically as
the prevention of realistic goals of raiding being diverted into
nonrealistic channels.

An example is provided by the 'Anaza code of raiding conduct:
they regard night attacks as treachery, for, as Burckhardt writes,
'during the confusion of a nocturnal assault, the women's
apartments might be entered and violence offered, which would
infallibly occasion much resistance from the men of the attacked
camp, and probably end in a general massacre' (1830:80) (cf.
also Musil 1928:523). In other words, the Bedouin recognize
that the subjective value with which they vest the sexual shame
of women is (as I shall show in the next chapter) an eminently
nonrealistic goal of conflict. They therefore do their best to prevent the admixture of this nonrealistic element in the pursuit of

[34] Similarly, Peters reports that in Cyrenaica 'a man who voluntarily
abandons his means of defence cannot be killed' (1951:277); and in
Somaliland, 'While livestock are seized as booty and many raids made
solely to loot camels, captives are rarely taken in battle since Somali have
little use for them and do not seek to humiliate their adversaries in this
fashion' (Lewis 1961:242).

raiding for primarily realistic goals, in order that the conflict shall not become unnecessarily intensive and destructive.

In so far as nonrealistic factors remain of minor importance in this type of conflict they are nonetheless allowed to enter into the practice of raiding. For where raiding as a form of hostile relationship is more frequent than feud of the Cyrenaican type, it serves both as an economic leveller and as a means of acquiring honour and prestige. The booty brought back from a successful raid is mostly in the form of camels, she-beasts in milk being the most treasured prize. But if it is at all possible, young men trying to prove their worth and gain prestige will also attempt to seize a horse, the supreme symbol of wealth and status among the desert-dwelling nomads.[35] Now a large part of the value attached to horses is due to their intrinsic uselessness; they are extremely difficult and expensive to keep in the desert and serve almost no practical purpose. They are occasionally taken on raiding expeditions and led by the halter until they are mounted only in the final attack, when their speed and manoeuvrability in battle are thought to be greater than that of riding camels. But they are generally regarded as an adornment and are little used other than for visiting in nearby camps. I suggest that the very uselessness of the horse as a prize and the extra difficulty involved in bringing it back to base constitute highly nonrealistic factors in an otherwise realistic conflict for resources.

Other nonrealistic elements in raiding are discernible in the competition which is engaged upon, once the successful expedition has returned to camp, to show who is the most generous of the victors: raiders vye with one another to demonstrate their largess by giving away portions of their booty (Sweet 1965:1146). Prestige goes to the most generous who is also canny enough not to divest himself entirely of his share of the spoils, so that by raiding he acquires wealth in kind *and* reputation. Lastly, resourceful command of the raiding party itself can increase the stock of a young man, making him eligible for the hand of a chief's daughter and future leadership of the group (Sweet 1965: 1146; Musil 1928:507).

Raiding in northern Arabia and the Syrian desert is a mecha-

---

[35] For evidence of the prestige attached to the ownership of horses in a semi-desert environment cf. Lewis 1955:67.

nism ensuring equality of economic opportunity in conditions of oecological scarcity and is thus undertaken for primarily realistic goals. But these goals have their nonrealistic concomitants which supply the criteria for differentiation in an egalitarian society and, in the form of prestige, represent the qualifications demanded of those aspiring to leadership. Thus, if Bedouin raiding can be said to have a political content, this is not, as Malinowski thought (cf. p. 6), because conflict for economic goals necessarily implies an effective political relationship between the contestants. For the political aspects of Bedouin raiding are almost exclusively confined to internal relations within the raiding party itself. The absence of an effective political relationship between the raiders and the victims is indeed almost a prerequisite for the raid to take place at all: Bedouin only launch *ghazw* raids against other noble tribes living at a considerable distance—several hundred kilometres by Murray's reckoning—in order that re-prisals should not be immediate and that the ensuing state of enmity between the two groups should not make their daily life impossible. The economic objectives in fact almost rule out any potential political ambitions of one group to dominate another, since the plunder acquired on such an expedition can only be enjoyed in the absence of those to whom it originally belonged. Moreover, the terminology employed by the Bedouin themselves (cf. p. 199) lends undeniable support to the contention that the raiders in no way confuse their expeditions for economic goals with others in which the objectives are the establishment of political dominance or territorial gains.

The nonrealistic concomitants of raiding for realistic goals, that is those factors which permit the acquisition of prestige, find expression among the Bedouin of northern Arabia and the Syrian desert in another form of conflict which closely parallels camel raiding, but is carried on by individuals or, at the most, by two men in association. This is a type of private raiding to despoil traditionally enemy camps living at some distance, which ob-servers, like Burckhardt and Musil, have rather inappropriately called 'theft'. This kind of theft is highly stylized and hedged around, like large scale raiding, by a corpus of rules indicating what can and what cannot be done on these private expeditions. However, unlike raiding, the objectives of theft are almost en-tirely nonrealistic: a man will prepare himself for weeks and undergo great hardships to obtain, not merely an economic asset such as a few milch camels, but a particular beast famed for its beauty or a particular horse belonging to an outstandingly pre-eminent *sheikh*. Men embark upon thieving expeditions almost exclusively to obtain prestige from the successful outcome of an exceptionally hazardous undertaking, for if they are caught they are held prisoner until a heavy ransom is paid over by their kinsmen. It may take months or even years for a group to collect together the necessary number of camels for the ransom, the pay-ment of which may so impoverish them that they lose as a group any prestige that the thief may have personally gained for his courage. It is interesting to note that although the *harramy* ('thief') enjoys great prestige and is admired above all men in the open desert plains of northeastern Arabia and those tracts of the Syrian desert which lie towards the Euphrates, he has no status at all and is regarded as dishonourable scum by the tribes of the Ḥidjāz, Sinaï and parts of Egypt which inhabit a moun-tainous terrain in which survival is relatively more precarious than elsewhere (Burckhardt 1831:326).

The oecological distribution of Bedouin theft and raiding, which both seem to occur in their most developed and institu-tionalized forms in conditions in which material scarcity and spatial constraints are minimal in comparison with those pre-vailing among other nomadic pastoralists in the Mediterranean and the Middle East, would seem to confirm Coser's hypothesis concerning the incidence of nonrealistic conflict and its relation to 'rigidity'. Among the Bedouin realistic conflict (i.e. raiding) is most frequent where 'rigidity', in the form of material scarcity, is least prevalent. Nonrealistic conflict on a very minor scale— i.e. theft as a means of acquiring status and prestige—is also rife in the same conditions to supplement the nonrealistic aspects of raiding, which cater for the creation of a system of leadership which parallels and contradicts the egalitarian ideology. Theft remains nonrealistic, and therefore feasible, as long as space and resources do not change its character from that of a harmless pastime to that of a socially disruptive act. Raiding itself is also countenanced as long as it does not threaten to destroy the material premises of subsistence.

But as soon as the pursuit of either looks as if it might place in jeopardy the continued existence of the society as a whole, the relationships of violence predicated by the nature of feuding societies in conditions of 'total scarcity' take on a somewhat different complexion. This might explain, for instance, why feuding relations among the Bedouin of southern Cyrenaica are apparently more intensive and less realistic (cf. Peters 1951:354) than the hostilities described among the Bedouin of northern Arabia. A comparison of hostilities in the two areas would seem to suggest that Cyrenaica is oecologically the poorer of the two. This, however, remains to be proved.

If the Bedouin of northern Arabia and the Syrian desert can be said to constitute the nomadic society in which nonrealistic elements in conflict are the least pronounced and the least conducive to the spontaneous intensification of hostilities, the tribesmen of northern Albania certainly represent the opposite pole as far as sedentary feuding societies in the Mediterranean and the Middle East are concerned. Nonetheless they were certainly not averse to raiding and theft of a kind very similar to that indulged in by the Bedouin. As the *Pre-invasion basic handbook* puts it, 'Raids, brigandage and vendetta murder (carefully regulated by custom) are regarded as honourable; ordinary theft and other crimes are rare' (Albania 1943:72). Mrs. Hasluck adds that, 'Though poverty is, and always has been, extreme in this mountainous land, hunger rarely made a man steal.' Raiding for sheep 'often took place on a grand scale between family and family, village and village or tribe and tribe. There are many popular tales of forays for fun or glory . . . There was a picnic atmosphere about such expeditions' (1954:203). They constituted a reciprocal relationship very like those described by Musil in Arabia, and 'The man who stole because he had been stolen from evoked universal admiration' (Hasluck 1954:203).

The nonrealistic content of such forms of conflict is plainly very high indeed. But whereas the Bedouin very consciously try to limit the extent of material damage to both man and beast in the course of these expeditions, the Albanians always carried rifles when raiding, did not hesitate to use them if resisted and frequently killed an animal on the spot and gorged themselves with its flesh if too much risk were involved in carrying it back to base (Hasluck 1954:203). The economic, realistic advantage to be gained from raiding was constantly minimized, while the nonrealistic factor of prestige derived from worsting an enemy was regarded as the principal objective of hostile interaction of this and any other type.

Unlike the Bedouin, the Albanians never gave nor ever expected quarter except in very specific circumstances stipulated by the rules of *besa* (cf. pp. 139–40). Theft itself, and in particular housebreaking which 'always implied that the men in it were weak or the womenfolk light' (Hasluck 1954:198), was dishonouring to the victims (1954:207). It was one of a large number of manners whereby an individual could acquire prestige at the expense of others, which were all liable to provoke violent reprisals and a subsequent feud, despite the existence of legislation theoretically conceived to punish offenders and bring about the restitution of property or its replacement by a substitute in kind.

I shall not repeat here the copious evidence, which I set out in the first section of this chapter, of the predominantly non-realistic forms taken by conflict in sedentary societies. Conflict among sedentary agriculturalists is, I have said (cf. pp. 193–4), invariably translated, whatever the original causes, into the language of honour, while nomadic pastoralists remain more concerned with the prosecution of hostilities for more directly realistic goals. Following Simmel, therefore, I suggest that it is partially for this reason that feuding relations among nomadic pastoralists are more frequently punctuated by truces sanctioned by the promised transfer of compensation. For as Simmel has pointed out (1964:114), where the prize of conflict is material in nature it can usually be divided, so that compromise is a feasible outcome. Compromise is also possible where the prize can be represented by a substitute value. But when the prize itself is regarded as unique and intrinsically superior to any other prize or substitute value, no such compromise solution is possible.

Applying this theoretical analysis to the facts, it becomes evident that where the prize of conflict between pastoralists is predominantly realistic—in the form of water, land or animals—deaths or injuries incurred during the struggle can be represented by a substitute value in kind. Hence the frequency and relative facility among nomadic pastoralists of 'composition' achieved by the actual or promised transfer principally of goods. But when the prize cannot be represented by a substitute value—as is the case in feuds fought for honour, in which the prize at stake is already a 'representation' of a series of more realistic objectives and, therefore, the most desired value of all—compromise is considerably more difficult to achieve (cf. p. 113). Hence the repeated assertions of sedentary agriculturalists to the effect that they are not prepared to 'sell' their honour (cf. pp. 11–12).

It is true that nomadic pastoralists do also make similar claims. But the frequent recurrence in the literature of references to compromise solutions to feud in nomadic societies would seem to suggest that the ideal of bringing vengeance is far less fiercely adhered to there than among sedentary agriculturalists. Nonrealistic elements in conflict among nomads are clearly not absent, but they are partially catered for by the stipulation in reconciliation agreements of payments specifically set aside to compensate for nonrealistic factors such as loss of 'face' (e.g. Kadhim 1957:62; Murray 1935:210).[36] Such supplementary stipulations are rarely mentioned in the occasional cases of reconciliation reported from sedentary societies, for the feeling that reconciliation is a mere palliative before the final bringing of vengeance is directly proportionate in its intensity to the number and relative predominance of nonrealistic elements in a given conflict.

Another reason for the infrequency of compromise solutions among sedentary agriculturalists is the fact, as Simmel intimates, that since primarily nonrealistic conflict is largely 'determined by subjective feelings, where there are energies which *can* be satisfied only through fight, its substitution by other means is impossible . . .' (1964:28). In other words, nonrealistic conflict, once engaged upon, is self-perpetuating until the energies which caused it are dissipated or are so diminished by the hostilities themselves that one of the parties can no longer continue to fight. A compromise cannot intervene where the conflict (for honour and prestige) 'is its own purpose and content' (1964:28).

Coser's analytical device of distinguishing between two basic ingredients of conflict which are always present is varying pro-

[36] Murray gives the details of one such indemnity over and above the customary *diya* of forty camels, which was traditionally levied on a murderer to 'whiten the face' of a man in whose tent the victim had been killed when in the act of seeking asylum: 'a negro [slave] riding on a white male camel, a negress riding on a white she-camel, and the building of a white cairn . . .'

portions in any relationship of mutual hostility has enabled me to establish tentatively why some feuding societies in the Mediterranean and the Middle East practise a more 'intensive' and, to all external appearances, less 'rational' form of feud than others. It has also made it possible for me to show how the combination within the same society of an egalitarian ideology and a minimal form of social stratification is not as self-contradictory as it might at first seem. In conditions of 'total scarcity', which necessarily imply the simultaneous involvement at a number of different levels of all members of a society in relations of co-operation and conflict, the nonrealistic concomitants of the latter provide the bases of leadership. Leadership is *both* the dynamic factor which regulates the interaction of co-operating and conflicting individuals *and*, at the same time, the prize or incentive for such co-operation and conflict. The struggle for leadership between individuals and groups is the pivot around which co-operation and conflict revolve. Changing patterns of domination and subordination developing out of this struggle constitute social process. Because in feuding societies no one can opt out of this struggle if he is to survive, feud, that is the struggle itself, is identical with the social system. It is therefore not '*an* institution', but a summary of all those institutions which in other circumstances go to make what is known as 'a society'.

V

Feud and Ritual

> Very lame and imperfect theories are sufficient to
> suggest useful experiments which serve to correct
> these theories, and give birth to others more per-
> fect. These, then, occasion further experiments,
> which bring us still nearer to the truth; and in
> this method of *approximation*, we must be con-
> tent to proceed, and we ought to think ourselves
> happy, if, in this slow method, we make any real
> progress (Priestley 1772:181).

I have constantly emphasized in my argument up to this point
that feud may be regarded first and foremost as a relationship,
that is, as a form of communicative behaviour uniting parts of
society in alliance and locking opposed groups in hostile competition over shared values which are exchanged and intensified
through such interaction. Feud, I have said, constitutes an all-
embracing network of communication the ramifications of which
are ultimately coterminous with those of the society in which it is
found. As a reciprocal relationship which may, at different times
and in different social contexts, be expressed in terms of either
conflict or co-operation it both separates and unites, differentiates
in the particular and engenders cohesion within a wider framework of value consensus.

This is one way of looking at feud. I may be wrong in my
interpretation of a number of details, but I doubt, in view of
the ethnographic data, whether it could be successfully argued
that feud is not primarily a form of communicative behaviour.
The approach I have adopted has, nonetheless, proved inadequate to bring out the full significance of several aspects of
the feud that I have touched upon. I have, moreover, been
obliged to ignore totally one ethnographically very important
feature of the feud which cannot be treated satisfactorily unless
another dimension is added to my possibly rather simplistic
equation of feud with communication.

The feature I am referring to is the role that women play in the prosecution of feud. The further dimension that I think it is necessary to investigate is that of ritual. I intend to show in this last chapter that an analysis of feud as a form of communication frequently suffused with a strong admixture of ritual concomitants will contribute to a better understanding of attitudes to women in feuding societies in the Mediterranean and the Middle East and provide a tentative interpretation of a variety of 'bizarre exaggerations' (cf. p. 146) associated with the practice of feud, which would at first sight appear to possess little or no intrinsic significance.

But before I begin, I must stress that, whereas most of what I have said in preceding chapters could be conclusively proved or disproved by empirical observation in the field, none of the ideas I put forward from now on have anything but the most tenuous connection with the existing factual evidence. I shall be making some largely intuitive suggestions as to the manner in which future investigators might approach a number of problems related to the feud. Only experience and further research can definitively show whether these suggestions are at all valid.

(1) A RITUAL OF SOCIAL RELATIONS

A major stumbling block in any anthropological discussion of ritual is the definitional problem. I shall not review the opinions of all those who have written on this subject. Instead, I shall limit myself to a brief appraisal of those descriptive criteria proposed in recent years which I personally feel to be germane to the study of ritual. It has been variously held that ritual behaviour is characterized by (1) repetition, (2) standardization, (3) lack of a demonstrable relationship of the means employed to desired ends, and (4) reference to 'mystical notions'.

In his discussion of rites at the beginning of his book *Les rites et la condition humaine d'après les documents ethnographiques* (1958) Cazeneuve, for instance, emphasizes the first and third of these criteria, but still insists upon the flexible character of ritual actions, which can, in his opinion, be either individual or collective and should be able to accommodate a certain amount of improvisation. He does not see them as belonging to a rigidly circumscribed category of human behaviour; and while, for him, an important aspect of ritual is repetition, this criterion alone is insufficient to distinguish ritual from other kinds of action unless it is also expressed within the framework of a ceremony which 'n'est pas indispensable' and 'n'a pas une utilité observable'. He sums up his definition in three sentences: 'Un rite semble être une action qui se répète selon des règles invariables[1] et dont on ne voit pas que son accomplissement produise des effets utiles.' It is 'un acte dont l'efficacité (réelle ou prétendue) ne s'épuise pas dans l'enchaînement empirique des causes et des effets'; 'qui se répète et dont l'efficacité est, au moins en partie, d'ordre extra-empirique' (1958:2–4).

Expressed in somewhat different terms, Jack Goody's definition of ritual subscribes to the same emphasis as does Cazeneuve: 'a category of standardized behaviour in which the relationship between the means and the end is not "intrinsic", i.e. is either irrational or non-rational' (Goody 1961, quoted in Gluckman 1962:21). Although Goody insists, like Cazeneuve, that ritual action is invariably marked by the absence of an explicitly teleological relationship of cause to effect, his use of the word standardized adds precision where this quality was otherwise lacking in Cazeneuve's definition. For repetitive and standardized behaviour are not quite the same thing. The repeated performance of the same act by an individual cannot be described as standardized adds precision where this quality was otherwise lacking Standardized behaviour is shared either contemporaneously or subsequently by two or more individuals, that is, it is essentially social in character and is subject to the overt or tacit recognition of a shared body of rules. It is thus 'normative' or induces adherence to a norm, as opposed to repetition which merely demonstrates the statistical 'normality' of a situation in which social factors are absent or fortuitous.

Gluckman incorporates the same factors of standardization and non-rationality into his own definition of ritual, which he further qualifies ('following here Evans-Pritchard's view of magic') as 'referred to "mystical notions"', which are 'patterns of thought that attribute to phenomena supra-sensible qualities which, or part of which, are not derived from observation or cannot be logically inferred from it, and which they do not possess' (Evans-

---

[1] It might be said *en passant* that he thus inadvertently contradicts his own view, put forward earlier, that ritual practices must allow for 'une marge d'improvisation' (1958:2).

Pritchard 1937:12, quoted in Gluckman 1962:22). In counter-distinction to ritual thus defined, Gluckman posits a category, to which he gives the inelegant name of 'ceremonious', which he sees as identical to ritual in all details except that it is not 'referred to "mystical notions" '.

Gluckman's classification is unsatisfactory for a number of reasons which it would serve no purpose to state here. It is, how-ever, interesting to note that he allows for a certain overlap and admits that the categories of 'ceremonious' and 'ritual' 'shade into one another' (1962:22).

Although Gluckman's essay on 'Les rites de passage', in which he formulates this definition, constitutes a laudable attempt to refine and lend a greater degree of flexibility to an already exist-ing classification of ritual and ancillary phenomena, it is difficult to understand why he stops where he does. For ten years earlier Leach had already followed Gluckman's postulate of 'shades' of ritual and ceremonial behaviour to a much more logical and significant conclusion. In doing so he had furthermore managed to avoid the stipulation of such deceptively precise and superfluous categories as the 'ceremonious'. Recognizing, like Gluckman, that it is impossible to distinguish with any real accuracy between different types of action, Leach entirely rejects the Durkheimian dichotomy between the sacred and the profane and proposes that we regard *all* human actions as falling

> into place on a continuous scale. At one extreme we have actions which are entirely profane, entirely functional, tech-nique pure and simple; at the other we have actions which are entirely sacred, strictly aesthetic, technically non-functional. Between these two extremes we have the great majority of social actions which partake partly of the one sphere and partly of the other.
>
> From this point of view technique and ritual, profane and sacred, do not denote *types* of action but *aspects* of almost any kind of action. Technique has economic material consequences which are measurable and predictable; ritual on the other hand is a symbolic statement which 'says' something about the individuals involved in the action (1954:10–11).

I myself am very much in sympathy with this approach to

ritual, for, like Coser's realistic-nonrealistic analysis of conflict, it provides for an infinitely greater and more subtle range of interpretation than can be achieved by the establishment of any cut and dried typology relying for the precise classification of individual phenomena upon the pertinence of a whole list of necessarily arbitrary criteria. Nor, in my opinion, is the resemblance between Leach's treatment of ritual phenomena and Coser's realistic-nonrealistic scaling of conflicts purely co-incidental. There clearly exists a real congruence between Leach's notion of ritual action and Coser's characterization of nonrealistic conflict: both are marked by the absence of a pronounced teleological relationship between means and ends. Ritual actions are, moreover, in Leach's words, 'technically non-functional'; the intensity and form of nonrealistic conflict tend, says Coser, to bear little direct relationship to the covert goals of the contestants. I shall attempt to show later that nonrealistic elements in a particular sort of conflict— that is feud—are in fact identical with what in Leach's terms may be called the ritual 'aspects' of certain types of human action.

Though I agree with Goody and Cazeneuve that ritual action is inclined to be at least repetitive, if not standardized, I do not consider it necessary to include Gluckman's reference to 'mystical notions' as intrinsic to all forms of ritual behaviour: some rituals *may* make explicit reference to the supernatural, but this is by no means true of *all* types of ritual action. It is a general failure to appreciate this point which has bedevilled much of the work which has been done on the nature of ritual. 'Ritual' is a 'loaded' word. I think that a good deal of confusion would be avoided if ritual were conceptually dissociated from the supernatural or mystical and were instead merely regarded as a type of behaviour in which symbolic representation precedes and predominates over the desire to accomplish material ends.

This is the stance taken by Lienhardt in his book on Dinka religion (1961, cf. ch. VII). It has the advantage of isolating and stressing the only factor which is common to all the definitions of ritual I have quoted above: for, if ritual may be characterized in a large number of different manners according to the circumstances, one thing that it can *always* be said to do is to provide a symbolic (or indirect) representation of something else, which is outside and extrinsic to the particular situation in which a given ritual action is observed.

In the discussion of the ritual aspects of feud which follows I shall not be able to substitute the word 'symbolic' for 'ritual', because I shall be referring frequently to what Gluckman and Leach have written on the subject, and to change the word altogether would merely obscure their arguments and do little to advance my own. It should, however, be borne in mind that whatever else ritual may be taken to be on occasion, it is my opinion that it invariably serves to *symbolize* an act or an intention which is not necessarily eplicit in the ritual itself.

The apparent diversity of opinion among the different authors I have quoted as to the definition of ritual is no less pronounced in their views as to the functions which they believe ritual fulfils. But here again disagreement is largely superficial, and their arguments can ultimately be reduced to consensus over a single common denominator.

For Gluckman, *the* most important function of ritual is to clarify: by drawing or emphasizing lines of demarcation between different social categories it facilitates comprehension of a social system by the people who live within it. Ritual highlights differences between male and female, young and old, past, present and future. It acts, say Gluckman, in extremely homogeneous self-subsistence societies, in which 'each social relation ... tends to serve manifold purposes' (1962:26), to underline the division of labour and to separate out roles which the presence of multiplex, frequently self-duplicating ties of simultaneous affiliation might otherwise confuse.

In somewhat more sophisticated terms Lienhardt makes a similar point: symbolic actions 're-create, and even dramatize, situations which they aim to control, and the experience which they effectively modulate' (1961:291); that is, they represent or reproduce in symbolic form the inescapable and frequently unwelcome facts of social existence so that, by repetition, standardization and the confirmation of familiar patterns of behaviour, they act as a filter to slow down the individual's rate of perception, in order that only the right elements trickle through, at the right time and speed, to reinforce intentions without creating unbalance and confusion due to the simultaneous intrusion of an excess of factors. By canalizing the experience of empirical reality, symbolic—or ritual—action helps individuals and groups to come to terms with their natural and social environments, makes palatable the distasteful and acceptable that which is initially regarded as incompatible.

Both Gluckman and Lienhardt agree, then, that ritual or symbolic actions are performed in order to clarify and define situations and social relationships. Although he approaches the problem from another angle and therefore appears to be saying something quite different, Leach does not substantially depart from this view. But he is more interested in what Gluckman has called 'rituals of social relations' than in ritual practices in general. Since feud may be regarded as a social system (i.e. a network of social relations) in its own right (cf. pp. 168–72), it is principally on the 'relational' aspects of ritual that I shall be concentrating in the remainder of this chapter, and I shall consequently disregard rituals which do not refer to inter-personal and inter-group relations.

In common with Gluckman (and, ultimately, Lienhardt) Leach holds that those aspects of human behaviour which are to be found towards the 'technically non-functional' end of his continuum tend to demarcate, to separate out and make clear lines of cleavage between individuals and groups. He thus endorses the view that ritual constitutes a symbolic language the principal function of which is to clarify and make easily intelligible assertions about social situations and processes. But while ritual may serve 'to express the individual's [or group's] status as a social person in the structural system in which he finds himself for the time being' (1954:10–11), it can also be used to emphasize the unity of the wider society. Thus, in a society like that of the Kachin, of whom Leach was writing, where any form of centralized governmental control is entirely lacking and the 'chief works in his field side by side with his meanest serf' (1954:15)—that is, in a social system presenting the two major characteristics of feuding societies—'if anarchy is to be avoided, the individuals who make up [the] society must from time to time be reminded, at least in symbol, of the underlying order which is supposed to guide their social activities. Ritual performances have this function for the participating group as a whole; they momentarily make explicit what is otherwise fiction' (1954:16).

Leach considers ritual as an essentially ambiguous form of action: at the level of individuals or individual groups it may express uniqueness and difference *vis-à-vis* the society at large;

but at another level, by providing an opportunity for the participation of large numbers of people in a single highly standardized activity, it can underscore the unity of the whole, which is not always self-evident, and enable the different parts of a society to communicate with one another. It is, however, not always clear to all those involved on which level they are participating at a given moment. Some members of a society may even deliberately use rituals of collective solidarity to further their own private ends which are opposed to the interests of the majority.

It is precisely to this kind of ambiguity that I tried to draw attention in my discussion of honour in the preceding chapter: the differential interpretation of the exact meaning of 'honour' in a given context makes it possible for hostile groups to envisage the same situation in a manner which is simultaneously compatible with (1) their opposed aspirations, (2) the 'officially' non-violent ideology (e.g. 'canon') of the society in which they live and (3) the folk model which acknowledges that violence is the only effective answer to violence. Honour, it will be remembered, constitutes a predominantly nonrealistic prize of conflict. But conflicts for honour are rarely, if ever, engaged upon for the attainment of exclusively nonrealistic goals.

Now I suggested earlier (cf. p. 212) that there was some congruence between Coser's notion of conflict for predominantly nonrealistic goals and Leach's use of the term ritual. In both types of action there is a lack of directly perceptible functional orientation. This absence of a relationship between means and ends causes the purposes of both nonrealistic conflict and ritual action to be blurred or ambiguous; and it is this ambiguity which allows self-seeking individuals room for manoeuvre so that they can manipulate the social system to achieve their own largely realistic objectives. On one plane both ritual and honour separate individuals and groups insofar as they serve as media for the expression of personal status and social ambitions leading to material betterment. In Leach's words, as 'a symbolic statement' ritual '"says" something about the individuals involved in the action' (cf. p. 211). But, on another plane, ritual (as a standardized form of behaviour) and honour (as a summary of all that is socially valued) are shared by all members of the society in which they occur and serve as a focus for group identity and unity.

Like honour regarded as a nonrealistic goal of conflict in

Mediterranean and Middle Eastern feuding societies, ritual functions both to create and to dispel ambiguity. Leach believes—and in this I concur—that most social situations are 'full of inconsistencies' (1954:8). It is through manipulation of the ambiguities inherent in ritual, he claims, that these inconsistencies are surmounted and used by individuals and groups in the unceasing struggle for dominance, which Leach equates with the 'processes of social change' (1954:8). But he pushes his analysis even further and does not hesitate to state quite explicitly that he sees little if any difference between this 'process of social change' and what other social anthropologists have preferred to call social structure. For Leach holds that 'social structure in practical situations (as contrasted with the sociologist's abstract model) consists of a set of ideas about the distribution of power between persons and groups of persons' (1954:4).

Again, with certain reservations, I agree with Leach: throughout the preceding chapter I have tried to demonstrate how feud as a social system is identical with an incessant modification of the power structure in feuding societies. Yet I am not unsympathetic with the strictures pronounced by Firth in his 'Foreword' to the first edition of Leach's *Political systems of Highland Burma*. Firth taxes Leach with having oversimplified the relationship between power structure and social structure. The attention Leach pays to 'the concentration of power and status on the quest for esteem as leading to office', Firth writes, 'suggests either an undue restriction of the field of motivation or a re-interpretation of the power notion in terms so wide as to include any social action' (Firth, in Leach 1954:vii–viii). The latter alternative is, I think, correct if Leach's analysis of power and social structure is taken to be applicable without modification in *all* societies. It is indeed Leach's own contention that his analysis is universally valid. However, I submit that this is not so and that Kachin society, in the context of which he developed these concepts, *is* subject to what Firth calls 'an undue restriction of the field of motivation'; that is (if interpreted into the vocabulary I have been using in this book), the Kachin constitute a feuding society in my sense of the phrase and consequently exhibit a peculiar form of social structure in which the *only* motivation in social interaction is violence, or the threatened exercise of violence, inspiring fear out of which arises a surrogate social system to compensate for the absence of more sophisticated institutions.

If the general terms of Leach's analysis of ritual and its concomitants in the sphere of political action are regarded as valid and if it is further remembered that these theoretical considerations were originally developed to elucidate mechanisms observed in a feuding society, it is legitimate to surmise that the wider implications of Leach's argument hold also for other feuding societies. This is the reasoning I shall adopt in much of what follows.

To recapitulate for a moment, Leach believes, then, that ritual is essentially ambiguous: it both can and does operate on two or more levels at once to clarify intentions and make statements concerning the relative position of individuals and groups. It serves on one level to ensure that the parts of a society communicate with one another to maintain an ideal of unity and solidarity, which in practice not infrequently proves to be almost inexistent; on another level, it functions to delineate social groups and express rival ambitions for the acquisition and retention of power and status.

I have shown that feud functions in precisely the same manner, and in so far as certain types of feud are strongly suffused with nonrealistic elements—that is, are not oriented towards the attainment of manifestly material goals—they may be said to constitute a ritual 'performance'. Nonrealistic feuding is furthermore characterized by the presence of a considerable amount of invariable and repetitive (or standardized) detail, which for most authors is an important indication of the ritual content of certain forms of human behaviour. Such details are particularly in evidence in acts of violence ostensibly carried out in defence of the sexual 'shame' of women or to wipe away the slur cast upon a family's reputation by the 'shameless' behaviour of one of its female members.

I affirmed earlier that honour, an exclusively masculine attribute, is the cause of feud *par excellence*. This is on the whole true. But I have up to this point been treating feuding societies almost as if they compromised only men. Another pre-eminent 'cause' of feud is women. Women are involved in feuds, though mainly in a passive capacity. Yet, however minimal their active participation, they play an extremely important role by providing an unimpeachable pretext for violence whenever it can be held that a woman's reputation has been compromised. My treatment of the feud as an all-male pursuit is nevertheless justified by numerous statements reported from feuding societies to the effect that 'Women don't have blood feuds' (cf. p. 137 note 9). For a man 'to be called weak woman' (cf. p. 15; e.g. also Barth 1965:82) implies, moreover, that his behaviour is the very antithesis of that expected of a man of honour, who, by definition, must be actively involved in the network of feuding relations.

Women have no honour. But they do have 'shame' or sexual modesty, the feminine counterpart of and complement to honour, which both they and their menfolk must do their utmost to defend. The failure of a woman or her family to maintain her shame inviolate exposes her to death at the hands of her agnates. A woman's shame summarizes her public reputation and social position in much the same manner as honour does for men. But whereas honour is positive and cumulative, shame is negative, absolute (a woman either has it or does not—there are no degrees of shame), cannot be increased and can be demonstrated, as it were, only in the breach. A woman is not said to 'possess' shame in the same way as a member of the opposite sex may boast of his honour or praise that of a man of importance and power. All women (unless bastards) are born with shame, whereas honour must in general be earned through action. Shame is a latent virtue which only becomes manifest if assaulted. Shame is to a large extent coterminous with the sexual vulnerability of women. It is the means whereby they combat their innate sensuality or propensity to evil, which stand as a constant threat to the purity of the masculine ideal of honour.

Women are therefore frequently—in sedentary societies, at least—regarded as 'devils' (Durham 1909:198) and 'very wicked' (1909:184). Consequently, it is not surprising if, in Albania, 'blood feuds' were said to be 'almost all the fault of women' (Durham 1909:184). Stirling confirms that much the same opinion prevails in certain village communities of Central Anatolia (1965). An early twentieth-century source quoted by Andromedas (p. 14) states that 95 per cent of the crimes of violence recorded in the Mani area of southern Greece were committed at the instigation of women. Thus, although women stand, as it were, outside the system of reciprocal prestations in violence which is feud (cf. pp. 84–5), they are nonetheless thought of as one of the main factors contributing to the continuation of hostilities between groups. According to the Albanian 'canon', 'Women do not have rifles' (Hasluck 1954:223). Only in exceptional circumstances are they known to kill.[2] Furthermore, in no feuding society in the Mediterranean and the Middle East are they regarded as legitimate targets for vengeance. Yet they are feared by men lest they bring dishonour upon the family, may in this one circumstance be killed and are said to be a major cause of feud.

An understanding of this paradoxical attitude towards women in feuding societies may be reached through an analysis of the feud in which the two themes of communication and ritual are combined.

If women are viewed, following Lévi-Strauss' suggestion, as messages circulated through a network of reciprocal communication channels between permanently constituted 'all-male' groups (Lévi-Strauss 1958:68–9) it is evident that the position of women in any society is highly ambiguous: as sisters and daughters on the one hand and wives and mothers on the other they are in most societies subject to a fundamental conflict of loyalties. Now, the authors quoted above agree that one of the foremost functions of ritual is to clarify and affirm intentions in situations where ambiguity occurs or, in other terms, to make clear the significance of different messages in circumstances in which confusion is likely. But whereas marriage rites and various other *rites de passage* or

---

[2] Even if a woman did occasionally bring vengeance in Albania, it might be held, as in one case reported by Mrs. Hasluck, that 'a kill by a woman did not count' (1954:256). The only activity connected with feud in which women could legitimately indulge was incitement to vengeance: it was the womenfolk of the victim whose duty it was to keep his memory alive by singing funerary dirges, lacerating their faces until they bled (Busquet 1920:100; Hasluck 1954:157; Andromedas 19) and keeping relics, such as a blood soaked shirt, to show provocatively to the heirs of the victim when they were grown old enough to bear a rifle (cf. pp. 78–80; p. 14). Kabyle and Rwala Bedouin women also play the role of cheer-leaders when their menfolk meet in pitched battle (Bourdieu 1965:201–2; Musil 1928:540). These aspects of the behaviour of women in the feud are, in Coser's terms, obviously highly nonrealistic. The reason for this will become apparent later in the present chapter (pp. 227–8).

d'aggrégation, supplemented by a relatively strong framework of
apposite political and legal institutions, are in the majority of
societies sufficiently compelling to make a reasonably unequivocal
statement dispelling any ambiguity which may arise out of the
transfer of rights over women from one group to another, this is
rarely if ever the case in feuding societies in the Mediterranean
and the Middle East, where the allegiances of women remain
more than usually divided between the agnatic and affinal groups
after marriage and the wife is most often regarded as a member of
her own lineage on conditional loan to the affinal group. Thus
the position of women in Mediterranean and Middle Eastern
feuding societies is more than usually fraught with ambiguities.

I suggest that their importance as the object or focus of violent
interaction is best understood if feud is seen as a ritual performance designed to bring about a *selective* minimization of the
ambiguities inherent in messages (women) transmitted from one
group to another. For, like all words or signals of any sort, women
are the bearers of a number of simultaneously conflicting meanings, and feud is employed to extract or select the meaning which
is politically expedient at a given moment to a given group. In
other words, women, and marital alliance in general, constitute
one of the spheres of social existence which Leach refers to as
'full of inconsistencies'. These inconsistencies are manipulated in
the feud to provide one of the bases of effective political power.

Before I attempt to show the workings of this mechanism I
shall review some of the ethnographic data pointing to the ambiguous position of women in feuding societies.

The most succinct statement on the position of married women
I have encountered in the literature on Mediterranean and
Middle Eastern tribal societies is given by von Hahn, who says
that the Albanian wife

> wird auch während der Dauer der Ehe stets als Mitglied des
> Stammes betrachtet, in dem sie geboren worden. Daher steht
> nicht ihren angeheiratheten, sondern ihren leiblichen Ver-
> wandten die Blutrache zu, wenn sie getödtet oder verletzt wird,
> und muss sich sogar ihr eigener Mann hüten, sie, wenn er sie
> prügelt, blutig zu schlagen, oder schwerer zu verletzen, weil er
> sonst mit ihren Verwandten in Blutfeindschaft geräth (1854:
> 180).

This pattern is repeated with slight variations throughout the Mediterranean and the Middle East. In general, it is the woman's agnates who remain responsible for the welfare of their kinswoman even though she be married at some distance from her natal camp or village. They invariably maintain close contacts with women who have married out to ensure that they are well treated by their husbands' groups. In some areas, like Albania, there even exist stipulations in the customary 'canon' which uphold the bride's inalienable right to return home to visit her agnates at least once a year (von Hahn 1867:340; Hasluck 1954: 31–2). This residual attachment of women to the agnatic family after marriage is so strong in other parts of the Balkans—in Montenegro, for instance—that women quite openly confess to loving their brothers with far greater affection and intensity than their husbands, for, they say, a husband can be replaced, whereas a brother cannot (Durham 1928:148).

On the rare occasions when a woman commits murder, it is her agnates who are held responsible and upon whom vengeance will be visited, not her husband (Hanoteau and Letourneux 1893: 64; Lewis 1962:32). It is also normally her agnates who receive compensation for the killing of their married kinswoman (Peters 1967:270; Lewis 1962:32), although Musil asserts that in similar circumstances among the Bedouin of the Syrian desert an agnate—usually a brother—will bring vengeance against the killer, but will compensate the woman's husband for relinquishing this privilege in favour of those having prior rights (1928:494).

The maintenance of agnatic ties with women who have married out is, however, most frequent and forcefully expressed, not in matters concerned with the murder of or by a married kinswoman, but in the assumption of responsibility for her bad conduct. For when married women are unfaithful to their husbands or commit any other act which may be interpreted as 'shameless', it is in the first instance the woman's own agnates, and not her husband's group, who consider themselves to have been dishonoured.[3] It is consequently nearly always thought that she should be killed by her own agnates in order that they may 'regain face'. In societies which practise preferential father's brother's daughter marriage the executioner designate is often the father's brother's son (whether or not he is also the husband of

[3] E.g. Burckhardt 1831:110; von Hahn 1867:339; Murray 1935:222.

the woman in question) (e.g. Abou Zeid 1965:257). Elsewhere it may be any close agnate of the woman or even, as in some regions of Albania, the husband himself providing he has formally requested the permission of his wife's father or brothers (e.g. Durham 1909:34; Hasluck 1954:213).

It is thus clear that married women in Mediterranean and Middle Eastern feuding societies occupy a social position between two groups, which is considerably more ambivalent than is usual in small scale societies and which is likely to make them subject to an exceptional degree of emotional strain. They live with, work and bear children for one group, but remain heavily dependent upon their group of origin whose authority over the woman constantly rivals that of her husband. In Lewis' words, Somali women, for instance, are 'only lightly attached to their husbands' group' (1961:136). This phrase aptly describes the condition of married women throughout the area under consideration.

In such circumstances it is not surprising if marriages are apparently unstable and there is, among nomadic pastoralists at least, a fairly high incidence of divorce. Unfortunately, few accurate figures are available for comparison. But statements attesting the prevalence of divorce among nomadic pastoralists are not lacking. Burckhardt, for example, notes that '... divorces are very frequent among all Bedouin' (1830:154), but 'Instances of conjugal infidelity', he thinks, 'are very rare' (1831:187). Burckhardt was referring to the camel herding nomads of Sinaï and northern Arabia. A century later Murray was able to confirm Burckhardt's observations and described divorce among the same people as 'very common' (1935:225). A similar trend was noticed by Lewis during his work on the pastoral Somali among whom 'Divorce is frequent' (1961:138). Among Somali cultivators Lewis found, on the other hand, that marriage was considered a much more binding contract than among pastoralists, and that the community would go to some lengths to heal a rift between man and wife (1961:236–7).

Although there is no statistical material whatsoever by which to judge the stability of marriage among sedentary agriculturalists such as the Albanians or the Kabyles, it would appear from the literature that, while divorce seems to have been a possibility (e.g. Hasluck 1954:213), it was rarely resorted to by husbands.

Mastery of a recalcitrant wife with threats and blows was preferred to repudiation of a woman of whom it might be said that
her husband had not been man enough to make her do his
bidding. It is doubtless for this reason that the flight of married
women back to their families of origin, adultery and the murder of
husbands by their wives are commonplaces of the ethnography
on Albania and Kabylia, whereas none of these appear to be at
all common among nomadic pastoralists, who attach little or no
stigma to divorce.[4]

Whatever the outward manifestation—whether frequent
divorce or marital disharmony resulting in homicide—it would
seem, however, that in both nomadic pastoral and sedentary
agricultural societies in the Mediterranean and the Middle East
marriage is on the whole extremely unstable. I submit that the
instability of marriage in these feuding societies may be imputed
to the highly ambivalent position that women occupy between
two social groups. I shall investigate the reasons for this ambivalence later.

It is, however, not only married women who occupy this
interstitial position and are consequently regarded with apprehension by their menfolk who, as agnates, fear that their daughters
and sisters will be illtreated by their affines and, as husbands,
are anxious lest their wives commit adultery or abscond back to
their family of origin. The same attitude of general apprehension
is extended by the male members of feuding societies to the
whole of the female sex, with the possible exception of very
young infants and very old women (who are regarded as sexless).

The intensity of the fear evinced by men as regards women,
which is expressed in the ferocity with which adulterous or
immodest behaviour on the part of women is sanctioned, is
clearly to be associated with folk ideas about 'shame'. Shame,
I have said (cf. p. 218), 'is to a large extent coterminous with
the sexual vulnerability of women'. Like women themselves,
shame is ambivalent, for the elements of behaviour which

---

[4] The relative facility of divorce which is found in many islamic communities and its proscription in principle by the catholic church do not
account for this disparity between attitudes to divorce in sedentary and
nomadic societies. For a large proportion of the Albanian mountain tribes
are nominally catholic, while the Kabyles are equally nominal muslims.
Yet both societies shun divorce.

constitute shamelessness and qualify the woman who so behaves for death at the hands of her agnates, are, in another context, entirely consonant with the role properly played by women in the society: shamelessness is sexual behaviour outside marriage; but a woman who exhibits this same behaviour towards her husband is acting in accordance with social expectations. The difference between shamelessness and socially accepted behaviour on the part of women is only in the context in which sexual behaviour occurs.

In this respect the notion of shame is almost identical with the notion of taboo as analyzed by Franz Steiner (1965) and developed by Mary Douglas in her recent book *Purity and danger* (1966). Shame, like taboo, is simultaneously an ambivalent concept and a way of demarcating or separating out zones of behaviour by the application of concomitant sanctions which act as diacritical marks to point up different meanings in different contexts. Ideas about shame in feuding societies symbolize the discreteness of women *vis-à-vis* the male members of society and, by placing a strong emphasis upon the conjugal fidelity of women and premarital virginity, serve to reduce the degree of ambiguity inherent in their position as wives or potential wives.

Taboo beliefs are invariably found in conjunction with rituals which, it has been suggested, function to underscore the social or generic distinctions which are implicit in the taboo: ritual clarifies in social situations in which ambiguity is liable to obscure the nature and quality of communications between individuals and groups. Working on much the same lines, but employing different terms of reference, Gluckman has proposed that the incidence of ritual actions is directly proportionate to the profusion of 'undifferentiated and overlapping roles' which ritual is intended to distinguish from one another (1962:34).

If this hypothesis is applied in feuding societies to the position of women whose roles are blurred owing to the unusual degree of ambivalence inherent in their marital status, it becomes immediately obvious that feuds ostensibly begun to punish the behaviour of a woman or, alternatively, to vindicate an innocent woman's shame, constitute ritual actions. For such hostilities conform to all the criteria I have so far advanced for the recognition of ritual actions:

(1) They are standardized, that is they are a repetitive and socially accepted form of behaviour.

(2) They are 'technically non-functional', i.e. they are mainly nonrealistic in content and are not predominantly oriented to the attainment of objective material goals.

(3) They serve to clarify the role of the woman who was the original cause of the conflict and to establish the exact nature of the relationship (affinity, dominance, submission) which links the opposed parties.

As a ritual performance or 'symbolic statement' concerning the shame of women the outcome of feud determines their role as wives or daughters: if a woman flees from a brutal husband to return to her own family, the husband will attempt to reclaim his wife by force, and the wife's agnates will seek to defend her (unless they consider her defection an unwarranted and therefore shameful act reflecting unfavourably upon their honour). A feud will be declared the latent purpose of which will be to make it quite clear whether the woman's role is to be henceforward that of a wife or a daughter.

Although it is not absent from nomadic pastoral societies in the Mediterranean and the Middle East, feuding for the shame of women appears to be more frequent in sedentary agricultural communities. This type of feud constitutes a form of conflict in which nonrealistic factors predominate over realistic ones. The greater prevalence and intensity of feuding for shame in sedentary societies conforms to a pattern which might be expected on the grounds of my analysis in the preceding chapter of the 'dichotomy'. Divorce is possible in both types of society, but sedentary agriculturalists seem to prefer to engage in feud rather than accept the more peaceful solution to an unsatisfactory marriage which is provided by divorce. I suggest that the explanation of this particular aspect of the 'dichotomy' and the greater emphasis on shame in sedentary societies is once again to be sought in the interpretation of oecological differences.

For if I am correct in my hypothesis that the rate of increase in flocks or herds in nomadic pastoral societies can never exceed the birth rate of the human population (cf. pp. 166–7), the amount of pastoral wealth to which an individual will have access at any given moment will remain roughly constant; and people will tend to regard the number of offspring born to them with a certain amount of fatalism or resignation, because there is no one-to-one relationship between control over larger numbers of children and greater *per capita* productivity in the pastoral sphere. Nomadic pastoralists, moreover, are always obliged to engage in military and economic alliance outside the extended family if they are to survive in a harsh environment. These two factors of oecology and alliance make the question of actual numbers in a given extended family less important than among sedentary agriculturalists, since pastoralists can always seek the protection of numbers in alliance, whereas agriculturalists can rarely count on military or economic aid from beyond the vengeance group, which is identical with the extended family. Nomadic pastoralists sometimes actually fear a rapid increase in numbers within the vengeance group, because they are painfully aware of the fact that oecological pressures will eventually cause the group to segment and that segmentation is not infrequently accompanied by bloodshed (cf. Peters 1967). The foremost ambition of sedentary agriculturalists, on the other hand, is to see their vengeance group blessed with an ever increasing number of sons who, as they grow older, will prove themselves able riflemen and supporters of the group's claims to power and wealth. I am not suggesting that nomadic pastoralists are unconcerned with the number of male offspring they produce, but merely that oecological conditions make this a less compelling preoccupation for them than for sedentary agriculturalists, for whom a small vengeance group is almost synonymous with political impotence.

I propose, then, that it is this strategic importance attached to the birth of (male) offspring which lies behind the emphasis which is laid upon the shame of women in sedentary feuding societies. The sexual integrity of women is vested with extreme value, since the misuse of the reproductive powers of women results in the 'waste' of an affinal tie and, if pregnancy ensues, a potential misappropriation of manpower. In the first case, loss of virginity or adultery imply the forfeiture of a brideprice which would normally have been used to acquire a woman to bear sons (i.e. riflemen) to the vengeance group. In the second case, the woman who bears a bastard son is of no use to anyone: she can no longer be used to obtain a bride to replace her in her own agnatic group; and her son belongs to no group, has no kinsmen and is therefore by definition without honour (cf. p. 181), that is, he is barely a human being. Bastards are, however, but rarely born in sedentary feuding societies in the Mediterranean and the Middle East, since their mothers are invariably killed before they can give birth.

To sum up the argument so far: the ambivalence of women in feuding societies is symbolized by their shame. Feuds declared in defence of or to punish a transgression of female shame may be said to have the function of clarifying the role of the woman concerned. As ritual performances, feuding activities centring upon women determine their position and their significance as messages at different points in the network of affinal alliance. This function of feud is made necessary by the absence, owing to conditions of 'total scarcity', of adequate institutions to fulfil the same purpose. Shame, like honour, is a nonrealistic or subjective goal of conflict; and like honour, its very subjectivity makes possible a number of inconsistent and mutually contradictory interpretations. Thus what constitutes and what does not constitute 'shameless' behaviour on the part of a woman depends to a very large extent upon the political status of her agnatic group, the influence and military strength of her husband and his group, and the current of public opinion at a given moment. The shame of women is manipulated in feuding relations, in very much the same manner as 'face' and honour are also used as nonrealistic pretexts for conflict and for the demonstration in realistic terms of effective political power.[5]

I have interpreted the intensity of feuding for shame—particularly in sedentary societies—as a function of the strategic desirability of women as the ultimate source of manpower. Campbell has ingeniously pointed out that at least one of the reasons for the intensity of feuding for shame is that women are regarded by their menfolk as the 'weakest links in the chain' (1964:199): the violation of shame, seen as a sort of mirror image of masculine honour, constitutes a public assertion of the weakness of a woman's agnates who, by allowing such a thing to happen, have shown their ineptitude and lack of manly virtues. The sexual integrity of women is a symbolic representation of the political integrity of the group. As a symbol of honour, which is already itself a nonrealistic or symbolic prize of conflict, shame is doubly nonrealistic. It is for this reason also that the violation of

[5] E.g. the Albanian case of Grimës and Gjelosh (cf. pp. 142–3). Mrs. Hasluck's reference to the 'honour' of Grimës' wife should, in my terminology, read 'shame'.

shame provides such an infallible cause of conflict and women are commonly cited as the harbingers of feud (cf. note 2), for it will be recalled that the less predominantly nonrealistic conflict is mitigated by the presence of realistic elements the more liable it is to spontaneous intensification. Of all conflicts which occur in feuding societies those which arise over women and shame are among the least adulterated by realistic factors. They are consequently those in which hostilities are the most intense.

If feuding for shame is more 'technically non-functional' than feuding for honour, it can be said that, regarded as a ritual performance, it is even nearer to the 'sacred' end of Leach's 'continuous scale' of human actions. However, like feuds undertaken for the acquisition or retention of honour, conflicts for shame also ' "say" something about those involved in the action'. They constitute a symbolic statement of inter-group relations in conditions characterized by what Firth has called 'an undue restriction of the field of motivation' (cf. p. 216) and a weak development of institutions designed to ensure non-violent communications between the parts of a society. In so far as feuds can be said to express the tenor of relationships by nonrealistic means, they may be described as rituals of social relations.

(2) INTRA-GROUP KILLING

If this be accepted, then it can be seen that marriage and feud are two different forms of communicative behaviour which achieve very similar results: both are ritualizations of extra-group ties expressed, respectively, in terms of alliance and defiance. They are two aspects of precisely the same process. The ambiguities inherent in marital alliance often cause feuds, just as feuds are also frequently the 'cause' of marriages contracted to 'conclude' hostilities.

Now, I would argue that this similarity between the nature of feud and affinal relations has most important consequences for the explanation of one feature of feuding societies which I have previously only touched upon. The feature I refer to is the attitude adopted by all feuding societies to intra-group killing.

Murder within the vengeance group is never treated in the same manner as murder without—that is, feud. The killing of

near agnates, and in some cases of other near associates living
in the same household or camp, always arouses sentiments of
profound public indignation and is spoken of as a 'sin' (e.g.
Peters 1951:263; 1967:264), which, unlike a crime, cannot be
punished by human agency. For this reason the only[6] sanction
visited upon intra-group killers is exile from the community (cf.
pp. 117–18).[7] But they are sometimes allowed to remain (e.g. Durham 1909:216–17) and, if exiled, they are even then, as I have
already mentioned (cf. p. 118), frequently permitted to return after
a suitable period of time has elapsed. Peters has reported a single
case in which a Cyrenaican Bedouin intra-group killer was
banished for ever from his vengeance group (1951:256–7). But
the general feeling is that homicide within the tertiary section
'is a great pity, but it is a double pity to lose two members'
(1951:255; cf. also 1967:264). The banished intra-group killer
is therefore eventually reintegrated into his group of origin, if
this is his wish.

The apparent reluctance of the group to apply to one of its
members the very sanction of violence which it does not hesitate
to use in its relations with other groups calls for some explanation.
Schapera merely eschews the problem when, quoting as evidence
the biblical story of Cain, he asserts that the exile of the offender
in a hostile desert environment is tantamount to eliminating him
permanently from the group (1955:38). This is almost never true,
for, as I have said, there is ample evidence to show that the
intra-group killer is usually accepted back into his vengeance
group after a lapse of months or years. Peters is nearer a con-
structive solution when he suggests that temporary exile is the
only possible way of dealing with an intra-group homicide, because for him to remain within the group he would have to pay
diya; but this would be impossible, as the payment of compensation is a criterion of political discreteness which characterizes
inter-group relations only, and would necessarily imply fission if

---

[6] In Albania, if in exceptional circumstances a man killed his brother's
son or father's brother's son *with malice aforethought* in order to inherit his
land, he might be condemned to death and executed by the community.
But this was very rare (Hasluck 1954:211).

[7] E.g. Palestinian Bedouin: Hardy 1963:92; Bedouin of the Syrian desert:
Musil 1928:495; Pastoral Somali: Lewis 1961:257; Anglo-Saxon 'tribal
law': Seebohm 1902:30.

paid by an intra-group killer (1967:263). In support of this view he quotes the Bedouin themselves who say that an intra-group killer 'destroys the lineage' and 'corrupts the family' (1967:264). If these dire consequences are to be avoided, he *must* be exiled. In this manner he is eliminated until such time as passions have cooled and he may return with impunity, so that there arises neither the question of his paying compensation for his crime nor the perplexing problem of the community being obliged to collect and hand over to his near agnates the *diya* outstanding were he to be collectively condemned to death.

Peters has examined the question from a practical angle; and his conclusions are no doubt, at a practical level, correct. I would, however, suggest that there is a more fundamental reason for the consistent reluctance on the part of feuding societies to sanction intra-group killing with the violence which is customarily employed in intra-group relations. For if Lévi-Strauss' view of society as a network of communications based on the principles of reciprocity and exchange is accepted (Lévi-Strauss 1949: *passim*; 1958:68 ff.) and it is further conceded that feud and affinity both constitute a ritualization of *extra*-group ties, intra-group killing may be regarded as strictly equivalent to incest:[8] incest and intra-group killing both constitute a duplication of ties where these already exist, a 'waste' of a potential extra-group relationship normally created and maintained through an exchange of, respectively, women and homicides; they are consequently both subject to the same prohibition and are therefore treated alike, when they occur. This would explain why intra-group killing, like incest, is frequently regarded as a 'sin' (e.g. Nadel 1947:303), that is a crime so enormous that it strikes at and negates the fundamental premises of social existence, which is inconceivable without some form of communication between biological families and larger groups. To kill a close agnate of the same sex is equivalent, in a purely masculine idiom, to seducing

[8] I am aware that a certain amount of criticism (e.g. Fox 1967:57) has been directly and indirectly levelled against Lévi-Strauss' proposal that the incest taboo and the rule of exogamy be regarded as 'the same thing, merely negative and positive statements of the same rule' (Hart 1950:392). The reasoning involved in this criticism is sound but, in my opinion, beside the point: it does not show that Lévi-Strauss' basic postulate is 'wrong'; but merely that some caution and subtlety should be observed in the application of Lévi-Strauss' theory to the ethnographic facts.

an agnate of the opposite sex: both actions, unless strongly proscribed, would result, firstly, in the isolation of the agnatic group from other groups and, subsequently, in its structural disintegration owing to the progressive confusion of roles and loss, as a consequence of the cessation of external exchange activities with similar groups, of a discrete identity as a unit within the wider society.

Inter-group feuding, I have said, clarifies the status of groups *vis-à-vis* each other. By providing an opportunity for the acquisition of honour and prestige by individuals it also serves to establish a hierarchy of dominance within the group. Without this hierarchy the group would be deprived of a focus for the orientation of co-operative action in the economic and political spheres. In other words, where 'total scarcity' inhibits the development of efficient secular institutions, feud supplies a ritual framework for social relations without which feuding societies would lapse into a state of unalleviated confusion or *anomie*. This analysis of the situation is interestingly confirmed by a few ethnographic details.

In the first place, one of the verbalizations that the Bedouin of Cyrenaica make about intra-group killing is that it 'brings confusion' (*khabaṣ*) (Peters 1951:262; 1967:264). Now these are precisely the same terms as those used by the Chinese to refer to incest.[9] The idea of confusion is also inherent in the biblical Hebrew notion of *tebhel*, which describes any complex of related categories or concepts, including incest, in which confusion might obtain (Douglas 1966:53). Other sources would suggest that this association of the notion of incest with an abhorrence for the confusion of social categories is widespread throughout the world. Peters himself does not mention what word the Cyrenaican Bedouin use to refer to incest, although he does unambiguously state that incestuous relationships are relatively common among them. It is therefore tempting to infer from the comparative material quoted that the Cyrenaican Bedouin word for incest (if there is one) is also *khabaṣ*, the same as that employed to describe the structurally disruptive effects of intra-group killing.

The probability that this conjecture squares with ethnographic fact is further reinforced by the details that Peters reports of a

[9] Beattie states that the Chinese characters which stand for the concept of incest can be translated as 'confusion of relationships' (Beattie 1966: 127).

marriage which was arranged, without transfer of bridewealth, between an incestuous girl and a close kinsman who had shot his sister (1965:125): according to Bedouin logic, the union of these two delinquents could hardly have constituted a more grotesquely suitable match, since the structural conseqences of the mis-demeanors they had committed were identical; both ran counter to the vital premise of external exchange—in women and homicides—with other groups. In Peters' own words: the two acts were equated! The absence of bridewealth from the transaction (which in a narrowly legalistic sense bore the implication that this was not a real marriage at all) and the fact that the couple subsequently went to take up residence in an enemy tribal section further serve to emphasize the almost punitive nature of the whole affair. For hardly had this doubly aberrent couple attained, through a parody of marriage, a position of social maturity, than all their newly acquired rights were cancelled and they were relegated to the status of outlaws in retribution for their different, yet analogous, crimes. The group to which they belonged per-ceived these same crimes as identical threats to its internal cohesion and as a common source of confusion impairing the orderly pursuit of its external relationships of feud and affinity.

A single case in which incest and intra-group killing are quite patently treated as analogous acts is, of course, hardly sufficient, on its own, to prove the general validity of my proposition that in feuding societies the two constitute structurally identical events. My contention is, however, corroborated by two further ethno-graphic details. The Cyrenaican Bedouin not only say that the intra-group killer 'destroys the lineage' and 'corrupts the family' by bringing confusion, but they also liken him to a 'dog' which 'defecates in the tent' (1967:264). In more than one society this simile is used to characterize the behaviour of incestuous couples too.

Brenda Seligman reports, for instance, that 'An Ababdah (a nomad Arab tribe living in Egypt) hearing a Shilluk say that it was customary among them for a man to marry his father's widows (other than his own mother), spat upon the ground and said: "*You* marry your mothers". The Shilluk retorted, "You worse than dogs—marry your sisters!" (ortho-cousins)"[10] (1950:

[10] The 'Abābda, like most Arabs, maintain a tradition of preferential father's brother's daughter marriage.

309). The same equation of incest with dog-like behaviour is current in northern Thailand (Wijeyewardene 1968:86).

If my tentative analysis of feud as a ritual of social relations is correct, the parallel I have drawn between incest and intra-group killing is logically consequent upon it, and it is not difficult to understand why intra-group killing should be said to 'bring confusion'. The leap to talk of dogs does, however, require some explanation.

Lévi-Strauss has postulated that observation of the incest taboo and the circulation of women outside the nuclear family, which results from it, stand on the line of demarcation between nature and culture and thus distinguish social from subsocial forms of life. I will not here discuss the merits of this argument.[11] But if Lévi-Strauss is right, then to behave 'like a dog' is to deny the existence of society and to identify oneself with nature. Both incest and intra-group killing may thus be said to constitute 'unnatural' behaviour in the fullest sense of the word. They are a negation of the communicative premise of social existence.[12]

---

[11] Lorenz's work on the mating habits of a particular species of geese would seem to invite the formulation of certain strictures as regards Lévi-Strauss' postulate: according to Lorenz, siblings among the geese in question almost invariably avoid mating with each other ('. . . sich so gut wie nie verheiraten . . .'), i.e. observe an incest taboo (1935:175).

[12] To abuse a man, to call him a dog, or any other 'inhuman' name, is, as Leach has pointed out (1964: *passim*; 1967:130), to diminish his social potency by reducing him to *sub*-human proportions. Similarly, in most societies, it is insulting—i.e. it reduces his status or social potency—to tell a person that he is a 'real bastard'. It is thus not surprising that slayers of kinsmen among the Cyrenaican Bedouin are branded as *walad ḥarām* or illegitimate sons (Peters 1951:259; 1967:275). The same terminology is used in Albania for parricides (Hasluck 1954:211). This appellation not only disculpates the agnatic minimal lineage for having spawned such an unnatural scion by placing the onus of responsibility on the immoral conduct of the mother, who frequently belongs (even in societies practising preferential father's brother's daughter marriage) to another group altogether, but it also serves to emphasize the anti- or sub-social character of the intra-group killer's act.

As witches throughout the world are not uncommonly said to be bastards too and since witchcraft, like feud, is regarded as a means of diminishing the potency of enemies, it might be interesting to make a comparative study of witchcraft and feud to find out whether there is any real sociological congruence between the two. A rich terrain upon which to begin such a study is provided by Leach's and Evans-Pritchard's books on the

While *intra*-group killing is the complete antithesis of social behaviour and brings confusion, *inter*-group killing, or feud proper, demarcates, separates and confers order upon social relations, that is, the channels of communication which link one group to another and provide the moral and material bases which make it possible for a given number of individuals to think of themselves as constituting a 'society'.

(3) MYTHOLOGY AND HISTORY

If feud as a ritual performance clarifies relationships as a whole and generally fosters social cohesion by acting as a standardized symbolic representation or 'reminder' of shared values (cf. p. 214), it nonetheless serves, as I have already frequently had occasion to show, at a more specific level, to express individual values and aspirations, and as a means to the attainment of goals which run counter to the immediate interests of other members of the society. Feud both unites and separates, conveys consensus and divergence. It is thus to be expected that the statements which members of feuding societies make about current and past feuds, whilst evincing an overall adherence to the same generally accepted scale of values, will nevertheless differ radically in their presentation of the facts according to the degree of involvement of the speaker and his structural relationship to the principals: a man whose brother has been killed will naturally try to justify his desire to bring vengeance, whereas the killer's group will in all probability either claim that the homicide was an accident or else that the victim acted in a manner so provocative that to kill him was the only 'honourable' solution. Similarly, an impartial observer unrelated to either of the principals will produce a less biased version of the facts which will be at variance with the stories of both the conflicting parties.

Since feud is an essentially diachronic phenomenon it is usually

Kachin and the Azande, where even a cursory glance is sufficient to suggest a variety of correspondences. Unfortunately, there are very few witchcraft beliefs in the Middle East. But this in itself might prove revealing in view of the intensity and prevalence of feud in the area: might not feud in a certain type of society be regarded as fulfilling a social function similar to that played by witchcraft in different, but in some respects analogous social surroundings?

impossible to observe a whole feud at first hand. Much of the material on feud presented by anthropologists has consequently been gleaned from conversations with tribesmen or from stories told about great feuds of the past. Such material is naturally fraught with contradictions stemming from the desire of opposed individuals and groups to exonerate themselves and justify their position in a feuding relationship. But in the absence of written records this is the only possible method of investigating feud. Obliged therefore to adopt it, Peters found that Bedouin tribesmen, whilst being eager to talk with relish about their own hostilities with distant secondary sections and other people's feuds, were much more reticent as regards acts of violence against collateral tertiary sections and remained of an invincible discretion in all that touched upon intra-group killing within their own section. If Peters had not been a good fieldworker, he might well have come away with the idea that intra-group homicide never took place.

It might thus be said that the Bedouin of Cyrenaica cultivate a mythology of feud 'by omission': their deliberate silence on a number of issues is intended to enhance in the eyes of an outsider the reputation that they, at least, (i.e. the informants' vengeance group) do not commit intra-group homicide. In fact, this is rarely the case and, as Peters discovered, the history of numerous tertiary sections in Cyrenaica is marked by the murder of close kinsmen, which the descendants go to considerable lengths to dissimulate. Successful feuds with distant sections were, on the other hand, frequently quoted as evidence of the honourable conduct and military strength of the speaker's group.

Such behaviour is nothing remarkable *per se*. A tendency for self-justification is a trait common to all human beings. However, in view of my general agreement with Leach's ideas on the nature of ritual and my own analysis of feud as a ritual of social relations, it might be interesting to interpret the inconsistencies which characterize different structural 'anglings' of the facts of any given feud in the light shed by the rider which Leach develops from his initial postulate of a sacred-profane continuum. Implicitly building upon Malinowski's theory of myth as a 'charter' for political and structural reality,[13] Leach has come to the

[13] I am indebted to Professor Maurice Freedman for this insight into the epistemology of Leach's ideas on ritual.

conclusion that '. . . myth and ritual are essentially one and the same. Both are modes of making statements about structural relationships' (1954:264): '. . . myth regarded as a statement in words "says" the same thing as ritual regarded as a statement in action' (1954:13–14). Seen in this manner, the stories told about feud in, for instance, Bedouin camps and Albanian villages can—in Leach's terms, at least—be said, quite literally, to constitute the mythology of feuding societies.

Like ritual, myths shared by a whole society function to stress the unity of the whole and its discreteness *vis-à-vis* other social groups which do not have the same mythology. But like ritual again and taken at a less general level, myths tend to be employed by smaller groups and individuals for the furtherance of their own ends against those of their rivals. Myths translate into words the political and structural processes expressed in ritual actions. As symbolic narratives they describe social structure and the changing patterns of dominance and alliance. I therefore agree with Leach that, in certain circumstances, myth 'is not so much a justification of ritual as a description of it' (1954:172) and believe that it is not unreasonable to argue that all the histories of feud given to anthropologists by members of feuding societies may be seen as 'myths' (in Leach's sense of the word) deriving from the necessity in which the informant finds himself to vindicate his structural position in a society in which feud itself is the very stuff of relationships and provides the only idiom for internal communication between parts, the only record of the passage of time.[14]

As a mythology in its own right, the history of feud is thus 'a language of argument, not a chorus of harmony' (Leach 1954: 278). In as much as at least some of the tales of famous feuds told during leisure hours in nomadic camps and tribal villages are related by individuals so far removed in time and structural distance from the original participants that a fair measure of

[14] The idea that the history of feud is synonymous with the history of feuding societies is a commonplace of the literature on feud in the Mediterranean and the Middle East. Peters states, for instance, that, in Bedouin eyes, a 'history of the tribe is a history of what they consider to be the feuds that have occurred between groups in the past' (1951:375). E.g. also Müller 1931:158 (quoted in Sweet 1965:1132); Durham 1909: 218; von Hahn 1867:47.

impartiality can be expected, they may be said to describe actual events. But if the events, or a good proportion of them, are of ritual significance and serve symbolically to determine the precise nature of relationships of inequality, the history of feud describes ritual.

(4) CONSPICUOUS CONSUMPTION AND 'DENIAL OF THE DEBT'

In the context of feud, myth and ritual are both public statements about social process. They both make explicit to the society at large the changing state of inter-group ties and individual aspirations. In so far as actions must be subject to a certain degree of standardization to qualify as ritual, feud postulates the existence of a framework of shared expectations which make it possible for the members of feuding societies to apprehend the social significance and even forsee the occurrence of acts of violence in a given set of circumstances. But feud, like all other systems of communication, enjoys a certain amount of built-in flexibility: as long as it is not done too frequently and the framework of shared expectations is not irreparably damaged, messages can occasionally be transmitted by a reversal of the normal communicative process—silence when articulate protest is expected, can sometimes serve to transmit a more telling message than positive reaction. Or, as Mauss has put it, 'Ne pas faire est encore une action, un acte d'inhibition est encore un acte' (1939:192, quoted in Cazeneuve 1958:4). Negation can at times be as, if not more, effective than affirmation when it is desired to establish the exact tenor of relationships.

In the light of these comments I should like to suggest briefly that feud may, in more than one respect, be usefully compared with the *potlatch* (or similar institutions like the southeast Asian feast of merit and the Latin American *fiesta*) and that such a comparison makes it possible to interpret a number of details in feuding behaviour which are otherwise not readily intelligible.

In his *Essai sur le don* Mauss describes the *potlatch* as a 'prestation totale de type agonistique' (1950:153). Now it would, I think, be difficult to find a more succinct phrase to characterize the feud as I have analyzed it. But parallels between feud and the *potlatch* do not cease here, for in one of the earliest serious attempts to apprehend the underlying significance of the *potlatch* Boas pointed out that the Kwakiutl *potlatch* ceremonial was the culmination and *public* avowal of a whole network of debt relationships which ultimately constituted the very fabric of Kwakiutl society. In Boas' opinion it was necessary for the ceremonial to take place in order that debts might be *publicly* placed on record in the memories of those present. This procedure conveniently compensated for the absence in Kwakiutl society of other more sophisticated methods of drawing up and keeping accounts of loans (Boas 1898:54–5, quoted in Mauss 1950:198).

The debts contracted in the *potlatch* proved that the debtor was worthy of the creditor's confidence, or, alternatively, that the debtor possessed sufficient political ascendancy over the creditor to force the latter to lend him capital which would aid him in his struggle for status and power. Although the situation in the feud is not quite the same (for no one in a feuding society willingly parts with capital in the form of blood), feud nevertheless exhibits a very similar mechanism: the greater the loan an individual or group can float (i.e. the larger the number of homicides it can commit without incurring retribution), the greater their political ascendancy. But like the *potlatch* again—and in this the feud resembles Foster's and Wolf's analysis of the *fiesta* in Latin American peasant societies too (Wolf 1959:216, quoted in Foster 1967:141)—the more a man acquires in feud the more he is obliged to redistribute both in the form of wealth (cf. pp. 183, 201) and risk to himself and his agnates. For the more debts a vengeance group accumulates the greater the risk that vengeance will be brought by the creditors.

The *potlatch* and feud both provide, in the first instance, a means of acquiring wealth and the status attached to material possession. But they both also ensure that inequality in terms of wealth and status cannot reach excessive proportions. For the obligation, in feuding societies, to redistribute wealth through gifts and hospitality and, in societies having *potlatch*-like practices, to expend wealth by conspicuous consumption, sets a limit on what can be acquired in material terms. The same obligation, if not manipulated with extreme circumspection, also exposes the incautious individual to a loss of status, as does too—but only in the feud—the numerical depletion of the group whatever its material gains.

There are obviously a number of points at which a comparison between the *potlatch* and feud becomes arduous, if not impossible. One of these is the fact that *potlatch*-type societies are normally (but not always) endowed with a fairly pronounced form of social stratification, while feuding societies are not. I would nevertheless argue that the comparison *is* valid as far as it goes and that some interesting further results might be obtained were Bohannan's development of Firth's theory of spheres of exchange (e.g. Bohannan 1963:248–59) applied to the feud with a view to discovering whether honour can be regarded as a medium for 'conversion' between distinct spheres of value culminating in the sphere of prestige out of which no further conversion can be made.

Whatever the points of divergence between the *potlatch* and feud, it is clear that both function, as social systems based on a 'prestation totale de type agonistique', to provide a framework for the public 'registration' of changing structural relations expressed in terms of debt. I have already quoted Peters to the effect that the denial of a debt of blood (1951:iv) is regarded by the Cyrenaican Bedouin as the most ineluctable cause of protracted hostilities between groups. Peters suggests that the reason for this is that, if the debt is not recognized, there is no possibility of 'concluding' hostilities by the promised payment of *diya*, for it is not possible to exact payment for a debt the existence of which the debtor is unwilling to admit. This is perfectly logical. But it does not adequately explain why in many feuding societies—not only among the Bedouin of Cyrenaica—throughout the world the covert killing of an enemy always gives rise to public outrage and converts what might have been a normal feuding relationship into a ferocious conflict in which the 'rules' cease to be observed and multiple vengeance is frequently brought for a single initial homicide.

In general, feuding societies explicitly distinguish between what the Scots lawyer Skene termed 'two kindes of slaughter; ane quhilk is called murther, quhilk is committed quyetlie, na other man seing or knawing the samine, except onely the man-slayer and his complices...' and the other, 'simpill man-slauchter' (1609:67v). Until the end of the twelfth century English and Norman law maintained the same distinction between ordinary homicide and *morth*, or homicide with concealment of the corpse

(Lancaster 1958:371; Maitland and Pollock 1895: vol. II, p. 484). The covert murderer in the tribal districts of Iraq who attempts to hide the body of the victim is regarded, if indentified, as the author of a more heinous deed than he who kills and declares publicly what he has done (Kadhim 1957:72). The same emphasis on the necessity for the killer to declare his guilt and bear the consequences is found among the Nuer (Howell 1954: 52), in the Norse saga (Njal 1955:362) and in Albania, where it is ' "held dishonourable" to kill and not to tell' (Hasluck 1954: 228). According to Wallace-Hadrill, the *Lex Salica* and *Lex Ribvaria* of the Merovingian period also make it quite clear that the body of a man killed in feud must on no account be hidden or buried by the killer (Wallace-Hadrill 1962:141).

I would suggest that this widespread prohibition in feuding societies upon concealment of the corpse and the concomitant stress upon a public affirmation by the killer of his guilt are not merely to be ascribed, as Peters intimates, to the impossibility of paying compensation and 'concluding' a feud, if the debt is denied. This is certainly partly the answer. But I think that the ethnographic facts are better explained if covert homicide is seen as a deliberate break in communications, as a negation of existing relationships which, by the introduction of an element of 'surprise', is designed to galvanize the adversary into frenzied reprisals. In this manner the two opposed groups are forced to adopt, or to resume, hostile attitudes towards each other which express, respectively, either a hitherto latent necessity for fission, or a renewal of contact after a prolonged period of mutual indifference in the course of which the two have grown apart to such an extent that they almost no longer recognize the fact that they belong to the same moral community.[15]

Concealment of the corpse is, if it remains a relatively rare occurrence, a standardized ritual means of exacerbating feuding relations to achieve fission or reaffirm ties which have lapsed. It does not constitute 'normal' practice, but is 'normal' enough to be recognized as a 'customary anomaly', falling within the general language of violence—like an anachronistic or rare word in a

---

[15] This analysis is implicit in Peters' statements relative to covert homicide. I have sought merely to lay a greater stress than he has done upon the communicative aspects of the problem.

modern text, which, whilst remaining intelligible, nonetheless makes the reader sit up and pay closer attention.

This is also the role of the 'fouls' I referred to in the first chapter (cf. p. 26), the character of which varies from the killing of a minor or of a fugitive who has sought asylum in the tent of a third party (Peters 1967:269) to mutilation of the corpse (Peters 1967:268; Musil 1928:495) or removal of the victim's rifle[16] (Durham 1909:198). By occasionally demonstrating the accrued intensity of hostilities when the rules of the game are ignored and by affording a glimpse of what a permanent departure from the feuding norm could portend, 'fouls' serve finally as a ritual 'reminder', not of the underlying unity of feuding societies, but of the dire consequences that would ensue were all constituent groups to abandon the self-buttressing system of violence which is their only defence against the onset of *anomie*. Even when it flouts its own rules the ritual 'language' of feud succeeds in conveying the messages of cohesion and superordination without which social existence in conditions of 'total scarcity' can have no meaning.

[16] The theft of the victim's rifle is probably thought to be synonymous with an act of symbolic castration, i.e. the removal of the outward sign of a man's virility and force, the diacritical mark which differentiates him from womankind. If this diagnosis is correct, the act of stealing a rifle from a dead man is very similar to the more obviously significant mutilation of the corpse.

Bibliography

(A) *Titles quoted in the text and notes:*

ABOU-ZEID, A. M. 1965. 'Honour and shame among the Bedouins of Egypt', pp. 245–9, in PERISTIANY, J. G. (ed.)

AFRICAN SYSTEMS OF THOUGHT 1966. *African systems of thought: studies presented and discussed at the Third International Seminar in Salisbury,* December 1960, pp. viii, 392, Published for the International African Institute, Oxford University Press: London, New York, Toronto

ALBANIA 1943. *Albania: basic handbook, part I—Pre-invasion, Secret 595,* August, p. 73 [British Museum shelf mark: BS 14/84]

AMERY, Julian 1948. *Sons of the Eagle: a study in guerilla war,* pp. xii, 354, Macmillan and Co. Ltd.: London

ANDROMEDAS, J. N. no date. 'Women, vengeance and unilineal descent groups, in Mani southern Greece', p. 19 [mimeographed]

ANONYMOUS 1814. *The Feud, a Scottish story: in seven cantos,* pp. ii, 153, John Cumming: Dublin [British Museum shelf mark: 11642.d.5]

ARENSBERG, Conrad M. 1937. *The Irish countryman: an anthropological study,* pp. xi, 216, The Macmillan Co.: New York

BARTH, Fredrik 1953. *Principles of social organization in southern Kurdistan,* p. 146, Universitets Etnografiske Museum Bulletin no. 7, Brødrene Jørgensen A/S, Boktrykkeri: Oslo.

— 1965. *Political leadership among the Swat Pathans,* p. 143, University of London, the Athlone Press and Humanities Press Inc.: London and New York

BEATTIE, John 1966. *Other cultures: aims, methods and achievements in social anthropology*, pp. xii, 283, Routledge and Kegan Paul Ltd.: London

BOAS, Franz 1898. 12th Report on the North-Western Tribes of Canada, British Association for the Advancement of Science

BOHANNAN, Paul James 1963. *Social anthropology*, pp. viii, 421, Holt, Rinehart and Winston Inc.: New York

BOURDIEU, Pierre 1965. 'The sentiment of honour in Kabyle society', pp. 193–241, in PERISTIANY, J. G. 1965 (ed.)

BRITISH NATIONAL BIOGRAPHY 1921–1922. *The dictionary of national biography*, 22 vols. + Supplement, reprinted by the Oxford University Press from plates furnished by Messrs. Spottiswoode and Co.: London

BRYSON, Frederick Robertson 1935. *The point of honour in sixteenth-century Italy*, p. 129, Publications of the Institute of French Studies, Columbia University: New York

BURCKHARDT, John Lewis 1830. *Notes on the Bedouins and the Wahabys*, pp. ix, 439, Published by the authority of the association for promoting the discovery of the interior of Africa, Henry Colburn and Richard Bentley: London

— 1831. Volume I of another edition, in two volumes, of BURCKHARDT, John Lewis 1830

BUSQUET, J. 1920. *Le droit de la vendetta et les paci corses*, p. 703, A. Pedone, Editeur: Paris

CAMPBELL, John K. 1963. 'The kindred in a Greek mountain community', pp. 73–96, in PITT-RIVERS, Julian 1963 (ed.)

— 1964. *Honour, family and patronage: a study of institutions and moral values in a Greek mountain community*, pp. xi, 393, Clarendon Press: Oxford

CAZENEUVE, Jean 1958. *Les rites et la condition humaine d'après des documents ethnographiques*, p. 500, Presses Universitaires de France: Paris

CHAMBERS, R. W. 1921. *Beowulf: an introduction to the study of the poem with a discussion of the stories of Offa and Finn*, pp. xii, 417, Cambridge University Press: Cambridge

COHEN, Abner 1965. *Arab border-villages in Israel: a study of continuity and change in social organization*, pp. xiv, 194, Manchester University Press: Manchester

COLSON, Elizabeth 1962. *The Plateau Tonga of Northern*

Rhodesia: social and religious studies, pp. xv, 237, Published on behalf of the Rhodes–Livingstone Institute by Manchester University Press: Manchester

COSER, Lewis A.   1956 (reprinted with the same pagination 1965). *The functions of social conflict*, p. 188, Routledge and Kegan Paul Ltd.: London

DICKSON, Harold Richard Patrick   1949. *The Arab of the desert: a glimpse into Bedawin life in Kuwait and Sau'di Arabia*, p. 648, Allen and Unwin: London

DOUGLAS, Mary   1966. *Purity and danger: an analysis of concepts of pollution and taboo*, pp. viii, 188 Routledge and Kegan Paul Ltd.: London

DRAKE-BROCKMAN, Ralph E.   1912. *British Somaliland*, pp. xvi, 334, Hurst and Blackett, Ltd.: London

DU BOIS-AYMÉ [DUBOIS, Aimé, known as] 1809. 'Mémoires sur les tribus arabes des déserts de l'Egypte', pp. 577–606, in *Description de l'Egypte ou Recueil des observations qui ont été faites en Egypte pendant l'Expédition de l'armée française publié par ordre de sa Majesté Napoléon le Grand: Etat Moderne*, tome premier, A Paris, de l'Imprimerie Impériale [British Museum shelf mark: 1899.k.1]

DURHAM, Mary Edith   1909. *High Albania*, pp. xii, 352, Edward Arnold: London

—   1928. *Some tribal origins, laws and customs of the Balkans*, p. 318, George Allen & Unwin Ltd.: London

ELIOT, Thomas Stearns   1950. *Selected essays*, pp. xiv, 460, Harcourt, Brace and Company: New York

ENCYCLOPAEDIA OF ISLAM   1913–1938. *The Encyclopaedia of Islam: a dictionary of the geography, ethnography and biography of the Mohammadan peoples*, 4 vols. + Supplement, Late E. J. Brill Ltd. and Luzac and Co.: Leyden and London

EVANS-PRITCHARD, Edward Evan   1937. *Witchcraft, oracles and magic among the Azande*, pp. xv, 558, Clarendon Press: Oxford

—   1940. *The Nuer: a description of the modes of livelihood and political institutions of a Nilotic people*, pp. viii, 271, Oxford University Press: Oxford

—   1949. *The Sanusi of Cyrenaica*, pp. V, 240, Oxford University Press: London

FIRTH, Raymond 1954. 'Foreword', pp. v–viii, in LEACH, Edmund R. 1954

FORTES, Meyer 1949. *The web of kinship among the Tallensi: the second part of an analysis of the social structure of a Trans-Volta tribe*, pp. xiv, 358, Published for the International African Institute, Oxford University Press: London, New York, Toronto

FORTES, Meyer and EVANS-PRITCHARD, Edward Evan 1940 (eds.). *African political systems*, pp. xxiii, 301, Published for the International African Institute, Oxford University Press: London

— 1940. 'Introduction', pp. 1–23, in FORTES, Meyer and EVANS-PRITCHARD, Edward Evan 1940 (eds.)

FOSTER, George M. 1967. *Tzintzuntzan: Mexican peasants in a changing world*, pp. xii, 372, Little, Brown and Company: Boston

FOX, Robin 1967. *Kinship and marriage: an anthropological perspective*, p. 271, Penguin Books Ltd.: Harmondsworth

FRANCE, Anatole 1908. *L'île des Pingouins* (many editions)

GALY, Charles 1901. *La famille à l'époque mérovingienne, étude faite principalement d'après les récits de Grégoire de Tours*, pp. iii, 429, Larose: Paris

GELLNER, Ernest A. 1961. *The rôle and organization of a Berber Zawiya*, pp. vi, 479, Unpublished Ph.D. thesis: London

— 1969. *Saints of the Atlas*, pp. xxiii, 317, Weidenfeld and Nicolson: London

GLUCKMAN, Max 1955. *Custom and conflict in Africa*, pp. ix, 173, Basil Blackwell: Oxford

— 1962. 'Les rites de passage', pp. 1–52, in GLUCKMAN, Max 1962 (ed.)

— 1962 (ed.). *Essays on the ritual of social relations*, pp. vii, 190, Manchester University Press: Manchester

GOODY, Jack 1961. 'Religion and ritual: the definitional problem', pp. 142–64, in *The British Journal of Sociology*, vol. XII, no. 2, June, Routledge and Kegan Paul Ltd.: London

GOPČEVIĆ, Spiridion 1881. 'Die albanesische Blutrache', pp. 71–4, in *Globus: illustrirte Zeitschrift für Länder- und Völkerkunde mit besonderer Berücksichtigung der Anthropologie und Ethnologie*, Bd. 39: Braunschweig

GOULD, Julius and KOLB, William L.   1964 (eds.). *A dictionary of the social sciences*, compiled under the auspices of the United Nations Educational, Scientific, and Cultural Organization, pp. xvi, 761, Tavistock Publications (1959) Limited: London

GREGORY OF TOURS   1927. *The history of the Franks . . .* Translated with an introduction by DALTON, O. M., 2 vols., Clarendon Press: Oxford

HAHN, Johann Georg von 1854. *Albanesische Studien*, 3 Hefte, Friedrich Mauke: Jena

—   1867. *Reise durch die Gebiete des Drin und Wardar im Auftrage der k. Akademie der Wissenschaften*, pp. ii, 365, kk. Hof – und Staatsdruckerei: Wien

HANOTEAU, A. and LETOURNEUX, A.   1893. *La Kabylie et les coutumes kabyles, deuxième édition revue et augmentée des lois et décrets formant la législation actuelle*, 3 vols., t. III, Augustin Challamel, Editeur: Paris

HARDY, M. J. L.   1963. *Blood feuds and the payment of blood money in the Middle East*, p. 106, E. J. Brill: Leiden

HART, C. W. M.   1950. Review of LÉVI-STRAUSS, Claude 1949, pp. 392–3, in *American Anthropologist*, vol. 52, no. 3, July–September

HARTLEY, John G.   1961. *The political organization of an Arab tribe of the Hadhramaut*, p. 212, Unpublished Ph.D. thesis: London

HASLUCK, Margaret   1954. *The unwritten law of Albania*, edited by HUTTON, J. H. (and ALDERSON, Mrs. J. E.), pp. xv, 285, Cambridge University Press: Cambridge

HONIGMANN, John J.   1964. 'Tribe', pp. 729–30, in GOULD, Julius and KOLB, William L.   1964 (eds.)

HOWELL, P. P.   1954. *A manual of Nuer law, being an account of customary law, its evolution and development in the courts established by the Sudan Government*, pp. xv, 256, Published for the International African Institute, Oxford University Press: London

JOHNSON, Alvin   1935. 'War', pp. 331–42, in vol. XV, SELIGMAN, Edwin R. A.   1935 (ed.)

KADHIM, M. Noori   1957. *Homicide in Iraq: a criminological study based on a survey of all homicide cases before the Session Courts in the year 1955*, Unpublished B.Litt. thesis: Oxford

— 1961. *Reaction to crime under tribal law and modern codification in Iraq*, Unpublished D.Phil. thesis: Oxford
KENNETT, Austin 1925. *Bedouin justice: laws and customs among the Egyptian Bedouin*, pp. xiv, 158, Cambridge University Press: Cambridge
KLUCKHOHN, Clyde K. M. 1944. *Navaho witchcraft*, pp. x, 149, Papers of the Peabody Museum of American Archaeology and Ethnology, vol. 22, no. 2: Cambridge, Mass.
LANCASTER, Lorraine 1958. 'Kinship in Anglo-saxon society', pp. 230–50 and 359–77, in *The British Journal of Sociology*, vol. IX, nos. 3 and 4, Routledge and Kegan Paul Ltd.: London
LAROUSSE, Pierre 1873. *Grand dictionnaire universel du XIXᵉ siècle*, 15 vols. + supplementary vols., Librairie classique Larousse et Boyer: Paris (1866–1888)
LEACH, Edmund R. 1954. *Political systems of Highland Burma: a study of Kachin social structure*, pp. xii, 324, for the London School of Economics and Political Science, G. Bell and Sons, Ltd.: London
— 1964. 'Anthropological aspects of language: animal categories and verbal abuse', pp. 23–63, in LENNEBERG, Eric H. 1964 (ed.)
— 1967. A letter published (p. 130) in *Man: the Journal of the Royal Anthropological Institute*, New Series, vol. 2, no. 1, March
LENNEBERG, Eric H. 1964 (ed.). *New directions in the study of language*, pp. ix, 194, Massachusetts Institute of Technology Press: Cambridge, Mass.
LÉVI-STRAUSS, Claude 1949. *Les structures élémentaires de la parenté*, pp. xiv, 639, Presses Universitaires de France: Paris
— 1950 (ed.). *Marcel Mauss: sociologie et anthropologie*, pp. lii, 389, Presses Universitaires de France: Paris
— 1958. *Anthropologie structurale*, pp. ii, 452, Librairie Plon: Paris
LEWIS, Ioan Myrddin 1955. 'Peoples of the Horn of Africa: Somali, Afar and Saho', pp. ix, + 11–200, in FORDE, Daryll (ed.)—*Ethnographic survey of Africa*, pt. I: 'North Eastern Africa', International African Institute: London
— 1961. *A pastoral democracy: a study of pastoralism and politics among the northern Somali of the Horn of Africa*, pp.

ix, 320, Published for the International African Institute, Oxford University Press: London, New York, Toronto

LEWIS, Ioan Myrddin 1962. *Marriage and the family in northern Somaliland*, p. 51, East African Studies, no. 15, East African Institute of Social Research: Kampala, Uganda

—— 1966. 'Shaikhs and warriors in Somaliland', pp. 204–23, in AFRICAN SYSTEMS OF THOUGHT 1966

LEYTON, Elliott 1966. 'Conscious models and dispute regulation in an Ulster village', pp. 534–42, in *Man: the Journal of the Royal Anthropological Institute*, New Series, vol. 1, no. 4, December

LIENHARDT, Peter A. 1957. *Shaikhdoms of eastern Arabia*, Unpublished D.Phil. thesis: Oxford

LIENHARDT, Ronald Godfrey 1961. *Divinity and experience: the religion of the Dinka*, pp. viii, 328, Clarendon Press: Oxford

LOCKE, John 1690 [published anonymously]. *Two Treatises of Civil Government: In the former, . . . The latter is an Essay concerning the True Original, Extent, and End of Civil Government*, p. 271, Awnsham Churchill: London

LORENZ, Konrad 1935. 'Der Kumpan in der Umwelt des Vogels. Der Artgenosse als auslösendes Moment sozialer Verhaltungsweisen', pp. 137–213 and 289–413, in *Journal für Ornithologie*, vol. 83, Hefte 2 and 3, April and July

MAITLAND, Frederic William and POLLOCK, Sir Frederick 1895. *The history of English law before the time of Edward I*, 2 vols., pp. xxxviii, 678 and xiii, 684, Cambridge University Press: Cambridge

MALINOWSKI, Bronislaw 1941. 'An anthropological analysis of war', pp. 521–50, in *The American Journal of Sociology*, vol. XLVI, no. 4 January

MANN, Thomas 1961. *The holy sinner*, p. 228, translated by LOWE-PORTER, H. T., Penguin Books in association with Secker and Warburg: Harmondsworth

MAUSS, Marcel 1950. 'Essai sur le don: forme et raison de l'échange dans les sociétés archaïques', pp. 143–279, in LÉVI-STRAUSS, Claude 1950 (ed.)

MERIMÉE, Prosper 1840a. *Notes d'un voyage en Corse*, p. 236, Fournier Jeune, Libraire: Paris

—— 1840b. *Colomba* (many editions)

MIDDLETON, John and TAIT, David 1958 (eds.). *Tribes without rulers: studies in African segmentary systems*, pp. xi, 234, Routledge and Kegan Paul: London
— 1958. 'Introduction', pp. 1–31, in MIDDLETON, John and TAIT, David 1958 (eds.)
MONTEIL, Vincent 1966. *Les tribus du Fars et la sédentarisation des nomades*, p. 156, Mouton et Co.: Paris, La Haye
MÜLLER, Victor Marie Pierre 1931. *En Syrie avec les Bedouins*, pp. xii, 347, C. Leroux: Paris
MURRAY, G. W. 1935. *Sons of Ishmael: a study of the Egyptian Bedouin*, pp. xv, 344, George Routledge and Sons, Ltd.: London
MUSIL, Alois 1928. *The manners and customs of the Rwala Bedouins*, pp. xiv, 712, American Geographical Society Oriental Explorations and Studies no. 6, edited by WRIGHT, J. K.: New York
NADEL, Siegfried Frederick 1947. *The Nuba: an anthropological study of the hill tribes of Kordofan*, pp. xiv, 527, Oxford University Press: London
NIMKOFF, M. F. 1965 (ed.). *Comparative family systems*, pp. x, 402, Houghton Mifflin Company: Boston
NJAL 1955. *Njal's saga*, translated from the Old Icelandic with introduction and notes by BAYERSCHMIDT, Carl F. and HOLLANDER, Lee M., pp. xvii, 389, New York University Press: New York
PALGRAVE, William Gifford 1868. *Personal narrative of a year's journey through central and eastern Arabia (1862–63)*, pp. vi, 421, Macmillan and Co.: London
PERISTIANY, J. G. 1965 (ed.). *Honour and shame: the values of Mediterranean society*, p. 266, Weidenfeld and Nicolson: London
— 1968 (ed.). *Contributions to Mediterranean sociology: Mediterranean rural communities and social change*, p. 349, Mouton & Co.: Paris – The Hague
PETERS, Emrys L. 1951. *The sociology of the Bedouin of Cyrenaica*, pp. xii, 408(9), Unpublished D.Phil. thesis: Oxford
— 1960. 'The proliferation of segments in the lineage of the Bedouin of Cyrenaica', 'Curl Bequest Prize Essay' (1959), pp. 29–53, in *Journal of the Royal Anthropological Institute*, vol. 90, pt. I, January–June

PETERS, Emrys L.   1965. 'Aspects of the family among the
Bedouin of Cyrenaica', pp. 121–46, in NIMKOFF, M. F.
1965 (ed.)
— 1967. 'Some structural aspects of the feud among the camel-
herding Bedouin of Cyrenaica', pp. 261–82, in *Africa*, vol.
XXXVII, no. 3, July
— 1968. 'The tied and the free: an account of a type of patron-
client relationship among the Bedouin pastoralists of Cyrenaica', pp. 167–88, in PERISTIANY, J. G.   1968 (ed.)
PHILLPOTTS, Bertha Surtees   1913. *Kindred and clan in the
Middle Ages and after: a study in the sociology of the Teutonic
races*, pp. x, 302, Cambridge University Press: Cambridge
PITT-RIVERS, Julian   1963 (ed.). *Mediterranean countrymen*,
p. 236, Mouton and Co.: Paris et La Haye
— 1965. 'Honour and social status', pp. 21–77, in PERIS-
TIANY, J. G.   1965 (ed.)
PRIESTLEY, Joseph   1772. *History and present state of dis-
coveries relating to Vision, Light, and Colours*, 2 vols., J.
Johnson publ.: London
ROBIQUET, F.   1835?. *Recherches historiques et statistiques
sur la Corse*, 2 vols. (text + plates), Chez Robiquet et Chez
Duchesne: Paris et Rennes
SCHAPERA, Isaac   1955. 'The sin of Cain', pp. 33–43, in
Journal of the Royal Anthropological Institute, vol. 85, pts.
I and II, January–December
SCHNEIDER, Joseph   1950. 'Primitive warfare: a methodo-
logical note', pp. 772–7, in *American Sociological Review*,
vol. 15, no. 6, December
SEEBOHM, Frederic   1902. *Tribal custom in Anglo-saxon law*,
pp. xvi, 538, Longmans, Green and Co.: London, New York
and Bombay
SELIGMAN, Brenda Z.   1950. 'Incest and exogamy: a re-
statement', pp. 305–15, in *American Anthropologist*, vol. 52,
no. 3, July–September
SELIGMAN, Edwin R. A.   1935 (ed.). *Encyclopaedia of the
social sciences*, 15 vols., The Macmillan Company: New York
SHAKESPEARE, William. *Romeo and Juliet* (many editions)
SIMMEL, Georg   1955 (reprinted with the same pagination
1964 and 1966). *Conflict*, translated by WOLFF, Kurt H.,
and *The web of group-affiliations*, translated by BENDIX,

Reinhard, with a foreward by HUGHES, Everett C., p. 195, The Free Press of Glencoe, Collier-Macmillan: London

SKENE, Sir John 1609. *Regiam Majestatem. The auld lawes and constitutions of Scotland faithfullie collected . . .* etc., Printed by Thomas Finlason: Edinburgh

SMITH, Alfred G. 1966 (ed.). *Communication and culture: readings in the codes of human interaction*, pp. xi, 626, Holt, Rinehart and Winston: New York, London

STEINER, Franz 1956. *Taboo*, with a preface by E. E. Evans-Pritchard, p. 154, Cohen and West Ltd.: London

STIRLING, Paul 1960. 'A death and a youth club: feuding in a Turkish village', pp. 51–75, in *Anthropological Quarterly*, vol. 33, Catholic University of America Press: Washington D.C.

— 1965. *Turkish village*, pp. xiii, 316, Weidenfeld and Nicolson: London

SWEET, Louise E. 1965. 'Camel raiding of North Arabian Bedouin: a mechanism of ecological adaptation', pp. 1132–50, in *American Anthropologist*, vol. 67, no. 5, pt I, October

TACITUS, Publius Cornelius. *Germania* (many editions)

THURNWALD, Richard 1930. 'Blood vengeance feud', pp. 598–9, in vol. II of SELIGMAN, Edwin R. A. 1935 (ed.)

TOZER, Rev. Henry Fanshawe 1869. *Researches in the Highlands of Turkey . . .* etc., 2 vols., John Murray: London

TYLOR, Edward Burnett 1889. 'On a method of investigating the development of institutions: applied to laws of marriage and descent', pp. 245–72, in *Journal of the Royal Anthropological Institute*, vol. 18, Trübner and Co.: London

WALLACE-HADRILL, J. M. 1959. 'The bloodfeud of the Franks', pp. 459–87, in *Bulletin of the John Rylands Library*, vol. 41, no. 2, March: Manchester

— 1962. WALLACE-HADRILL, J. M. 1959 reprinted as chapter 6, pp. 121–47, in the same author's *The long-haired kings and other studies in Frankish history*, p. 261, Methuen & Co Ltd: London

WHITELOCK, Dorothy 1952. *The beginnings of English society*, p. 256, Pelican History of England, vol. 2, Penguin Books: Harmondsworth

WIJEYEWARDENE, Gehan 1968. 'Address, abuse and animal categories in northern Thailand', pp. 76–93, in *Man:*

the Journal of the Royal Anthropological Institute, New Series, vol. 3, no. 1, March

WOLF, Eric R.   1959. *Sons of the Shaking Earth*, pp. viii, 303, University of Chicago Press: Chicago

(B) *Titles not quoted in the text or notes, but listed* either *because they contain further ethnographic data relevant to feud-like phenomena, not only in unilineal but also in bilateral societies, or because they represent a contribution to the epistemology of earlier attempts to analyze social mechanisms of the type discussed in the present book:*

ALBERGATI, Fabio   1583. *Trattato . . . del modo di ridurre à Pace l'inimicitie priuate etc . . .*, p. 272, Francesco Zannetti: Roma

'ĀREF EL–'ĀREF   1938. *Die Beduinen von Beerseba: ihre Rechtsverhältnisse, Sitten und Gebräuche*, translated from the Arabic by HAEFLI, Leo, p. 231, Verlag Räber & Cie.: Luzern

ASBÓTH, J. de   1890. *An official tour through Bosnia & Herzegovina, with an account of the history, antiquities, agrarian conditions, religion, ethnology, folk lore, and social life of the people*, pp. xx, 496, Swan, Sonnenschein & Co.: London

BARTH, Fredrik   1954. 'FaBrDa marriage in Kurdistan', pp. 164–71, in *Southwestern Journal of Anthropology*, vol. 10, no. 2, summer

— 1964. *Nomads of south Persia: the Basseri tribe of the Khamseh confederacy*, p. 159, Universitetsforlaget, Allen & Unwin Ltd., and Humanities Press Inc.: Oslo, London and New York

BLUNT, Anne   1879. *Bedouin tribes of the Euphrates . . . edited, with a preface and some account of the Arabs and their horses, by W. S. B.*, 2 vols., John Murray: London

— 1881. *A pilgrimage to Nejd, the cradle of the Arab race— a visit to the court of the Arab emir, and "our Persian Campaign"*, 2 vols., John Murray: London

BOUSQUET, Georges-Henri   1956. 'Le droit coutumier des Aït Haddidou des Assif Melloul et Isselaten (Confédération des

Aït Yafelmane): notes et réflexions', pp. 113–230, in *Annales de l'Institut d'études orientales*, t. XIV, Faculté des Lettres de l'Université d'Alger: Alger

BOUVAT, L. 1921. 'Le droit coutumier des tribus bédouines de Syrie', pp. 27–45, in *Revue du monde musulman*, vol. 43, Editions Ernest Leroux: Paris

BRUNNER, Heinrich 1882. 'Sippe und Wergeld nach niederdeutschen Rechten', pp. 1–87, in *Zeitschrift der Savigny-Stiftung für Rechtsgeschichte*, Germanistische Abtheilung, Bd. 3, Hermann Böhlau: Weimar

CARETTE, E. 1848. *Etudes sur la Kabilie proprement dite*, 2 vols., t. IV & V in Exploration scientifique de l'Algerie pendant les années 1840, 1841, 1842, Imprimerie nationale: Paris

DAHN, Felix 1879–1884. *Bausteine: gesammelte kleine Schriften*, 6 vols., Verlag von Otto Janke: Berlin

— 1880. 'Fehde-Gang und Rechts-Gang der Germanen', pp. 76–128, in DAHN, Felix 1879–1884, Zweite Reihe

DEVAUX, C. 1859. *Les Kebaïles du Djerdjera: études nouvelles sur les pays vulgairement appelés la Grande Kabylie*, pp. XIV, 468, Camoin Frères, libraires éditeurs & Challamel: Marseille & Paris

DOZIER, Edward P. 1966. *Mountain arbiters: the changing life of a Philippine hill people*, pp. xx, 299, University of Arizona Press: Tucson

EBERT, Max 1924–1932 (ed.). *Reallexikon der Vorgeschichte*, 15 vols., Verlag Walter de Gruyter & Co.: Berlin

FARÈS, Bichr 1932. *L'honneur chez les Arabes avant l'Islam: étude de sociologie*, pp. XIV, 226, Librairie d'Amérique et d'Orient Adrien-Maisonneuve: Paris

FRAUENSTÄDT, Paul 1881. *Blutrache und Todtschlagsühne im Deutschen Mittelalter: Studien zur Deutschen Kultur- und Rechtsgeschichte*, pp. XI, 250, Verlag von Duncker & Humblot: Leipzig

GJEÇOV, Padre Stefano Costantino 1941. *Codice di Lek Dukagjini, ossia Diritto consuetudinario delle Montagne d'Albania* tradotto dal DODAJ, Padre Paolo, a cura di FISHTA, Padre Giorgio e SCHIRÒ, Giuseppe. Introduzione de PATETTA, Federico, p. 327, Reale Accademia d'Italia, Centro Studi per l'Albania: Roma

GLOTZ, Gustave 1904. *La solidarité de la famille dans le droit criminel en Grèce*, pp. XX, 621, Albert Fontemoing, Editeur: Paris

GODIN, Marie Amelie Freiin von 1953–1956. 'Das albanesische Gewohneitsrecht (Kanun i Lek Dukagjinit)', in *Zeitschrift für vergleichende Rechtswissenschaft*, Bde. 56–58, Ferdinand Enke Verlag: Stuttgart

GOEBEL, Julius 1937. *Felony and misdemeanour: a study in the history of English criminal procedure*, vol. I, in Publications of the Foundation for Research in Legal History, Columbia University School of Law, 'The Commonwealth Fund' and Oxford University Press: New York and London

GRÄF, Erwin no date. *Das Rechtwesen der heutigen Beduinen*, p. 198, Bd. 5 of Beiträge zur Sprach- und Kulturgeschichte des Orients, Verlag für Orientkunde Dr. H. Vorndran: Walldorf-Hessen

HADDĀD, Elias N. 1917. 'Die Blutrache in Palästina' pp. 225–35, in *Zeitschrift des deutschen Palästina-Vereins*, Bd. XL, J. C. Hinrichs'sche Buchhandlung: Leipzig

HARTLAND, E. Sidney 1924. *Primitive law*, p. 222, Methuen & Co. Ltd.: London

HENNINGER, Josef 1943. 'Die Familie bei den heutigen Beduinen Arabiens und seiner Randgebiete: ein Beitrag zur Frage der ursprünglichen Familienform der Semiten', pp. 1–189, in *Internationales Archiv für Ethnographie*, Bd. XLII, E. J. Brill: Leiden

HEUSLER, Andreas 1911. *Das Strafrecht der Isländersagas*, p. 246, Verlag von Duncker & Humblot: Leipzig

JUYNBOLL, Th. W. 1910. *Handbuch des islāmischen Gesetzes nach der Lehre der schāfi'itischen Schule nebst einer allgemeinen Einleitung*, pp. XVI, 384, E. J. Brill and Otto Harrassowitz: Leiden and Leipzig

KIRK, John William Carnegie 1905. *A grammar of the Somali language with examples in prose and verse and an account of the Yibir and Midgan dialects*, pp. xvi, 216, Cambridge University Press: Cambridge

KRAUSS, Friedrich S. 1885. *Sitte und Brauch der Südslaven nach heimischen gedruckten und ungedruckten Quellen*, pp. XXVI, 681, 'Im Auftrage der anthropologischen Gesellschaft in Wien', Alfred Hölder k.k. Hof- und Universitäts-Buchhändler: Wien

LEWIS, Ioan Myrddin 1961. 'Force and fission in northern Somali lineage structure', pp. 94-112, in *American Anthropologist*, vol. 63, no. 1, February

MARCAGGI, J. B. 1898a. *Les chants de la mort et de la vendetta de la Corse publiés avec la traduction et des notes*, pp. 351, Perrin et Cie Libraires-Editeurs: Paris

— 1898b. *Fleuve de sang: histoire d'une vendetta corse*, p. 330, Perrin et Cie, Libraires-Editeurs: Paris

MIKLOSICH, Franz 1888. 'Die Blutrache bei den Slaven', pp. 127–209, in *Denkschriften der kaiserlichen Akademie der Wissenschaften*, philosophisch-historische Classe, Bd. 33, F. Tempsky: Wien

NOPCSA, Franz 1910. *Aus Šala und Klementi: albanische Wanderungen*, pp. II, 115, Heft 11 in PATSCH, Carl 1904–1919 (ed.)

— 1923. 'Die Herkunft des nordalbanischen Gewohnheitsrechtes, des Kanun Dukadžinit', pp. 371–6, in *Zeitschrift für vergleichende Rechtswissenschaft*, Bd. 40, Verlag von Ferdinand Enke: Stuttgart

OSENBRÜGGEN, Eduard 1863. *Das Strafrecht der Langobarden*, pp. XII, 168, Verlag der Fr. Hurter'schen Buchhandlung: Schaffhausen

PATSCH, Carl 1904–1919 (ed.). *Zur Kunde der Balkanhalbinsel*, 3 Series (1st Series: 'Reisen und Beobachtungen', 20 Hefte; Heft 11, published by Daniel A. Kajon: Sarajevo—cf. NOPCSA 1910): Wien & Leipzig

PETIT-DUTAILLIS, Ch. 1908. *Documents nouveaux sur les moeurs populaires et le droit de vengeance dans les Pays-Bas au XVe siècle—Lettres de rémission de Philippe le Bon*, pp. VI, 226, in Bibliothèque du XVe siècle, t. IX, Honoré Champion, Editeur: Paris

PROCKSCH, Otto 1899. *Über die Blutrache bei den vorislamischen Arabern und Mohammeds Stellung zu ihr*, p. 92, in Leipziger Studien aus dem Gebiet der Geschichte, Bd. 5, Heft 4, B. G. Teubner: Leipzig

ROTH, R. 1887. 'Wergeld im Veda', pp. 672–6, in *Zeitschrift der deutschen morgenländischen Gesellschaft*, Bd. 41, F. A. Brockhaus: Leipzig

SICARD, Emile 1943. *La zadruga sud-slave dans l'évolution du groupe domestique*, pp. X, 705, Editions Ophrys: Paris

STEINMETZ, S. R.   1928. *Ethnologische Studien zur ersten Entwicklung der Strafe nebst einer psychologischen Abhandlung über Grausamkeit und Rachsucht*, 2 vols., pp. XLV, 478 and VII, 407, 2nd edition, P. Noordhoff: Groningen

THURNWALD, Richard   1925. 'Blutrache', pp. 30–41 and 'Busse', pp. 231–42, in EBERT, Max 1924–1932 (ed.), Bd. 2

VALENTINI, Giuseppe   1945. 'La famiglia nel diritto tradizionale albanese', pp. 9–212, in *Annali lateranensi: pubblicazione del Pontificio Museo Missionario Etnologico*, vol. IX, Tipografia poliglotta Vaticana: Città del Vaticano

WESNITSCH, Milenko R.   1889 and 1891. 'Die Blutrache bei den Südslaven', pp. 433–70 and 46–77, in *Zeitschrift für vergleichende Rechtswissenschaft*, Bd. 8 (1889) and Bd. 9 (1891), Verlag von Ferdinand Enke: Stuttgart

Index

NOTE: *The following authorities are quoted frequently throughout the book and are listed here to avoid overburdening the index.*
Burckhardt, J. L.; Coser, L. A.; Durham, M. E.; Evans-Pritchard, Prof. E. E.; Gellner, Prof. E. A.; Hasluck, Mrs. M.; Leach, Prof. E. R.; Lewis, Prof. I. M.; Peters, Prof. E. L.

270 *Index*

Vengeance—*cont.*
  close agnates of victim   50,
    125, 134–7
  group, Bedouin   44, 46, 55
    recruitment of   37–44, 53
    size of   226
    solidarity with   36–7, 38–54
    Somali   49–50
    structure of in pastoral
      societies   44, 48
  incitement to by funerary
    dirges and mnemonics
    78–80, 110, 116
  killing, definitions of   28–9,
    30
    occurrence of   29, 30–2, 51,
    88
  within Cyrenaican tribes
    21–3, 228–9
  as redemption of debt   20
Vicinage and agnation   61–2
  over-riding contract   61
  in vengeance group   125
Village, organization of   61–2
  Turkish, feuding in   77
  vengeance group in   50, 52
Violence in defence of women's
  reputation   200, 217–18
  disproportionate, examples of
    130–41, 144
  and political structure   23–32,
    171–2
  as solution to conflict   18, 215
  typology of   1–32, 19
Virginity, premarital   224, 226
Vllazni (brotherhood)   40

Wallace-Hadrill, J. M.   15, 51,
  240
War, warfare   4, 5, 6; *see also*
  Conflict, Hostility
  definitions   23, 28, 30–1
  distinction from feud   2–4, 8,
    9, 12, 22

  intertribal   57
Watan (home territory), share of
  18
  leaving   47
Water, equal access to   55, 145
  necessity of   165, 193
  scarcity of   164–6
  temporary access to in crisis
    47, 62
Wealth, prevention of long-term
  accumulation of   122,
    155–6, 168, 192, 199
  of tribal leaders   182–3
  recirculation of   183–4
Well(s), access to, conflict over
  144
  rights to   49, 73
Whitelock, Prof. D.   116
Witches as bastards   233n
Women, accidental death of
  112
  agnatic and affinal allegiances
    of   220–2, 225, 227
  concessions given to, after
    raids   199
  as devils   218
  execution of   221–2, 227
  incitement to feud by funerary
    dirges   78–9, 219n
  vengeance   80, 218–19
  male apprehensions with
    regard to   223–4
  protection of honour in raids
    200–1
  ritual actions with regard to
    224–5
  role of in feud   208, 217–20
  sexual honour of   181, 218
  shame of   217–18, 221
  transfer of, in reconciliation
    92

Yakays (punishment)   152–3

Zriba (clans)   42